£3

BUT NO BRASS FUNNEL

BUT
NO BRASS FUNNEL

CAPTAIN JAMES DOUGLAS STEWART

Whittles Publishing

Published by
Whittles Publishing Limited,
Roseleigh House,
Latheronwheel,
Caithness, KW5 6DW,
Scotland, UK
www.whittlespublishing.com

Typeset by
Samantha Barden

ISBN 1-904445-10-1

Printed by
Bell & Bain Ltd., Glasgow

CONTENTS

———

For
Katie, Natasha, William,
James, Greg, Matthew, Camilla and Andrew

Chapter 1

HOW IT ALL STARTED

———

"You have a little Admiral, Mr. Stewart", said Dr. Mackintosh informing my father of my arrival. He was no doubt alluding to my father's wartime service on the staff of Admiral Sir David Beatty as his chef when he became Commander-in-Chief of the Grand Fleet in 1916. The good doctor's prediction was somewhat optimistic but I did in fact go to sea.

I was born in 1923 in Troon, a small seaport and holiday resort on the Firth of Clyde. It was a quiet town with little through traffic and, for a small boy who was a bit of a wanderer, the ideal place in which to grow up. The large sand dunes which bordered the wide safe sandy beach and the thick woods which edged the municipal golf courses provided plenty of opportunity for rambling, exploration and imaginative games.

Being a holiday resort Troon was well supplied with sporting facilities and several golf courses, tennis courts and a large well-appointed swimming pool provided the opportunity and encouragement to take an active interest in all sports and to lead a healthy outdoor life. There was no organized sport during junior school years but we made our own arrangements. Football was played on vacant ground near our homes, badminton at the British Legion Club, and the renewal of season tickets for the golf course, swimming pool and tennis courts was an annual event.

In senior school rugby football, cricket and athletics became the main sports with the goal being selection for the lst XV and lst Xl. I was fortunate to be given the opportunity to play for the cricket lst Xl before leaving Marr College in Troon and, later, for the lst XV at Royal High School in Edinburgh. Unfortunately I left school before the end of the season to go to sea so that I did not earn my cap.

The harbour became my favourite haunt. Although the Depression had an effect on the amount of traffic visiting the port there was usually a vessel of some description in harbour, a coal boat loading, or a small tramp freighter making a short visit. I enjoyed watching the cargo operations – how the derricks were rigged and operated, and how the various items of cargo were dealt with once they had been landed. Crew members were usually very good at allowing me to go on board to see over the ship and in answering my many questions. On one occasion I got as far as arranging to sail on a coal boat to Ireland which would be back 'in a day or two' and raced home to tell my father who, needless to say, put paid to my adventure.

The shipyard, which built and fitted out small cargo vessels and warships was very quiet during these years but two minesweepers, the *Jason* and *Franklin*, were completed in 1937 and I met them again in 1945 in Harwich when I was serving in minesweepers. The only activity would usually be in the shipbreaking berth where, over a period of a few weeks, a fine steamer would just be eaten away until it disappeared altogether.

I was given two books which became my favourite possessions and constant companions and which were a marked influence on my decision to be a sailor *The Wonder Book of Ships* and *The Wonder Book of the Navy*. The former was mainly concerned with ships of the Mercantile Marine or Merchant Service which were the terms then in use for the Merchant Navy of today. There were many pictures and illustrations of the different types of ships, the cargoes that were carried and the manner in which they were stowed. I learned about the ships that 'tramped' around the world carrying mainly bulk cargoes, such as coal and grain, on irregular routes and picking up cargoes where and whenever they could. And the ships of the liner companies which operated a regular service to the different parts of the world – the ships which Rudyard Kipting referred to as 'The swift shuttles of the Empire's loom.'

A good deal of attention was focused on the large passenger ships of the day especially those engaged on the transatlantic service. To give the reader some idea of the size of ships like the *Mauretania* or *Leviathan* they would be illustrated standing perpendicular against a New York skyscraper such as the Empire State building, and there were many pictures of massive engines and boilers. Many of these ships were termed 'luxury liners' and were noted for the splendour of their public rooms, state-rooms and the excellent service provided for the passengers. I had an early introduction to passenger ships when I was six years old and went with my parents to say goodbye to an aunt who was taking passage from Glasgow to America in the SS *Transylvania*, a medium sized Anchor Line vessel of about 14,000 tons. I remember looking into the first class dining saloon and seeing a long table loaded with food, the most prominent item being a large boar's head with an apple in its mouth. I turned to my father and said "What happens to all this when the ship goes down, Daddy?"

However it was the Navy which captured my imagination and eventually absorbed my complete interest. From the *Wonder Book* I found out all about the different types of warships, their various classes and the roles they played in war and peacetime. The book was full of pictures showing aspects of life on board a man-of-war, and various shipboard operations such as putting out torpedo nets (an early form of defence used by large warships against attack by torpedoes,) sleeping near the guns when closed up at actions stations, signalmen hoisting flag signals and torpedoes being loaded into their tubes. I read about the Navy's role in such things as fighting piracy in the China Sea, surveying the waters of the Persian Gulf or visiting foreign ports to show the flag.

I preferred the clean lines of the warships with their turrets and gun mountings to the untidy forest of derricks of a merchant ship, and loading general cargo, coal, grain or even railway engines could not compare with the possibility of being a member of a gun crew or a boarding party, or having command of a picket boat or whaler. I was also attracted by the smart uniforms worn by the officers and by the various customs and traditions of the service. It seemed that the more I read my 'bible' the more I was determined to go to sea and, if possible, to be a naval officer, and throughout my childhood I never wavered in this ambition.

My father had enjoyed his time in the Navy very much and he was very proud of having served with Admiral Beatty. When father left the Service the Admiral presented him with a signed photograph mounted in a silver frame and suitably inscribed. It was a prized possession. He had many interesting stories about his time in the service and, being a good raconteur, he could give a vivid account of the event or occasion. These yarns whetted my appetite and encouraged my enthusiasm.

Evidence of how quickly news could get around in the Navy is illustrated by the following story. In those days sailors were given a daily rum ration, and in order to ensure that they did not keep it to go on a spree on board, it was diluted with 2 parts of water to 1 part of rum (called grog) which ensured that the rum would not keep and had to be consumed after the issue. In big ships – battleships, cruisers etc. – Chief Petty Officers and other senior ratings were allowed to 'draw' their rum neat, and this privilege was also afforded to all ratings serving on 'hard-lying' ships – small ships such as destroyers and below.

Rum was the currency of the lower deck. Not that it was sold or traded in the conventional sense but if anybody wanted a favour or became obliged in any way, his tot would be used to repay the debt. There were three scales of payment – sippers, gulpers, or the whole tot. It had to be a very big favour to induce a sailor to part with his tot. Father's messmates and other senior ratings would sometimes bring him something to cook for them, and would give him 'sippers' which he put in a bottle to take home on leave.

On one occasion when he went ashore at South Queensferry in the Firth of Forth he was stopped by the customs officers who found him in possession of a bottle of rum and some tobacco, both items of contraband and not allowed to be brought ashore. This was a serious offence and he found himself in considerable trouble.

However when he told the officers that his ship was the *Queen Elizabeth*, the Flagship, and that he was the Admiral's chef they decided that the situation required further discussion and that they should all retire to the Hawes Pier Inn to consider the matter. Needless to say all was settled in a convivial manner and father proceeded on leave with his rum and tobacco.

Returning from leave in Kilmarnock a few days later he shared a compartment on the train with another sailor who told him that he had overstayed his leave by fourteen days, whereupon father remarked that there would be a 'big dinner' (punishment) waiting for him when he arrived onboard. The sailor agreed but in turn asked my father if he had heard about the chap from the 'Q. E.' who had been caught trying to take tobacco and rum ashore. He had heard about father's escapade whilst he was on leave!

Unfortunately warships did not visit Troon harbour but whenever there was one calling nearby, and likely to be open to the public, we would go to see it. On one occasion HMS *Hood*, at that time the largest and most powerful warship in the world, was known to be at Rothesay and we went there in the hope of being able to go on board. After waiting for a considerable time on the jetty a boat from the *Hood* came alongside and we were disappointed to learn that she would not be open to visitors.

There was better luck when HMS *Nelson*, one of the latest battleships, called at Gourock for several days and it was advertised she would be open to the public. When we arrived on the jetty at Gourock there was a long queue waiting to be taken out to the ship, which was anchored offshore. We joined the queue and had a long wait of several hours watching the boats ferrying the visitors to and from the ship, and. moving slowly round the jetty until we finally arrived at the embarkation gate. By this time it was late afternoon and the last boat for the day was about to leave. As we moved to go through the gate the Chief Petty Officer in charge held up his hand and said "Sorry, the boat is full up – that's all for today." I was bitterly disappointed to have come all that way and to have waited for so long only to be turned away at the last minute. However all was not lost father's appeal to the Chief, "I was in the Andrew myself and the boy is very very keen," resulted in my being squeezed in whilst father had to wait on the jetty.

It was the first time that I had been on board a warship but I was familiar with the main features from what I had seen in my *Wonder Book*. I remember being puzzled by the shape of the *Nelson* compared to the other battleships of the day. The latter had their big guns mounted both at the fore-end and after-end of the vessel whilst the *Nelson's* big guns were all mounted on her foredeck. I found out later that this was because, during her building, a Naval Treaty had been signed with other nations which limited the size of battleships. Instead of being completed to her original designed length she was cut off at the stern and all her big guns were mounted in three turrets on the foredeck.

I had a wonderful time wandering round the ship and looking at the equipment and spaces which had been specially designated for visitor inspection. The visit on board was all too short and the time soon came to return to shore. I returned in the ship's picket-boat, a steam-driven pinnace with a tall brass funnel, in the charge of a Midshipman. I went up to the front of the boat and was standing up at the bow when I heard a bellow and turned to find him shouting at me to sit down. I had been given my first lesson – do not stand up in a boat!

Charge of the ship's boats was a Midshipman's first experience of command, and as I watched the young officer handling his boat and giving his orders confidently and with authority I was more than ever determined to be a Midshipman and to drive a boat with a brass funnel.

The British India Company, which I joined eventually, operated troop-ships which carried servicemen to India and other parts of the Empire. During the monsoon period, when it was too hot for trooping, some of the ships would be used for schoolboy cruises and I was fortunate to go on two cruises in the MV *Dilwara*. In 1936 the cruise was to the Baltic where we visited Copenhagen, Gothenberg, Stockholm, Helsinki and Danzig. In 1937 Norway was the destination and during the fourteen days we called at Oslo, Bergen, Stavanger, Narvik and Arendal.

The cruises were a good introduction to seafaring and, to some extent, the discipline of a service life. We slept in hammocks which we had to sling ourselves, ate at long mess tables and responded to the various bugle calls such as 'reveille ', 'lash up and stow,' 'cookhouse,' etc. There was no bullying that I recall although the senior boys from each school made sure we youngsters behaved and looked after ourselves properly. On one occasion I heard a bit of a commotion in the washroom and looked in to find a young lad being held down and scrubbed with a hard brush. Evidently he had failed to heed several warnings about keeping himself clean so his seniors had decided to teach him a lesson.

Visiting the foreign ports was a new adventure. At each port there were excursions to places of interest such as a glacier, or to the museum in which was displayed the equipment used by Amundsen, the famous Norwegian explorer, on the first trip to the South Pole. In Danzig harbour we saw what was said to be the oldest crane in Europe. It was a big building, shaped like a windmill and with a large, heavy beam protruding from the top storey. The mechanism inside was linked by wood gearing to a large treadmill which, in by-gone days, had been operated by prisoners.

My father had kept in touch with Mr. Woodley, the Admiral's steward and valet and Chief Petty Officer Walter Beer, his cox'n. In 1936, when the *Dilwara* returned to Tilbury Docks in London, it was arranged that I should travel down to Plymouth to spend Navy Week with Mr. and Mrs Beer.

Mr. Beer had been a senior Chief Petty Officer and had been Admiral Beatty's personal cox'n since the outbreak of the war, and was at the Admiral's side on the bridge of his flagship, HMS *Lion*, at the battles of the Dogger Bank, Heligoland Bight and Jutland. In 1917 King George V visited the fleet and stayed for a week onboard the *Queen Elizabeth* which was the flagship of the Grand Fleet. During his stay he visited many of the ships in the fleet, using the Admiral's barge of which Mr. Beer was the cox'n. At the end of the war the King and Queen Mary went on board the *Queen Elizabeth* for lunch with the Admiral. Mr. Beer was closely involved in various aspects of these visits at the end of which his Majesty showed his appreciation by presenting him with a small gift – I was shown a large silver watch and chain and a case of pipes. On each occasion my father received twenty pounds from the King's steward which he shared with his galley staff.

Picket boat with a brass funnel.
Photograph courtesy of the National Maritime Museum, Greenwich.

Troopship MV Dilwara.
Photograph courtesy of the National Maritime Museum, Greenwich.

I could not have wished for a more kind and knowledgeable person with whom to spend a Navy Week. Mr. Beer took great care to make sure that I saw everything of interest during my stay and was untiring in answering and explaining my constant questions. We hired a boat on two occasions and explored the dockyard and the Hamoaze – a stretch of water off Devonport. On these excursions he taught me the proper way to row a boat – I already had experience in rowing through lending a hand with the boats that were for hire on the beach at home. However this proper instruction stood me in good stead when, on my first trip to sea, I had to take Lascar seamen away for practice in a steel lifeboat capable of carrying 90 persons.

There were ships of every description in the dockyard – battleships, cruisers, destroyers and submarines. One battleship was undergoing an extensive refit which entailed the fitting of an armoured deck and alterations to the design and lay-out of the bridge superstructure. Mr. Beer told me that the reason our ships had blown up during the battle of Jutland was their lack of protection against plunging shell-fire. Armoured decks were required to stop the shells penetrating the decks and exploding inside the hull and possible hitting the magazines. HMS *Hood* was due to be altered in the same way, but when it was her turn to go into dock she could not be taken out of service due to the international situation at the time and she was never given the necessary protective armour. It was this weakness which was the cause of her loss during her action with the German battleship *Bismark*.

The cruiser HMS *Norfolk* was in the dockyard and I remember being attracted by her white hull and yellow funnels which was probably in preparation for the Far East station. Little did I know at that time that I was to meet her again 13 years later under very different circumstances.

I was based in Malta and serving in HMS *Chameleon* when the *Norfolk* called in on her way home from the Far East bound for the scrap-yard. One Sunday morning our Engineer Officer told me that I had an appointment with the dentist in the *Norfolk* at 11 am. I had been complaining of toothache and, as he had met the dentist during a run ashore the previous evening, he had taken the opportunity to make an appointment for me. I was not too happy about the arrangement, being inclined to put off visits to the Toothie for as long as possible, however it would have been bad manners not to have kept the appointment.

When I arrived in his cabin I became rather uneasy when I noticed a large collection of miniature bottles of various wines, spirits and liqeuers some of which had already been opened and consumed. It seemed to me that he had had a good run ashore the previous evening and had not been 'feeling any pain' when he went to bed. I only hoped that I would be in the same condition when he had finished with me. He arrived looking slightly bleary eyed and I would not have been surprised if he had not had any recollection of making the appointment. He turned out to be a very nice chap and an excellent dentist, pulling my tooth with the minimum of fuss and then inviting me to the wardroom, where any possible subsequent pain was deadened by several large gins.

In the dockyard there were many stalls where souvenirs could be purchased and some items were made from the wood taken from the decks of various ships which had undergone repair. I bought my father a pen and ink stand made from the wood taken from the deck of HMS *Iron Duke* – Admiral Jellicoe's flagship at the Battle of Jutland.

A popular event was the fight between a U-boat and a Q-ship which took place in one of the harbour basins. At the beginning of World War 1 the only methods available for sinking submarines was ramming or gunfire as depth charges had not been invented. Whilst submarines invariably used torpedoes to sink their victims, in order to conserve their torpedoes for more important targets such as large merchantmen and warships, they would often surface and use gunfire when engaging smaller and slower merchant vessels. To combat this practice the Admiralty armed selected merchant ships to act as decoys, the guns being mounted in a collapsible housing in order to conceal their presence from the enemy.

A large trawler played the part of the Q-ship and as the U-boat (a small coastal submarine) surfaced then fired a shot at the decoy, the 'panic party' complete with the Captain's wife and child, put on a performance of abandoning ship. Sometimes the life-boat would be made to tip the occupants into the water – a not uncommon occurrence on ships when a fall could jam while a boat was being lowered in haste in an emergency situation. Then the Q-ship's guns would be revealed, the White Ensign would be hoisted, and a cheer would go up from the spectators on the quayside as the Q-ship opened fire. Thunder flashes would be let off on the U-boat's hull indicating hits and there were more cheers as it slowly submerged mortally wounded.

It was a holiday and experience to remember and I was so grateful to my father and Mr. Beer for making it possible. I returned home more determined than ever to join the Navy.

Chapter 2

SPECIAL ENTRY

———

There were two methods of officer entry into the Royal Navy. The primary method was for a boy to enter the Royal Naval College at Dartmouth at about 13 years of age where he would spend four years acquiring the education that a public school would give and, in addition, receive early training to prepare him for an exacting and specialized profession. The annual fees were about £400 and also the costs of uniform and other expenses had to be borne. The second method was the Public School or Special Entry when boys entered Dartmouth straight from school. The primary method provided the minimum officer requirements for the service and the entry flow was kept at a steady level. The Special Entry numbers could be regulated according to demand, i.e. if an expansion was anticipated the numbers could be increased, but if a contraction in the fleet seemed likely the numbers could be reduced accordingly. It was easier to forecast future requirements 4 years hence rather than 8 years.

There was a great deal of competition in both cases. Holding a commission in one of the services was a top career and the Navy, being the Senior Service, was extremely popular. Entry was by written examination and interview; the latter was said to be the hardest part as, with many applicants to choose from, those who made the best impression on the selection board stood the best chance. Many applicants came from families with a naval tradition and it was only to be expected that, provided they were equal in other respects with their competitors, they would be given preference.

Notices giving the dates of entry examinations and the exact dates between which applicants had to be born, together with other relevant information, were inserted in the newspapers periodically. There was no large scale advertising and these notices, being small in size, could easily be missed unless a close watch was being kept for their appearance.

Unfortunately that is what happened in my case. By the time my future career in the Navy had been discussed with my headmaster when I entered senior school and it was decided that I should try for Dartmouth, I found that I had missed the last opportunity for my age group and that I was too old to apply. All that remained was to wait until I was 17 and eventually try for Special Entry.

In 1938 the family moved to Edinburgh where I attended the Royal High School, a boys' school, one of the oldest in Scotland with long traditions dating back to the beginning of the 16th century, and with the reputation of being one of the top rugby schools in the country. It was quite a change for me. Marr College, which I had just left, was a coeducational school which had only been open for three years and I had been one of the 'originals' starting in the 1st Form.

I did not look upon the change of schools as an upheaval but as an adventure – making new friends, learning of the school's traditions and its rivals and taking up new activities and interests. In common with the other boys' grammar schools in the city Royal High had an Officers Training Corps which all boys over a certain age were expected to join although there was no compulsion to do so. The Corps was affiliated to the Royal Scots Regiment and wore a kilt of Hunting Stewart Tartan and the Glengarry cap. I joined the Corps and when I left school to go to sea, like other boys of my age, I could handle a rifle and bayonet, drill a platoon and understood military discipline – all of which was to help me in my future career.

I was in church with my family on the morning that war was declared. There was a stir amongst the congregation as the beadle was seen to hurry down the aisle carrying a piece of paper which he handed to the young assistant minister, at the same time whispering in his ear. Because of the political events which had been taking place the announcement which followed was not totally unexpected, but it was a bit of a shock to hear for the first time that the country was at war. The minister brought the service to a close and I felt sorry for him that it should have ended in such a way. He certainly would not forget his first day in charge.

Being young and not knowing any better I was quite excited at the turn of events and at the prospects of the Navy being in action with the German Fleet. But my father was very grave and thoughtful as he brought me down to earth, explaining that things were not going to be easy and that difficult times for the country lay ahead.

During the winter of 1939 I began to get a little bit anxious about my chances of success in the Special Entry examination. I was only average at school work and by this time I had learned that many boys were given special preparation for the examination at their schools or at a crammer thus increasing their chances of success. I was anxious to get to sea and looked around for another way to enter the Navy as an officer, but the Chief Petty Officer in the recruiting office could only repeat what I already knew.

However I had a stroke of luck. I heard that an apprentice in the Merchant Service could apply to join the Royal Naval Reserve as a Midshipman after serving a minimum period of one year at sea. Although there was no immediate way of confirming that the scheme existed it seemed to be a possible way of entering the Navy and, as I was keen to get to sea, going away as an apprentice was the next best thing. Once again my father consulted the headmaster as to what would be best for me and once again he was told that I was ideally suited for a career at sea.

As I had no preference for any particular company I sent letters of application to several whose addresses I obtained from the many shipping advertisements in the newspapers. I chose only well known companies such as Cunard Line, New Zealand Shipping Company, and the British India Steam Navigation Company. As I recall Cunard had no vacancies, New Zealand Shipping Company required entrants to have the English Common Entrance Certificate or the Scottish Higher Leaving Certificate as a condition of entry. However I was successful with the British India Company who asked me to attend for interview accompanied by my father at the Company's agents in Glasgow.

I have often wondered just what took place at that interview. Father was asked to go in first and it seemed that he was away for a long time before he reappeared and it was my turn to be interviewed. This did not take long – I was asked why I wanted to go to sea, what games I played – and it appeared to me that everything had already been arranged and I had been accepted, which has led me to think that, maybe, the interviewer and my father had found something in common. Knowing my father, who was a most honest and straightforward man, this is unlikely as he would never have used such things to advantage, but in my fancy it is nice to think that he wanted to give me just a little help going out into the world.

Father duly received a copy of my indentures and a list of the items of uniform which would be required. During my four year apprenticeship the Company would also be responsible for my moral education and welfare, and one condition in my indentures stated that I would not be allowed to 'frequent ale-houses and taverns.' My pay would be one pound per month for the first year, two pounds for the second, three pounds for the third and four pounds for the final year. To be indentured cost fifty pounds so that over the four years there would be a gain of seventy pounds. As it turned out I received an extra fifty shillings per month it being 50% of the war bonus which was awarded to merchant seamen and other seafarers.

I was fitted out with my uniform and sea-going kit at Paisley's, an old established department store in Glasgow.

There was a long list of items to be purchased: 2 caps and badges, a naval officer's topee and a working topee, a bridge coat, 2 blue uniforms, 2 pairs of shoes, 6 socks, 6 uniform shirts and 6 sets of underwear, 12 stiff collars, leather and woollen gloves, balaclava helmet, scarf, oilskins seaboots and sou'wester, white square, grey flannel trousers, gym shoes, housewife and other odds and ends. Then there was the tropical uniform – 6 white tunics and trousers, shorts and shirts, stockings and shoes. There was a shortage of white gear and I had to make do with outsize tunics, which were subsequently altered by a stewardess, and other bits and pieces until the first port of call in India – Madras. There the tailor came onboard at 8 a.m. took my measurements and by evening I was fully kitted out. The kit was packed into a large blue cabin trunk.

Off to sea – 'first tripper'

All that remained was to have news of my first appointment and I was very excited when the letter arrived and I found myself directed to join the SS *Mulbera* at the Royal Albert Docks in London on the 31st of March 1940. I was off to sea at last!

My grandparents lived in London so I stayed with them for a couple of nights before joining my ship. Before we left to go to the docks grandfather took me aside and gave me an envelope and told me that as long as I had this I would never drown. Inside was a small bundle of what appeared to be dried skin – it was in fact a caul, the skin that sometimes surrounds a baby's head when it is born. My aunt had been born with one and grandfather had kept it.

I was very lucky to be given one. Cauls were much prized by seamen who, being a superstitious breed, had great faith in the belief that anyone born with a caul or possessing a caul would never drown at sea. I carried it in a chamois leather body belt which I wore all the time at sea until I lost it later in the war.

The railway terminus was right outside the dock gates and grandfather was able to wait in the train with my large trunk whilst I went to report on board. The ship appeared to have completed loading as there was not a great deal of activity taking place and nobody at the gangway when I arrived on board. I eventually found an entrance into the accommodation (the doors were masked by concrete protective blast screens) and found someone to take me to the Chief Officer who, after giving me a friendly welcome and making me feel at ease, took me up to introduce me to the Captain. Again there was nothing perfunctory about my reception and I began to feel less nervous. I did not feel strange in my new environment having read so much about ships, and having been on board and been to sea I was quite familiar with my surroundings.

I went back to the train to collect my trunk and say goodbye to my grandfather. He was an old man and I was very fond of him. Fortunately the train was about to leave so that there was no long leave-taking. As he shook my hand and wished me luck and said the usual things, I saw the tears in his eyes and I began to feel a tightening in my throat for the first time. I had never felt before that sensation when leaving home and I put it down to seeing my grandfather so upset.

I gave him a last hug and then turned around and went off to meet my new shipmates and to see the world.

Chapter 3

FIRST SHIP – SS *MULBERA*

———

The British India Steam Navigation Company was founded in 1857 by two Scotsmen, McKinnon and McKenzie. It was in some respects a continuation of the old East India Company whose Charter had ended about that time, as it subsequently developed other interests in India and neighbouring countries in addition to shipping. At the outbreak of war the fleet consisted of 112 ships making it the largest cargo/passenger line in the world. One could seldom enter any port east of Suez without seeing the black funnel with two white bands of a BI ship.

The company operated many services: the 'Home Line' run between the UK and India (the *Mulbera* was a 'Home Line M'), Bombay to ports in the Persian Gulf, Bombay to East and South Africa, Calcutta to Rangoon mail run, and Calcutta to Japan and Australia to name but a few. In addition to several troop-ships the company had two cadet-ships, *Nardana* and *Devon*, which each carried 40 Cadets. As each voyage lasted one year Cadets were referred to as first trippers, second trippers etc. The cadet-ships were discontinued as soon as war was declared, the Cadets being sent to join their fellows already serving throughout the fleet. I later learned that I was fortunate to miss the cadet-ships – life could be made quite hard for new boys who were made aware of their station by Cadet captains not averse to using a rope's end.

The SS *Mulbera* was a three island cargo passenger ship of about 9,000 tons built in 1923, having a forecastle and poop each separated from the midship structure by well-decks with two cargo hatches on each deck. There was accommodation for about 100/150 first and second class passengers.

SS Mulbera.
Photograph courtesy of the National Maritime Museum, Greenwich.

The crew were Indian seamen known as lascars, the senior rating being the Serang or Boatswain. The Petty Officers, of whom there were a similar number in the engine department, comprised two Tindals (boatswain's mates), a Cassab (storekeeper) and a lamptrimmer. Each department had its own Cook or Bhandarry. The Serangs wore bright red sashes and silver chains whilst the Seacunnies (quartermasters), who steered the ship and attended the gangway in port, were easily recognized in their blue cotton tunics which they embroidered in bright coloured patterns using the most delicate needlework. A British Chief Steward was in charge of the catering department with an Indian Butler responsible for the stewards. Among other British crew members were the baker, carpenter, hairdresser and deck quartermasters. A corporal of the Royal Marines Reserve was the ship's gunner responsible for the armament and for training the guns' crews, the ship being armed with a 4 inch gun for surface action and a 12 pounder anti-aircraft gun.

The deck officers comprised the Master, First, Second and Third Mates and two Radio Officers. The engine department consisted of the Chief Engineer, Second, Third and Fourth Engineers and several Junior Engineers. I was to learn that 'Captain' was an honorary title in the Merchant Service although it had now been adopted and was the name by which all Shipmasters were known and addressed. In the bigger and more reputable companies the term 'Officer' was used rather than 'Mate' which was the actual 'office' to be performed. In reality the only people who signed on the ship's articles under the term 'Officer' were the wireless operators.

In line with other major companies BI officers wore the Company's cap badge and insignia of rank instead of the official Merchant Navy uniform, for many companies had their own cap badges which often displayed the Company house-flag. I think BI had the most attractive cap badge of them all – Britannia sitting on her throne holding a trident and a shield showing the Union Flag. Senior officers wore their insignia on their shoulders. Instead of the normal collar patch of gold cord and button, the Cadets wore three buttons on each sleeve similar to those worn by Naval Midshipmen wearing full dress, from which they were termed 'snotties.' It was said that this had been a special privilege awarded by Queen Victoria to BI Apprentices.

When I returned to the ship I met the other Cadets and found that there were to be five of us. Three already serving in the ship and two first trippers – myself and a chap who was eventually known as the Bishop. Eustace French, known as Stacey, who was in his second year, had been born in India and had attended the Queen Victoria School in Darjeeling. The Bishop and myself were quickly introduced to the class structure in India when the Bishop referred to Stacey as being an Anglo-Indian, meaning an englishman born in India. It transpired that Anglo-Indian meant a person of mixed race and some people were very touchy on the subject. The two remaining Cadets were seniors – Isaac in his third year and Roy Le Lievre, the senior Cadet, in his last year. For some forgotten reason Roy was always known as Angus. He was a tall, good-looking chap who came from the Channel Islands where he was a swimming champion.

The Cadet cabins were on the boat deck behind the navigating bridge, the cabin doors opening directly on to the deck. The cabins accommodated three persons, the juniors in one whilst the two seniors shared the other. Conditions were quite cramped, on entering there was a bunk six feet long down one side with drawers underneath and a wardrobe at the far end. Along the back of the cabin were two bunks, one above the other, with drawers underneath, and on the other side a settee with drawers and adjacent to the door a folding wash-basin cabinet. Thus I learned that one had to be tolerant, considerate and understanding in order to get on with people and be happy when living and working together in a confined environment.

We were soon busy unpacking our cabin trunks and it was a wonder that we found space for all our belongings. Whilst doing this it was discovered that I had no text books for study so I was hurriedly taken to the ship chandler at the dock gates who, fortunately, had the necessary items, the Cadet's bibles – *Nicholl's Concise Guide for Navigation, Norie's Nautical Tables* and *Nicholl's Seamanship Manual*. I had been given five pounds to start me on my journey but there was not a great deal remaining by the time I left the chandler.

As the ship was sailing first thing in the morning the seniors decided on one last run ashore, and so I was given an early introduction to the night life in the dock-side area of East Ham. I do not recall very much about the evening except that we finished up at a dance hall and I remember that I had a sherry. I have a feeling that, in my brand new uniform, I must have looked very much like a chicken ready for plucking but we all returned on board safely.

Next morning we were awakened at five o'clock to get ready for 'stations' at six. My station was on the foc'sle with the Chief Officer, manning the telephone to the bridge. Whilst waiting for the tugs to arrive I was sent to chase up the carpenter who had not yet arrived to operate the windlass. I found him still in his bunk, fast asleep and surrounded by empty bottles. I had a difficult job in waking him and learned another lesson, that in such a situation it is no use tapping on the door and politely announcing that it is six o'clock. I also saw the results of too much drink and had early experience of the problems encountered when dealing with drunks.

The telephone was an ancient contraption which I came to hate and led me to dread the prospect of entering and leaving port. It was contained in a steel box and consisted of two arms, similar to ear trumpets, which were held to the ears and a small mouth-piece to speak into. The connection to the bridge was very poor and it was hard to distinguish clearly what was being said which resulted in my first 'bloomer.' A mooring wire ran from the foc'sle back along the jetty to a point just opposite the bridge its purpose being to prevent the ship surging ahead whilst it was alongside. A similar wire ran forward from the poop. These wires were known as springs. I received an order which sounded like, "let go the string!" and although I thought it an odd term I passed the message to the Chief Officer. Again another lesson – ignorance is no excuse and that a 'rocket' is given to ensure that the same mistake is not repeated, and then it is forgotten. And so I started to learn my trade.

We sailed on 1st April, sailing in convoy to Gibraltar and then unescorted to Malta and Port Said as Italy was not yet in the war.

I was put on watch with the Second Officer who kept the 12 – 4 watch (afternoon and middle) and immediately received my first instruction in navigation – how to take a bearing on the magnetic compass on top of the wheelhouse. If the ship was rolling and pitching in a seaway the magnetic compass card developed a considerable swing and skill and experience were required to obtain an accurate reading. Naval ships and some of the more modern liners and cargo ships had gyro compasses which were much more stable, and being not so much affected by the ship's movements were much easier to use. It was to be four years before I was shipmates with one.

A Cadet's duties on bridge watch were to help with the signalling – bending on flags to the signal halyards and hoisting signals (we had to learn quickly the flags of the International Code of Signals), writing down messages being received by lamp by the Officer of the Watch and keeping a look-out. This meant standing in the 'at ease' position – no slouching or leaning – and keeping a look-out for mines, torpedoes, periscopes and aircraft etc. During my first spell on watch I was in danger of letting my imagination run riot, seeing a periscope every time a wave broke and had to watch that I did not make any silly reports.

When the convoy had assembled it made an impressive sight. The ships had formed up in several columns with the Commodore of the convoy at the head of the centre column. The leaders of the other columns kept station on the Commodore and ships in column kept station on the ship ahead. I was to learn of the strain imposed on the Captains and Officers of the Watch on merchant ships when keeping station in convoy. Unlike Naval vessels merchant ships were not easy to manoeuvre and their engine controls were not designed to provide for small increases or decreases in speed, so that close co-operation and understanding was necessary between the engineroom and bridge to arrive at, and maintain, the exact engine revolutions required to stay in station.

At night there was only a small blue light at the stern of the vessel ahead, which in poor visibility towed a fog buoy astern, to indicate its position. There was often a zig-zag pattern to follow which required all ships to turn simultaneously on to each leg to maintain formation and avoid collision. All this was made more difficult in rough and stormy weather.

When zig-zagging the time to turn on to each leg was indicated by a bell ringing in a clock which had been pre-set for the pattern in use. One night the bell mechanism broke down and I had to spend three hours watching the minute hand creep slowly round, in order to make sure that I did not miss the exact moment it came into line with the marker which indicated the time to turn. I thought the watch would never end and it seemed to me, at that time, that my four years apprenticeship was going to be a long time in passing.

The officers did not mix with the passengers socially as was allowed, and was sometimes compulsory, in other companies. The Deck Officers, Cadets and Senior Engineer Officers dined in the first class saloon with the passengers, the rest of the Engineers had a working mess next to their accommodation.

The food was excellent, a three course breakfast with all the trimmings and five courses at lunch and dinner. Each officer had a steward to clean the cabin and to bring tea in the morning, during the forenoon and afternoon, also water in the morning for shaving. There was no running water in the cabins and only sea-water in the bathrooms where a bath could be taken using salt-water soap. During the night watches a steward would bring tea or coffee and toast to the bridge for the officers on watch.

We Cadets kept very much to ourselves and were not asked, and did not expect, to mix socially with our seniors who were always addressed as 'Sir.' It had not been necessary to give us instruction on this matter – in those days it came naturally having been taught at school. Although stewards brought us tea, etc. we were responsible for cleaning our cabins and one of the first things I was taught was to make up my bunk in the regulation manner which would have satisfied a hospital matron.

From Gibraltar we proceeded independently to Malta where we had a short stay with no shore leave. Several units of the Mediterranean Fleet were in harbour and I felt a tinge of regret when I saw the picket boats and barges plying between the various ships and the shore. However it soon passed as I settled into our new routine. We were looking forward to arrival at Port Said and the passage through the Suez canal.

Chapter 4

TO INDIA AND BACK

———

After the ship left Gibraltar and proceeded independently the Cadets were taken off bridge watches and put on day work which we all preferred because, apart from anything else, it meant that we had 'all night in' and did not have to get up in the middle of the night to go on watch.

We turned to at six a.m. in working gear and Angus, having already reported to the Chief Officer for orders, would give out the jobs to be done. At eight o'clock we had to change into uniform (after Port Said this meant full whites – tunic, trousers and shoes) to go to the saloon for breakfast after which we changed back into working gear. At about half past ten the steward would bring tea, or a pint of fresh lime juice in hot weather, and at twelve o'clock we changed back into uniform for lunch.

We were fortunate to be given the afternoons off for study and signalling instruction from the Second Officer, who rigged up a bulb in a cigarette tin and connected it to a morse key. There were no correspondence courses for Companies to monitor to keep track of a Cadet's progress or application, and many expected the Cadets to do all studying in their own time. I made good use of the navigation book I had bought and found that, with the spherical trigonometry that I had learned at school, I was able to work through the book by the end of the voyage.

I enjoyed day-work, being out on deck in the sun and salt air clambering in and out of boats, climbing sampson posts or masts, painting and greasing and usually covered in both. In white crew ships it was the practice for Cadets to work with the crew but with Indian crew we were given separate jobs to do and worked by ourselves. There was a great deal to learn and it was a case of keeping the eyes open and watching what was going on around me, and not being afraid to ask questions for fear of being asked the inevitable, "how long have you been at sea?"

And so I began to learn the basic skills and to do the variety of jobs that are required of a sailor and all of which come under the heading of seamanship. It is an old adage that a seaman does not need to be a navigator but a navigator must be a seaman.

The guns' crews were drawn from the Cadets, Junior Engineers and the British ratings. From the outset of the voyage the Marine gunner carried out training exercises several times a week when we would be made to perform the duties carried out by the various members of a gun's crew, such as layer, trainer, breech-worker, loader, sight-setter etc. This all stood me in good stead when I eventually went to the Gunnery School at Chatham during my naval training.

The ready-use ammunition for both guns was kept in lockers and shell racks on the gun deck, and before entering port it had to be taken down to the magazine for safe stowage whilst the ship was in harbour. This job was given to the Cadets and it was not one that we looked forward to. The 4 inch shells alone weighed about 40 pounds and there were a lot to be transferred by hand. However it all helped to develop our muscles and did not take the edge off our pleasure at the prospect of a possible run ashore.

Port Said was my first introduction to the East and little did I realise that, later in the war, I would spend over two and a half years in ships operating in the area. The scene was one of bustle, colour and noise. There were many ships at the buoys and landing stages along the water-front which teemed with people of every colour and nationality, engaged in business or shopping in the many stores. I had my first sight of Simon Artz, the local Harrods, which had a well-known reputation for stocking anything from a needle to an anchor.

The harbour was alive with small craft. I was particularly attracted by the smart launches of the shipping agents, port officials and pilots with their heavily varnished wood work, brass fittings and canopies. The pilots were quite a sight sitting aloof in their wicker chairs at the stem of the launch, seemingly very much masters of all they surveyed. It was hard to keep one's mind on the mooring operation with so much of interest going on round about.

No sooner had we moored in our berth than the bum-boats were alongside to do business with the passengers who lined the ship's side. I had been warned about buying souvenirs as much of the stuff was made in Birmingham; not for nothing had we been known as the workshop of the world. However I had no intention of wasting what money I had on what appeared to be mainly rubbish. Some of the bum-boatmen managed to get onboard and, like all first trippers, we found ourselves being pestered to buy 'dirty pictures' and 'Lady Chatterley's Lover.' The hawkers were not slow to spot the new boys. Like all first trippers we had a look at the pictures, searched the book for the juicy bits that we had heard about and then told the hawkers to "imshi," the first word that had to be learned in Egypt. It was then that I experienced the legendary persistence of the eastern trader. They would just not take no for an answer. It was not difficult to understand why, in their frustration, travellers sometimes treated them in a rough and peremptory manner. Angus soon got rid of them.

The Canal Pilots were mainly British and French. The ships proceeded through the canal as soon as they arrived in port or whenever they were ready to sail, as opposed to the later practice of proceeding in convoys which left at stated times from both ends of the canal. It was a very pleasant passage with the barren desert on one hand and the cultivated fields on the other where there was always something of interest taking place. I could not help feeling sorry for the little donkeys as they plodded round and round, turning the wheels that supplied water to the irrigation ditches, or the ones that could be seen carrying the big, fat farmers being followed home on foot by their wives.

Ismailia, a small town on the canal on the way to Suez, had a French hospital which was well-known in the area and an imposing memorial of the 1914-1918 war. I was to remember this first transit when I passed through the canal some 36 years later. Then, the land on either side could not be seen because of large earth-works constructed during the Arab-Israeli wars and Ismailia, the hospital, war memorial and the town of Suez had all been laid waste during the fighting.

I saw my first shark whilst we were at anchor at Suez. I was painting a lifebuoy on the poop when I happened to glance over the stem and saw two very large grey fish in the water directly below me. I got quite a surprise at the size of them and instinctively made sure I had a good grip of the rail before looking over to have another look.

After leaving Suez we called at Aden where we had to discharge cargo. I was down one of the holds giving a hand to discharge an ambulance; the space was very confined and not a great deal of room to move around. I wanted to get past one of the labourers – a Somali – and put my hands on the small of his back to push him away as I eased past. He turned round quickly and stared at me. He was straight out of Kipling, fuzzy hair, hooked nose and piercing black eyes; his father was probably one of the chaps who broke a British square. Bending down he turned again and pointed to his backside saying "you want?" I was out of the hatch without touching the ladder. I had heard vaguely about that sort of thing in schoolboy talk but found it hard to believe it actually went on. And so my education progressed.

A friend of the family, who was a Sub-Lieutenant in the RNVR, came on board and received permission to take me ashore where I saw the large wells named after the Queen of Sheba and a ship-yard, said to be the oldest in the world, where dhows were still built in the same way and to the same design as they had been for centuries. Later, whilst having tea in the mess, I was shown a beautiful example of Arab craftsmanship in the shape of a dagger with a silver handle and scabbard richly decorated with semi-precious stones, which had been bought from a desert tribesman. That was the type of souvenir I would have valued.

During the passage from Aden to Colombo an incident occurred which illustrated something of the Brotherhood of the Sea. Not far from the Island of Socotra a dhow was sighted showing distress signals, so course was altered to close and the ship stopped to allow the dhow to come alongside. On board were several natives who all appeared to be the worse for wear. It seemed that they had been becalmed for nearly 14 days and were practically out of food and water and had no firewood for the cooking stove. Their goatskins were filled with water and they were supplied with rice and other provisions whilst some old bunk boards and dunnage was broken up to supply them with firewood.

It was an interesting interlude and provided the passengers with a spot of drama. Later I was told that dhows sometimes made a practice of stopping ships, and pleading poverty and distress in order to obtain goods that would be sold when they reached port. However in our case they were definitely in need.

In Colombo we met the first troop convoy taking Australian troops to the Middle East and amongst the troopships was the Company ship *Dilwara*, my old cruise ship now engaged in her proper role. The decks were filled with bronzed, crew-cut, tough-looking Aussies in blue singlets and we heard that the ship had been out of beer for some time, a state of affairs that had not gone down well with the troops. When we went ashore we saw how they set out to enjoy themselves by commandeering gharries and racing each other up and down the wide streets.

The Grand Oriental Hotel which we visited was one of the top hotels in the East and we were dressed in our full whites and on our best behaviour when we went in for pints of fresh lime juice. The spacious rooms with their high ceilings, whirring fans and smart, polite and attentive servants combined with the general decorum of the other people present, gave me a brief insight into the high standards enjoyed by people who lived and worked in the East.

Our next port of call was Madras where I was finally kitted out with my white uniform. It was only a short stay and we did not go ashore. There was a similar short stay at Vizagapatam before we proceeded to our final destination – Calcutta.

The pilot station for Calcutta was at Sandheads at the mouth of the Hooghly river. In those days in India a Hooghly pilot was a 'Burra Sahib,' a top official and entitled to membership of the class 'A' clubs. When he boarded he was accompanied by his own servants, a bearer and a bhandary, and he struck me as having a rather imperious manner and that he would be hard on his inferiors. This was borne out in a later incident when he practically threw his bearer down the bridge ladder when he forgot to bring sugar with the tea.

Considerable knowledge and skill was required in piloting a vessel in the Hooghly River. The swift flowing river brought down great quantities of silt which caused frequent changes in the navigable channels. It was the expertise of the Hooghly pilots in knowing the vagaries of the river, and just how far they could go in driving vessels through the mud to keep the channels clear, that was the main reason for their superior status.

It took a couple of days to go up the river as we anchored during the hours of darkness – all very leisurely. As with all rivers it was full of interest, either with regard to the scenery and activities along the bank or in the various types of native craft plying to and fro. It was rather disconcerting to see the many animal carcases and the odd human body floating past as we steamed along.

At Calcutta the ship berthed in the Kidderpore Dock and cargo operations were started immediately, and continued round the clock whilst we were in port. The Chief and Third Officers and Cadets worked during the day whilst the Second Officer traditionally kept the night cargo watch.

We had been carrying a general cargo and I was able to see how the various goods and containers were handled. I suppose it was what might be called a text book cargo, it included steel rails, barrels, bales, sacks and packing cases. When the labourers boarded to begin discharge I was rather amused at the proprietorial attitude of the ones who operated the steam cargo winches. They set about rigging a canopy of dunnage matting to keep off the sun, fitted a piece of wood across the steam control handle to make for a more comfortable grip and generally got themselves settled before beginning work. The rattling noise of the steam winches as they hoisted the slings in and out of the hatches was known as the Clark-Chapman Symphony, the conductor being the hatchman who stood at the hatch coaming directing operations.

When the cargo had been discharged and the holds were empty, I was given the job of cleaning out the rose boxes in the bilges and helping to prepare the hold for loading. It was just as well that I was given these and other jobs to do, as it was the last time I was to have anything to do with general cargo work.

During the discharge we had a stroke of luck when we found that a large crate which had been damaged contained boxes of 'Outdoor Girl' face powder a popular cosmetic. The damaged goods were retrieved and taken to the dance at the Marine Club which was held every Saturday night, and we were an instant hit with the popsies when they found what we had to give away. These dances which were fairly formal affairs were for Officers and Cadets only and many of the girls were accompanied by their parents or chaperoned in some way.

The ship was in Calcutta for about six days and we were given the opportunity to go ashore and see something of the city. It was something of a shock to see a little girl of about ten years old with both arms taken off at the shoulders so that she could beg when she grew up, and there were so many other beggars with gross deformities. I found myself wondering what went through the minds of these people, and the pitiful labourers in their solitary loin cloths, when they saw other people so much better off with food and clothes and somewhere to rest their heads. It was hard to realise that many just slept in any corner they could find and that it was common for bodies to be found every morning under a bundle of dirty rags.

I enjoyed the bustle and colour of the city; and such sights as cows wandering about in the streets, the snake charmers giving a performance and a funeral where the procession included an elephant. I had a general feeling of adventure and of being out in the world and I knew I had picked the right career.

The return voyage home was made via Capetown, probably because of the situation in France. We arrived in Capetown in time to hear of the French capitulation and we thought the invasion of the UK was imminent. A rumour that the Second Officer had gone ashore to collect charts for America did nothing to dispel the feeling that we might not get home.

There was a supernumary Chief Officer onboard taking passage to the UK for leave and he suggested a competition amongst the cadets to see who could heave the lead the furthest distance. We had been having a spot of practice whilst at anchor. The lead itself weighed about 22 lbs and had a hole in the bottom into which tallow was inserted to obtain a sample of the sea bottom. The line was marked at various intervals with pieces of coloured cloth, rope and leather up to a length of about 120 feet. The operation was carried out from a small platform (called the chains) which folded out from the ship's side. The method was to swing the lead back and forward like a pendulum, at the same time lengthening the line little by little, then swinging it in a complete circle a couple of times before letting it go in a forward direction, so that it entered the water as far ahead as possible. In a moving ship the depth of water was obtained when the line was perpendicular and the lead could be felt hitting the sea bottom. It required skill to heave the lead and Bishop and myself had to take care that we did not land it on the deck amongst the onlookers.

The Chief Officer put up five shillings for the winner so we decided to have a party. Cadets were not allowed to buy beer or spirits so a Junior Engineer was asked to get us a bottle of gin and we supplied the lime juice. We had managed to go all the way to Calcutta without bothering about drinking but we had an excuse of sorts, we didn't know what the future held for us or if we would even get home. The officers too were drowning their sorrows.

I was to regret my father's advice, "if you must drink, stick to the beer and leave spirits alone!" I was 'under the weather' for the first time and I did not enjoy it – looping the loop backwards whenever I went to lie down.

We sailed independently from Capetown to Freetown in West Africa where we would join a convoy for the final leg of the passage home. Apart from the menace of submarine attack there was also the possibility of meeting up with an enemy surface raider so an extra sharp look-out was enforced and a watch was also kept from the gun platform. It was with considerable relief that we arrived safely and without incident at our destination.

When we finally sailed from Freetown it was found that the ship was having difficulty in maintaining convoy speed and it looked as though the Captain, eager to progress the voyage, had joined the fast convoy. We were eventually given the position of last ship in a column where we struggled to keep up with the rest of the ships. Once or twice the convoy had to slow down to allow ourselves and other stragglers to catch up.

Stragglers were a constant source of worry and caused considerable problems for the escort commander as the safety of the convoy depended on the ships maintaining a close formation so that the escorts could form a tight defensive screen around it. Stragglers dropping outside the screen could be picked off easily after the convoy had passed if the presence of the escorts prevented the main body being attacked. So we were not very popular with the escort commander and several times a destroyer came alongside and gave us a polite 'rocket' and exhorted us to close up and maintain position. As I looked at the destroyer with envy I did not realise that I was to have plenty of experience in the future of 'rocketing' and 'exhorting' when serving in corvettes on convoy duty.

We arrived in Liverpool about the middle of June and after the Marine Superintendent came onboard we were told that we could go home on leave for a week or so. Angus had nowhere to go as the Channel Islands had been occupied and his sister was nursing in one of the big London Hospitals, so I asked him to come home with me.

On returning to Liverpool after our leave had expired we were appointed to different ships. Angus joined the SS *Aska* one of the company's latest ships which had been on the Calcutta-Rangoon mail run before the war and was now to be employed in taking French troops, who had been evacuated at Dunkirk and who wanted to return home when given the choice, back to France. Shortly after he joined, the ship was bombed in the night and set on fire. Angus managed to slide down a rope to a lifeboat filled with French soldiers and they were adrift for two days before being picked up by a fishing boat which took them to Adrossan. There he was given five shillings, a scarf and a travel warrant and sent on his way. He made his way to Edinburgh and arrived at my home in the same state as he had got out of the lifeboat and already showing signs of delayed shock.

Angus stayed with my parents for about three months before he was fit to go back to sea and he was very grateful for the way they had looked after him and more or less taken him into the family. His father owned a large china shop in St. Helier and Mother was told that she would receive the finest dinner service after the war. Sadly he did not keep in touch for very long and, after the war, when friends on holiday in St. Helier inquired after him, his father said that he had become a wanderer and that even he was not sure of his whereabouts.

I had been appointed to the SS *Kenya* and when I arrived at the dock and saw the landing craft hanging from her boat davits I had a feeling of excitement and anticipation. It was apparent that I was not joining an ordinary merchant ship but one that was going to be engaged in a naval operation, and immediately I had hopes of being in charge of a landing craft. I could not have asked for a more suitable appointment to bring me closer to the service I had wanted to join and it seemed as though fate was playing a part in helping me to achieve my ambition.

Chapter 5

SS *Kenya* – Operation Menace

––––

The SS *Kenya* and her sister ship *Karanja* were two of the largest and latest ships in the company, being 10,000 tons and only three years old. They were designed to carry passengers on the Bombay to East Africa run and their spacious decks, which were used by the Indian deck passengers, their speed of 18 knots and electric winches for operating their lifeboats made them ideal ships for carrying troops and landing craft. They had been commandeered by the Admiralty to be converted to infantry assault ships and were in the process of being equipped for an operation at Dakar, West Africa. The destination was not known until after we had sailed.

There was one senior Cadet named Williams already onboard, and later another first tripper, Gus McNaughton, joined the ship for his first trip to sea. As I had been to sea for several months I would be senior to him and no longer junior boy. I had learned quickly that seniority was an important matter in my profession and counted a great deal in promotions and appointments, and when a question arose as to who should take charge. Officers who had been in the cadet-ships and in the Company for a long time all seemed to know each others position on the ladder and I noticed in *Mulbera* that, when entering port and passing a Company ship, the Captain always seemed to know which ship should dip the ensign first as being the junior officer.

The first unit to join the ship was the naval party which was to be responsible for manning the landing craft. They were under the command of Commander AH. Alexander RN and Lieutenant Paget RNVR Lieutenant Paget, a well-known barrister, was the brother of Dorothy Paget the famous owner of racehorses. Paget was a very nice chap but I think some of the sailors took him to be a bit of a softie. There was much amusement when he made enquiries about obtaining an insurance hawser, after being told that one would be required when the question of securing the landing craft in bad weather was being discussed. An insurance hawser was a wire rope of 6 inches circumference carried by ships in case they had to be towed. I was to meet Commander Alexander again on two occasions – when he was Naval Officer-in-Charge of Tobruk after it was re-captured following the Battle of Alamein, and subsequently when he was in command of the old battleship HMS *Centurion*, a radio controlled target ship, being used in a decoy role.

SS Kenya.
Photograph courtesy of the Imperial War Museum, London (neg. 8145).

The assault troops turned out to be the 2nd Battalion of the Royal Marines, the 5th Battalion going on board *Karanja*. I was very impressed as they came onboard with their equipment, the vast majority were regulars or reservists and their discipline and smart, confident bearing confirmed all that I had read about them. The commanding officer of the Marines was Lieutenant Colonel Williams who was to be very kind to Gus and myself in the months to come.

As the ship was no longer an ordinary merchantman I found our duties, and the work we were given to do, somewhat different to the *Mulbera*. At this stage of the war in ships carrying troops, the ship's officers had to liase and work with the officer commanding the regiment or the senior military, naval or air officer onboard, with regard to all administrative matters concerning the troops, e.g. accommodation allocation, victualling, posting look-outs, guns crews and inspections. This became the Chief Officer's responsibility and we Cadets became his assistants or, to quote a naval term given to Midshipmen, his 'doggies.' We had to show the troops to their allocated spaces on the mess-decks, issue hammocks and do rounds of the accommodation spaces, to mention a few the activities which brought us into contact with the Marines. In later years each troop-ship carried a permanent military staff who were responsible for all administrative matters concerning the troops onboard, thus relieving the ship's officers and any Service officers taking passage, regardless of rank, of any duty or responsibility except for disciplinary or domestic matters affecting their own particular unit.

We spent a great deal of time in the ship's life-boats, which in addition to the landing craft were also to be used for landing troops, checking and overhauling equipment to ensure it was in first class condition in case of emergency. It was not unknown during the war for dock workers to steal the tinned milk and provisions from ships' boats – a heartless and criminal act when the lives of seamen depended on them.

The boats were more like small barges each carrying 90 persons, ten boats double banked on each side of the ship. Two had been replaced by motor launches from a passenger liner to supplement our two motor boats as a means of towing the lifeboats. Water was to be carried ashore in petrol cans that were painted white and the petrol in cans painted red. In retrospect the arrangements seem primitive for a combined operation but that may have been due to an acute shortage of material and equipment after Dunkirk and insufficient experience of the type of operation which had been planned. When we eventually returned home and went to the Combined Operations Headquarters at Inverary, we were to find that landing troops had become a specialized operation.

We sailed from Liverpool for Scapa Flow where we stayed for several days before leaving on the 31st August 1940 to rendezvous with the rest of the expedition which, in addition to the *Karanja*, consisted of the *Westernland* (with De Gaulle on board), 'Penniand' carrying French troops, many of them Legionaires, and *Sobieski* and *Batory*, carrying Polish troops and the remainder of the British force. We had been told that the expedition was bound for Dakar, a French port in West Africa, where General De Gaulle would attempt to persuade the authorities to join the Allies instead of the Vichy government in France.

The voyage was fairly uneventful except for news that one of the escorting cruisers, HMS *Fiji*, had been torpedoed and had been forced to turn back, and the need for several burials at sea from the Dutch ships; the results of frequent outbreaks of fighting amongst the Legionaires. A naval signalman who transferred from one of these ships told how the Foreign Legion was a rough, tough outfit where men would pull out knives in an argument and use them without hesitation. He had landed himself in trouble and had been transferred because he had accidentally shot somebody whilst cleaning, or playing around with, a revolver.

During the voyage I gradually became acquainted with many of the marines and sailors whilst going about my duties and during rounds of the messdecks in the night watches. I was keen to get hold of a real naval duffel coat and I managed to get one through a bit of bartering with a Marine corporal. A Junior Engineer sold me a bottle of whisky for five shillings which I exchanged for the coat. The corporal's name was Andrews and he had quite an interesting story to tell. Before the war he was the Navy middle-weight boxing champion and in 1939 he was serving in HMS *Glasgow* which escorted King George and Queen Elizabeth during their visit to Canada and the United States. He deserted his ship in America and became a professional boxer and was doing very well until war broke out. When he heard that war had been declared he immediately surrendered himself to the police in Portland, Maine, and was returned to the UK. Instead of being court-martialled and punished on his return, the authorities considered that in his conduct in reporting immediately for duty, and his success whilst boxing, he had upheld the honour of the Corps and that it would be a waste of a good man to send him to detention when he was most needed.

The expedition stayed in Freetown for several days before proceeding to Dakar, arriving off the port on the morning of the 23rd September in a thick, damp tropical fog which had everything soaked in its dripping wetness. With the poor visibility it was difficult to see what was going on around us. There were several air-raid warnings, and in the late forenoon we came under shell-fire from the shore batteries which was answered by the warships covering the operation. Later that day we had to steam at full speed out to sea to avoid two French cruisers which were reported to have broken out from Dakar.

Next morning heavy gun-fire was heard well to the north of where we were cruising awaiting developments which indicated that the fleet was bombarding the port, but we had little idea of how the operation was progressing. Later we heard that during this action the battleship Barham had been hit four times with only slight damage, and the previous day the cruiser Cumberland had been hit and forced to retire, also two destroyers had been slightly damaged.

On the 25th September the transports were ordered to sail south and by the morning of the 27th we were back in Freetown. Later the battleship *Resolution* which had been torpedoed by a submarine on the 25th, arrived in Freetown under tow by the *Barham*.

There was little information given out as to what had gone wrong to cause the operation to be abandoned. We heard that De Gaulle's emissaries failed in their attempt to rally the Vichy authorities and that they had narrowly avoided arrest, being shot at and wounded as they made their escape. Also, the advantage of the fleet in gun power, which should have enabled it to pound the port well out of range of shore batteries, was much reduced by the presence of the new French battleship *Richelieu* whose 15 inch guns matched those of the *Barham* and *Resolution*. The late arrival in Dakar of a squadron of the latest French cruisers, which had left Toulon and had been allowed to pass through the Straits of Gibraltar, had been an unexpected set-back and may also have had an influence on the decision to withdraw.

Freetown was the main naval base in West Africa, and the extensive anchorage a port of call for all the troop convoys going to, and returning from, the Middle and Far East. We were anchored in the middle of the anchorage and remained there until January 1941, during which time I saw practically all the large passenger liners belonging to the well-known British companies in addition to several foreign ships belonging to the Allies, or which had been captured from the enemy. I went onboard the *Viceroy of India*, the flagship of the P&O fleet, and the first turbo-electric liner, also the Cap *Norte*, a German liner which was being operated by our company, and saw the magnificent painting of the North Cape which hung above her main staircase. The *Andes* of the Royal Mail line came in on her second voyage, she had just been built and had not completed fitting out for her peace-time role as a liner. The French liner *Pasteur* was easily recognized by her very large funnel. All the ships were painted grey and it became an interesting pastime trying to identify them as they steamed into the anchorage.

As it became obvious that the ship was going to be in Freetown for some time it was decided to use one of our motor life-boats as a liberty boat and for visiting Company ships which happened to be passing through. Merchant ship life-boats were designed for life-saving and not for every day use, and the average Merchant Navy Officer had little small boat experience compared to the Naval Officer whose first taste of responsibility was as Midshipman in charge of a picket-boat, barge or whaler. All the Senior Officers turned out to see the boat being lowered and I hoped that Gus and myself would be allowed to take it away. We were deeply disappointed when the Second Officer (Master's Certificate) and the Second Engineer (Chief Engineer's Certificate) were put in charge of the boat and its engine.

Whilst at the jetty during their first run to shore the steam picket-boat from the *Resolution* came alongside under the command of a Midshipman. That seemed to be enough for our senior officers. When they returned to the ship we were told that we would be in charge of the boat with a Junior Engineer on the engine.

The ship's officers were keeping anchor watches and I was put on watch with the Second Officer keeping the 12 to 4 watch; it was a most unpopular watch as there was no possibility of an afternoon 'zizz' or more than 4 hours uninterrupted sleep. Marine signalmen kept bridge watches and as we were positioned in the middle of the anchorage they were kept occupied as a relay station between the shore and other ships at anchor. Mead, Reid, Bendilow and Varley were the senior signalmen and I spent a lot of time in their company whilst on watch, receiving valuable experience when helping them in their duties. I enjoyed the night watches when there was little signal traffic and the time was passed listening to them spinning yarns about their experiences and adventures. Some thirty five years later my ship was in Whangarei, New Zealand, discharging crude oil to the refinery and a port official came onboard with papers requiring my signature. When he told me he came from Portsmouth, I asked if he had been in the Navy and he told me he had been a Royal Marine. When I told him where I had met the four signalmen it transpired he also had been a signalman in the *Kenya* and remembered the two cadets. For a short spell it was 'old home week.' Bendilow at that time was President of the Royal Marine Association.

There was not a great deal to do ashore in Freetown. There was an open-air swimming pool in an army establishment which we were allowed to use and sometimes we would see a film in a local hall which passed as a cinema. It was quite a sight to see the locals crowding around the entrance waving their tickets and all trying to get in at the same time. The order of entry appeared to be decided by the action of the door-keeper who would reach out and grab an arm holding a ticket and yank the attached body inside the door. Europeans entered by a side door and sat in a small balcony. Before the show started fire precautions were observed by the presence of two locals equipped with buckets of water and sand, who solemnly entered and took their seats at the front of the balcony. It was pleasant to go ashore and walk about the town looking at the native stalls and getting some idea of their way of life and culture. Fruit was very cheap with a large bunch of bananas costing only a shilling.

During our first visit to Lumley Beach Gus suffered a very bad dose of sunburn. He had been lying on his stomach and had dozed off, exposing his fair skin to the burning sun which resulted in a blister which completely covered his back from neck to waist, and left him in considerable pain and discomfort for some days. He received an imperial rocket from Mr. Bunn, the Chief Officer, who was responsible for his well-being. However the incident did bring home the need to guard against over exposure to the extreme heat of the sun. There was a great deal of malaria in the area – at that time it still had the reputation of being the white man's grave – and everybody on board had to take a daily dose of anti-malaria tablets. The hospital ship *Somersetshire* was stationed in the anchorage and at one time the marines were being transferred to her at the rate of twenty a day.

On one occasion I also received an imperial rocket; this time from a Marine sergeant. I was on Lumley Beach with a group of Marines which included a dispatch rider who had been riding his bike up and down the beach. When I asked the sergeant if I could have a ride on the bike he naturally asked me if I had been on a bike before. I told him I had, but what I did not tell him was that it was only on the pillion of my chum's bike and that I had never actually driven one. I had seen George drive his bike many times and I thought I would be able to handle the controls. I started off down the beach quite successfully and changed into top gear. When the time came to turn around I did change down, but I was going too fast when I started to turn and I ran out of beach finishing up in the South Atlantic with water up to the petrol tank. The sergeant was not amused and made his feelings known in a most emphatic manner.

From time to time the Sergeants' Mess would have a sing song and Gus and I were allowed to attend. I thoroughly enjoyed these evenings which were very well conducted; nobody was ever out of order and the words of the songs which were usually sung to well-known tunes, although often blue, were sometimes extremely funny. By the time I parted from the Marines I had quite a repertoire of party pieces.

I was doing rounds one evening when I came across a group of men standing around the bottom of the staircase leading up to the Sergeants' mess. Standing on the staircase were the two Marine buglers, one with a guitar and the other with a trumpet, who had just started to sing *Frankie and Johnnie*, the guitarist singing the words and the muted trumpet coming in at the appropriate time. The singer used exaggerated Cockney and American accents in different places when telling the story, the words of which had been slightly altered. All in all the setting and presentation were worthy of a scene from a film.

The two buglers, one short and stout the other tall and lean, had been the buglers in the Royal Yacht at the outbreak of war and they could practically make their bugles speak. When we eventually called at Gibraltar on the way home Force H was in port (the battleships *Nelson*, *Rodney*, etc.) and we could feel all eyes on our ship as our two buglers harmonised when playing Sunset at the ceremony when all ensigns are lowered at the end of the day.

I saw my first Service entertainment when the Marines put on a show at Christmas. The programme lasted for well over an hour with a variety of turns all of a very good standard. Lieutenant Devereaux, who had a very fine voice, sang the *The Soldiers Farewell* from *The White Horse Inn*. We were all amazed to see a beautiful blonde woman appear before us and after her performance there was a great deal of speculation as to where she had come from, nobody had seen her come on board. 'She' turned out to be a Marine who had been the understudy to Douglas Byng, the foremost female impersonator on the London stage.

The performance I enjoyed most was a parody of Captains Defaulters, the procedure where men on a charge are brought before the Commanding Officer for investigation and, if appropriate, punishment. It was very slick and well-timed with the words being sung to well-known operatic arias. Each defaulter was marched on, the charge made, The Captain asking if he had anything to say, the defendant giving his excuse, the Captain giving out the punishment, the defendant's opinion of the Captain and *vice versa*, the defendant being marched off to Laurel and Hardy's signature tune, to be quickly followed by the next defaulter.

With the abandonment of the operation the other troop-ships had left Freetown at different intervals, to return home or go to another theatre of operations, until only *Kenya* remained of the original force. During the four months at anchor (we had steamed round the anchorage several times in an attempt to keep the barnacles down) there had been very few, if any, 'buzzes' regarding our movements or what was being planned for the Battalion. However, at the beginning of January 1941 orders arrived for the Battalion to return to the UK and so, with considerable excitement and anticipation, the ship prepared to return home.

Chapter 6

HOME TO THE CLYDE

———

Before leaving harbour the live-stock had to be rounded up. Several monkeys had been brought on board during our stay and had happily taken up residence in and around the life-boats. For several reasons it was impossible to take them with us and they were put to sleep by the doctor.

A few nights before departure several Marine Officers carried out a well organized raid on the Freetown Golf Club when they 'cut out' a small brass cannon which was positioned at the doorway and brought it back on board. The general idea was to fire a farewell salute as they sailed out of Freetown harbour. Everyone on board knew about the 'prize' and all hands were on deck to see the firing of the salute. From the bridge we could see the Marines busy around the cannon which was mounted on the port side of the forecastle, loading it with a charge of powder said to have come from small arms cartridges, and making ready to fire as we left the anchorage. At the right moment the Marine's Medical Officer, who had been the leader of the cutting out party, fired the cannon but there was no bang nor did the cannon blow up as some had predicted. All that was heard was a bit of a hiss and a splutter which reduced the firing party to fits of laughter. The Marines intended to give the cannon to the St. Andrews Golf Club but for some reason or other they failed to take it with them when they disembarked. The cannon was still on board when I left the ship and I never found out its final destination. One of the cutting out party, Lieutenant Wakeling RM, subsequently became the Bishop of Southwell.

On the way to the UK a call was made at Gibraltar where the ship was put into dry-dock to have the bottom scraped. After such a long period at anchor the barnacles and marine growth on the hull were having a considerable effect on the ship's speed, reducing it by nearly two knots. The Marines were turned-to on the job, they worked alongside the dockyard labour and an element of competition was introduced to speed up the work.

Whilst in Freetown there had been little opportunity for sport and so I was delighted when I was given the opportunity for a game of rugby with the Marines. I had always carried my kit in case the opportunity should ever arise. It was my first game since leaving school nearly a year before but I found that I was not too rusty. The playing pitch was a bit rough, a mixture of grass and cinders with the odd piece of broken glass to be seen glinting in the sun but it was not allowed to spoil our game.

The passage from Gibraltar to the Clyde was uneventful except for extremely bad weather which may have helped to protect the convoy from enemy attacks. I had my first experience of really wild and stormy weather when we ran into the tail end of a hurricane which struck Lisbon and sank the flying boat *Clare* at its moorings in the harbour. I was pleased to note at the time that I stood up to the conditions and, being unaffected by the violent movements of the ship in the heavy seas, thought myself a real sailor.

On arrival in the Clyde the ship anchored at the Tail of the Bank where the Marines and naval party disembarked. I was sorry to see them go as I had made many friends amongst them, especially the Sergeants. About six years later, when I was playing rugby for United Services against the Marines at Eastney barracks, I unexpectedly came face to face with one of the Colour Sergeants as we arose from a ruck. When he saw me he said, "Good God, Jock, what are you doing here?" "I am in the Navy," I replied rather proudly, adding, "I am a Lieutenant now." At the end of the match we had a few beers and did a spot of reminiscing before he put me in a taxi back to my camp.

There was some delay whilst the authorities decided what to do with the ship and during this time my parents took the opportunity to pay a visit and bring me a portable radio; something which was much prized and which few Cadets possessed. Private radios could not be operated at sea but in port they provided much entertainment especially when there was little shore leave. I took the boat into Gourock Pier to bring them out to the ship. The sea was quite choppy and they got a bit of a 'heave' on the way out. Then of course the inevitable happened; the engine conked out and they found themselves bobbing around in the middle of the ocean. I saw my father looking at me and probably wondering if his son knew what to do next. His son was praying that the Fifth Engineer knew the answer, motor life-boat engines were not designed for hard and continuous running and this one could be temperamental. The engineer opened the casing and looked inside, fiddled with one or two things before taking up a hammer and giving the engine a couple of whacks, and then swung the starting handle a couple of times. Off she started and we proceeded on our way.

The Chief Engineer lived in Gourock and the ship's boat would sometimes be used to take him ashore. On one occasion the weather deteriorated as we were returning to the ship and it was decided to hoist the boat under the davits, clear of the water, as a safety measure. On arriving under the davits the sea was so rough that the movement of the boat made it very difficult to hook on the falls, and the engineer doubted whether he could keep the engine running much longer. It was therefore decided that the boat should be taken round to the entry port and secured there for the night with good ropes fore and aft. The engine lasted long enough for this to be accomplished and then the 'Fiver' and I were glad to get inboard out of the weather.

Next morning there was a flap on; the boat had disappeared during the night. The Fourth Officer, who was going on watch at 4 am, went back to sleep after he had acknowledged his call and the Officer who was on watch, believing the Fourth Officer to be awake, turned in without being properly relieved. It was never really established at what time the boat broke adrift, it may even have been stolen – it had been well secured and the weather had moderated somewhat – but the Fourth Officer seemed to carry the blame. He was a very nice chap named Francis Oliver Plunkett-Cole who had been to Dartmouth but did not want to carry on in the Navy at the end of his training. Instead he served his apprenticeship with the Canadian Pacific Line before joining BI. We all felt sorry for him when he was transferred to an old coalburning ship named the *Gogra* running between Bombay and the Persian Gulf, one of the worst appointments he could have been given.

Another boat was received from the P&O troopship *Ettrick* and I was delighted with it. It was much bigger than our old boat, diesel driven and with a steering wheel instead of a tiller. A bit of time was spent searching up and down the coast near our anchorage for the boat but it was never traced.

Transport to shore from the ships at anchor at the Tail of the Bank was provided by two brothers who operated two large motor launches from Gourock Pier. The launches called round the ships at anchor, putting off and taking on passengers. If a ship had people to go ashore flag 'R' was hoisted to attract attention, and they had to be ready to board when it came alongside as it would not wait. When going ashore I would stand at the gangway, all booted and spurred, for a couple of hours before the expected time to ensure that the boat was attracted to come alongside. It was this experience which, in future life, had me arriving well in advance for appointments, catching trains, etc. and left me with little patience for people who were late. In the Navy I heard a maxim from an old gunner's mate, "Them as is keen gets fell in previous!"

After a spell at anchor in the Gareloch word was received that our Indian crew were to be paid off and that their replacement by a British crew meant that the ship would have to proceed to Glasgow to have alterations made to the crew accommodation. We anchored at the Tail of the Bank preparatory to going up the river the following day and from the anchorage witnessed the first night of the Clydebank Blitz. The oil tanks at Dalmuir could be seen blazing in the distance and there was a dull glow over the north side of the river. There were one or two engineers from Glasgow on board and they were very worried about their families. When we docked in Glasgow the following day one chap found that his family had been bombed out and a relation killed. There was another raid that night when his family again suffered casualties. We stood to at 'stations' during the raid but, fortunately for us, we did not have much to do as Clydebank was again the target. From our berth we could see again the glow of the many fires and heard the terrible explosions of the bombing.

Whilst in Glasgow I was able to pursue my interest in dancing and became acquainted with some of the better class ballrooms in the city. Dancing and the cinema were the main recreations for service men and women during the war. A ballroom, with its warm friendly atmosphere, cheery and romantic music, was a good place to spend an evening improving one's dancing and, at the same time, making new friends. Many of the big dance bands visited Glasgow and performed at Green's Playhouse where I heard Ambrose and his Orchestra and Victor Sylvester, a well-known dancing teacher whose orchestra was noted for playing to a strict tempo. When I saw Sylvester he had just been found guilty of black market offences for dealing in commodities which were rationed.

When the alterations to the crew quarters had been completed we were ready to receive the new crew. Some of the Officers had only served with Indian crews and I think there was some apprehension as to how they would get on with a white crew, especially as the men had not been selected by the Captain which was the normal practice.

On the outbreak of war all merchant seamen were registered with the Merchant Shipping Establishment and ships requiring crews or replacements received them from pools of seamen in the major ports around the country. In major British companies with white crews the men often stayed with the same company, sometimes for many years, and continued to do so during the war providing the company had a ship for them. If for any reason they could not sail with the company of their choice they had to 'go on the Pool' and take whichever ship they were appointed to. They were allowed to refuse two ships but they had to take the third one that was offered.

From Glasgow we proceeded to the Combined Operations Headquarters which had been established at Inverary on Loch Fyne, under the command of Admiral of the Fleet Sir Roger Keyes VC. The Admiral had been awarded the Victoria Cross in World War 1 for his part in the combined operation which resulted in the blockade of Zeebrugge to prevent submarines from using the port. *Kenya* was to continue as an infantry assault ship and would be employed in training troops in landing operations. There were several other liners engaged in the same work and on one occasion the *Winchester Castle*, a Union Castle liner, had to take the drastic action of running her bows aground in order to avoid a collision with us. I heard later from someone who had been a Cadet on board at the time that all the troops had been sent down to the stem of the ship and told to jump up and down, in order to try and shake the bows free as the engines were put astern.

At Inverary it gradually became apparent that we had not been lucky with the new crew. The bosun was a Scot from the Isles and a good man, as were many of the sailors, but the engine room ratings and some of the stewards were a poor lot and we eventually had trouble with the former. Some of the stewards were gay and it was the first time that I had come into contact with effeminate men who painted themselves and put on women's clothes. I was to learn that in large passenger liners it was quite common for 'queens' to dress up in their quarters when they were off duty, and that they would quarrel and argue over boy-friends and other matters just like a bunch of women.

Different regiments came to the ship for training. The South Lancashire Fusiliers and the South Wales Borderers were two that I remember, especially the latter for their wonderful singing, and for the number of men with the same name which, on pay-day, resulted in men answering to 'Jones 8,' 'Davies 10' etc. Along with Gus I was kept busy helping the Chief Officer in liaising with the regimental officers, issuing and storing hammocks, doing 'rounds' and other duties about the ship.

During the landing exercises, when the ships would steam slowly in to Brodick Bay in Arran with the anchors practically on the bottom so that they did not make a racket when they were finally let go to anchor, Gus and myself were responsible for operating the brakes when the landing craft were being lowered. We had to ensure that they were lowered at an easy rate with no sudden stops or jerks and that they were not dropped into the water. When the craft were being hoisted after the exercise we had to guide the wire fails by hand on to the winch drums to ensure that there were no riding turns. These could result in the craft going down in a jerky and uneven manner the next time it was lowered. The exercises were often held at night and we put in long hours whilst they were going on, but I thoroughly enjoyed the work. The experience of being in close contact with soldiers and sailors and being able to witness the comradeship and *esprit de corps* that existed amongst them, was of considerable influence in my being convinced that I would enjoy the organized and disciplined life that a Service career would offer.

The first indication of the difference between an Indian and a white crew which affected Gus and myself came to light over the matter of refreshments during the night watches. It had been normal practice for us to go into the first class saloon where the night steward would serve us with either tea, coffee or cocoa, and toast or biscuits in the normal 1st class style, i.e. silver tray, teapot, etc. The first night I asked for tea the steward refused to serve me and said he wasn't there to serve 'bloody apprentices!' This was reported to the Chief Officer who took steps to ensure we were served in the future, but it did not go down well with the stewards and probably caused a bit of friction between the deck and catering departments.

As time went on there were indications of trouble amongst the crew and stories were heard of soup being poured over the cook and of a steward being assaulted with a broom handle. It became apparent that a group of engine-room ratings were more or less terrorising the rest of the crew and that, in the words of one officer, some of the dregs of the Glasgow and Liverpool pools had been sent to the ship. Men who, in peacetime, would have found difficulty in getting a ship and were not representative of the normal merchant seaman.

Matters came to a head when the crew refused to turn-to for work, probably after being threatened by the troublemakers. There was a battalion of Royal Marines on board at the time and the first indication I had that there was a serious situation was the presence of Marine sentries with fixed bayonets at various points around the ship. It looked as though the crew had mutinied.

Later in the day Gus and myself were in our cabin on the port side of the boat deck when we heard a bit of a commotion on the deck outside. On looking out of the large port-holes we saw about thirteen crew members being lined up facing outboard and being guarded by a large number of Marines with fixed bayonets. Shortly afterwards Admiral Keyes arrived accompanied by a Major and took up a position facing the men, thus giving us a first class view of the proceedings. The Admiral was an imposing figure, tall, with sharp, strong features and bushy eye-brows and a bearing denoting power and command. A sight to make any Cadet or Midshipman tremble.

The Admiral addressed the men and asked them to state their complaints, which they made in a truculent and disrespectful manner. They were unhappy about the landing craft and the type of operation that the ship was likely to be involved in, they wanted to know where the ship was going and for how long it would be away and complaints about their accommodation, were just some of their reasons for refusing to sail. Admiral Keyes endeavoured to reason with the men and explained that in time of war many peace-time customs and procedures had to be held in abeyance, and that every man should understand and accept this and that they should return to duty and serve their country. However the mutineers would have none of it; they interrupted the Admiral to plead with the Marines to support them, and then challenged the Marines that given rifles and bayonets they would fight them. The Marines showed not the slightest emotion as they stood with their long bayonets angled towards the men under guard, almost wishing that they would make a move.

Finally the Admiral brought the proceedings to a close by ordering the Major to, "Take them away." The men were put on board a landing craft and, surrounded by a guard of Marines, taken to shore where they were subsequently tried for mutiny and sentenced to 6 months imprisonment. It was later reported that when the men arrived ashore they could hardly walk, such was the treatment they received from the Marines.

It may have been as a result of the crew problem that the Admiralty decided to take over the ship completely and place her under the White Ensign with a full Naval crew, and so we returned once again to Glasgow where the crew was paid off and the ship handed over to the Navy. She was subsequently named HMS *Keren* and served as Headquarters ship at the landings in Madagascar.

A week before the ship paid off I became ill with pleurisy which, according to our sympathetic Indian doctor, was due to having been worked too hard and too long for my age. When the crew paid off I was sent home on sick leave and this provided an opportunity for me to make enquiries about joining the Royal Naval Reserve.

Chapter 7

THE NAVY AT LAST

———

When I left the SS *Kenya* I had been at sea for nearly sixteen months which was more than sufficient to qualify for entry to the Naval Reserve. My first step was to obtain permission from the Company to apply to join the Navy as a Midshipman in the Royal Naval Reserve and this was duly given. I was also given a report to accompany my application which said that I 'had always been reported on favourably by my Commanders.' I then wrote to the Admiralty to enquire if there was a scheme by which I could become a Midshipman and I was very pleased to receive an application form in which I was asked, amongst other things, if any of my family or other relations had served in the Navy. I was able to put down that my sister was serving in the Wrens (she had joined just after the outbreak of war) and mentioned my father's service with Admiral Beatty.

There was considerable excitement when I eventually received a letter from the Admiralty to say that I had been selected for an interview which would be conducted at Queen Anne's Mansions in London. I travelled down to London and stayed the night with grandfather which gave me the opportunity to have a good night's rest and spruce myself up for the interview. I do not think that I slept very well, I was rather nervous. An interview at the Admiralty, in my mind, would be totally different to an interview in a shipping office, after all I had seen Admiral Sir Roger Keyes in action.

At Queen Anne's Mansions I reported to the commissionaire who took my name and then directed me to an empty waiting room so it appeared that I was the only applicant at that time. I did not have long to wait before I was called into an adjoining office where a Rear-Admiral was seated at his desk with his secretary in another corner of the room. I was asked to sit down and I sat 'at attention' throughout the interview which seemed to last for a considerable time.

I had 'butterflies' when I entered the room but they gradually disappeared as I answered the Admiral's questions and his manner helped to put me at ease. He evidently knew about Troon and the golf facilities and enquired about my handicap and it became obvious that he had studied closely the details of my application. I was asked why I wanted to join the Service and when I told him of my life-long ambition he asked me several pertinent questions regarding classes of ships, their size and armament. The Admiral asked me questions about my service at sea and my – schooling he appeared to know about, the Royal High and its reputation – and also about my sporting activities. He did not ask any questions about academic achievements for which I was very grateful, I had left school without sitting my 'highers' and I was afraid that would count against me. He remarked on my father having served in the Navy and noted that it had been with Admiral Beatty which seemed to please him. At that time there was still a debate as to whether Admiral Jellicoe or Beatty had been the better officer, each having his supporters within the Service, and it looked as though the Rear-Admiral was a Beatty man.

At the end of the interview I was told that it looked as though I would be accepted and that I would be joining the Midshipmen's course at the Royal Naval College, Greenwich, starting on 15th September 1941. I would hear from the Admiralty in due course. Concluding the interview the Rear-Admiral said, "Good-morning" and it was here that I made my first and only mistake. Throughout the interview I had continuously addressed him as 'Sir' and I was confident that, in the words of Para Handy, 'my manners had been complete,' I got up from my chair, stood to attention and said, "Good-morning" and turned to leave the room. I had just reached the door when there was a roar. "Don't British India cadets say 'Sir' to Rear Admirals?" I was shattered! I could only stammer "Yes Sir", "Sorry Sir", Good-morning Sir", and as I opened the door and left the room he turned to his secretary and said, "Damned impertinence!"

My heart was in my boots as I left the building and I felt I had ruined my chance of being accepted. All my hopes had disappeared because of a careless slip, probably caused by a feeling of relief that the interview was over and that I had been successful. I wondered what my father would think when he heard what I had done.

I arrived early to board the train for Edinburgh and managed to get a corner seat. I was eventually joined by three Petty Officers and I could see they were intrigued by the three buttons on the sleeve of my uniform. Chief Petty Officers also wore three buttons on their sleeves and the naval men were obviously wondering how one so young could be a senior N.C.O. – they had not seen my Company cap badge. We started chatting and I was soon telling them about my interview, the Admiral's reaction to my slip-up and how I thought I had blown my chance of ever being in the Navy. The Petty Officers were very good in helping to raise my spirits by making light of the matter, telling me that Senior Officers were prone to blow their tops but once the reprimand had been given the matter would be forgotten.

Two Waafs (Womens Auxiliary Air Force) came into the compartment and their presence helped to make the journey pass more quickly. When it came to time for getting some sleep I gave my corner seat to one of the girls and awoke with an arm round each girl and a curly head on each shoulder. The only way to travel. The trains were crowded during the war and it was quite common for people to stand all the way on long distance journeys. There was usually a cheery comradeship and feeling of good-will amongst the passengers, and those people who were fortunate enough to obtain a seat would often get up and give their seats to others who had been standing for a long period to allow them to rest their legs.

It did not take long for the Admiralty, to come to a decision and about a week later the buff envelope arrived. It was opened with some trepidation but I gave a whoop of joy when I read that I had been appointed a Temporary Probationary Midshipman in the Royal Naval Reserve, and directed to report to the Royal Naval College, Greenwich on the 15th September 1941. At last I was in the Navy! The letter also contained information about uniform, etc. but as I already had a good kit all that I required was a new No. 1 uniform and a couple of cap badges and these were obtained from Gieves, the naval tailors.

Gieves was a very old firm which for many years had had a close association with the navy a the vast number of naval officers had an account with them. Gieves were reputed to be willing and able to carry out many services on behalf of their clients and did not dun officers with regard to unpaid bills, as long as something was paid from time to time they were reasonably happy. It was also said that if an officer was killed in action any debt was written off. On one occasion I was in London on a Saturday afternoon and ran short of money. I went to Gieves shop in Piccadilly and asked if they would cash a cheque. Whilst I was waiting two or three customers came in to make purchases. After about 15 minutes the assistant returned with my five pounds and apologized for keeping me waiting – they too had been short of money and had had to wait for someone to come in and pay cash in order to cash my cheque.

Another story was told concerning Gieves in Malta. When the Island became isolated and under siege the head cutter of Gieves and the stock of gold lace were taken to Alexandria, reputedly by submarine. In Alexandria all uniforms were made to measure; the gentleman from Malta did the cutting and fitting and local tailors did the sewing. The head cutter was looked upon as being one of the most important men in Alexandria, as far as the Navy was concerned.

Whilst I was waiting to report to Greenwich I sometimes went dancing and it was on one of these occasions that I met Isobel (Bobbie) Ness. Bobbie was in the WAAF and was stationed at Pitreavie Castle, across the Forth at Inverkeithing and, like myself, was fond of dancing. She was a lovely girl with golden hair and a lively, friendly personality and I became very fond of her. I still recall our first meeting whenever I hear the song *Frenesi* which the orchestra was playing when I first asked her to dance. Our first date was a day out at South Queensferry walking on the hills overlooking the Forth Bridge, and afterwards having tea in the crowded restaurant of the Hawes Pier Inn. It was the first time I had taken a young lady out for a meal and it was a pity that the best of the choices on offer was scrambled eggs made with dried egg. We managed to see each other on several occasions before the time came for me to leave for Greenwich.

Midshipman RNR

The Royal Naval College was originally erected as a hospital for maimed and aged seamen. It was designed and built by Christopher Wren on an old Royal property given to the Navy as a mark of appreciation by Queen Mary 11 for saving England at the battles of Barfleur and La Hogue in 1692. However it was not the single building that one might expect for a hospital for seamen, but a magnificent palace which emulated the beauty of the buildings for which Louis XIV, our enemy, had a passion for erecting. The great banqueting hall – known as the Painted Hall because of the magnificent painted ceiling – was not used for its original purpose until 1939 when it became arguably the finest Officers' Mess in the world. For many years it was a promenade for the old pensioners and in the 19th century housed a collection of naval portraits. The bodies of Nelson and Collingwood lay in state in the

Painted Hall before being taken to their final resting place. The hospital was at the height of its usefulness during the long Napoleonic wars and housed as many as 2,700 inmates, but the numbers greatly diminished during the 19th century in the long periods of peace and due to the practice of giving out pensions instead of insisting on residence. It was closed as a hospital in 1869 and reopened in 1873 as the Royal Naval College – the Navy's University.

I reported on a Sunday afternoon and soon found myself in the Gunroom (Midshipmen's mess) where the other course members were assembling as they arrived. There was a great deal of "What company are you from?" as we introduced ourselves and it soon became plain that many of the major shipping companies were represented, as well as Cadets from the Nautical College at Pangbourne and the training ships HMS *Conway* and HMS *Worcester*. The college and the training ships were public schools and trained boys primarily for entry into the Merchant Navy, and the boys had the rank of Cadet Royal Naval Reserve.

I became close friends with three Mids with whom I shared a room. 'Stumpy' Mason (he was short) from Blue Funnel Line, 'Shag' Lacey (he was tired) from Clan Line and 'Bandit' Crooks (Australian) from P&O. We eventually went everywhere together and had a good deal of fun. There were about 35 of us altogether aged between 17 and 20, the eldest being promoted to Sub-Lieutenant as Class Captain. His name was the Honourable David Hay, son of Lord Hay whom I believe was a government minister. David had been to Eton College and was reputed to have run away to sea to join Blue Funnel Line. When we arrived at Greenwich we found that he was a bit of a celebrity having just been awarded the Lloyds's Medal and Albert Medal for bravery at sea. When his ship was torpedoed he dived off a life-raft to go to the aid of a shipmate who was being attacked by a shark. The story was given away by reporters in a local pub when they came down to interview him.

Our training concentrated mainly on drill (square bashing) which most of us had experience of in the O.T.C. at school, signalling, navigation and seamanship. To begin with, the drill periods were held in the morning, but this was soon changed to the afternoon when it was found that we had difficulty in keeping awake in the class-room after a beer and heavy lunch. The food was excellent considering that it was war-time and there was plenty of it to satisfy our youthful appetites.

The instructors were mainly Chief Petty Officers who had to lick us into shape quickly and endeavour to impart some of their wide experience of Naval practice and tradition in the short time available. They were strict with us and we were made to learn the hard way when the occasion arose. One day during squad drill 'Bandit' was talking in the ranks and after receiving the customary dressing down from the Instructor he unfortunately made the mistake of replying with an attempted witticism. He was told to report in the quadrangle with full equipment for extra drill. 'Stumpy,' 'Shag' and myself had just finished our baths as 'Bandit' started his punishment which involved doubling around the quad carrying his rifle at the 'slope' position. We three were leaning out the window singing "She'll be coming round the mountain," when there was a knock at the door and a Petty Office came into the room. Pointing to each of us in turn he said, "You, you and you Sir, marching order on the square NOW!" Within minutes there were four of us doubling around, cursing ourselves for not keeping our mouths shut.

I enjoyed the periods that were spent in a cabin cruiser on the river gaining experience in taking the craft alongside the wharfs and barges in the sometimes strong tideway. At these times we were told about boat etiquette; juniors first to board and last to leave, asking a cox'n's permission before crossing his boat to get to another laying alongside, never to keep a boat waiting, and other tips of the trade. It was said that in peace-time it was not unknown for officers' wives to follow the same routine, and woe betide the junior officer whose wife got out of the boat before the wife of a senior officer.

On arrival at the College one of the first skills we had to learn was the tieing of a bow tie. Very few of the class had worn one and those who had were in great demand as instructors. A wing collar and bow tie was worn with normal uniform jacket as mess dress in war-time and at Greenwich it was worn on Guest Night which was held on Thursday.

The first Guest Night was a bit of an ordeal, there were the Mess customs to be observed and things to learn, such as the correct way to pass the port, and it was something of a strain watching one's Ps and Qs in front of the senior officers. However we soon learned the routine and how we were expected to conduct ourselves, and Guest Nights were usually lots of fun.

Usually there were not a great many ladies present on Guest Nights as most of the Officers were on courses and their relatives and friends probably some distance away, however those who did attend wore evening dress and looked upon the evening as something of an occasion.

During our training we were given plenty of PT and also taken to the local swimming baths for instruction. One day when marching off to the gym we saw a brewers dray standing outside the Gunroom door with a load of beer for the Mess. As we passed the dray some of us in the nearest file, managed to 'obtain' bottles of beer which we quickly tucked into our towels. As soon as we arrived in the gym dressing room the bottles were opened and passed around the class, unfortunately we forgot about our instructor. When he found out what we had been up to he gave us a real rocket, not so much for drinking the beer but for failing to keep some for him. We were made to suffer in the end when he put us through a very strenuous session. My sister received her Commission and attended the College some months later and when the PT instructor asked if she had a brother who was a Midshipman, she was left wondering what I had been up to, and if she was about to suffer for my misdeeds.

The rugby season had just started when we arrived and I managed to be selected for the College team. Most of the team were Midshipmen but there were several older officers amongst whom was an Engineer Lieutenant named Le Fluffy. He had played for Oxford University and was an extremely fast three-quarter. I learned a lot whilst playing with him – he made me stretch myself to keep up with him when I was playing at centre or making the extra man as full-back. We played some well-known clubs, and some of the team had the experience of playing against former school friends when we played the *Worcester* which they had left only recently.

Returning to the College after the matches which were held in Greenwich Park not far from the Observatory, at the entrance to our building we would find a long table with 15 pints of shandy at each end for the teams' refreshment. It was very welcome especially on a warm day, and whoever mixed the shandy got the proportions just right as it tasted like nectar. There was always a rush to get it down after looking forward to it throughout the match.

As young officers under training our leave was very much restricted and we had to be in the College by 7pm. If we wanted to stay out on Saturday nights a letter from a friend or relative had to be submitted to the Commanding Officer to obtain his permission and to show where we would be staying. During the week, by the time the day's training was over, we were usually too tired to want to go anywhere and any money we had was saved for the weekend. Our pay was five shillings a day and by the time we had paid mess and laundry bills there was not a great deal left over. My grandparents supplied me with the required letter and I spent my weekends with them or with the parents of one of my friends.

After six or seven weeks it was announced that the whole class would going to Dartmouth for instruction in boat-work under oars and sail, before going to Chatham to finish training at the gunnery school.

Chapter 8

TRAINING COURSES

———

During the journey to Dartmouth the train ran out of beer for which our class may have been largely responsible as we all arrived at the station in good spirits. Some of the class were taken up to the College by truck, but two or three of us went by car whose Wren driver scared the wits out of us as she raced through the narrow streets and round corners, as though she had a date and did not want to be late. She was the first Wren I had come into contact with whilst carrying out her duty (apart from the Wren stewards) and she certainly knew her business.

The College was an imposing building located on an elevated site overlooking the River Dart. Along the front of the building was a wide drive-way which, at each end, curved down to the large parade ground in front of the College. The class was allotted a large dormitory similar to the ones used by the Cadets and something of a change for us after the four bedded rooms at Greenwich. The Special Entry Cadets, who had joined at 17 straight from school, were known as 'Frobishers', the name of their term which was named after the Elizabethan sea-dog, and we were permitted to use their Gunroom and other facilities.

An incident occurred shortly after our arrival which showed the Cadets' early appreciation of rank and seniority. In the mess the Cadets sat at long tables with the Senior Cadets seated at a separate table at the top of the room, the Midshipmen's class and the College Officers had their own tables. The Cadets had their meals in two sittings with the first sitting having only 15 minutes or so to get it down before the Cadet Captain stood up and ordered, "Clear the mess." At this command the Cadets were up as one and out of the mess in quick order, without any delaying tactics in the event that they had not finished their meal. It was no wonder that they got tucked in with gusto, reminiscent of Burns, 'Hand for hand they stretch and strive, de'il tak the hindmost on they drive.' They were growing lads, some only 13 years of age, with good appetites and the food was not all that plentiful. At the end of the second sitting the same order was given and the Cadets reacted accordingly, but we Midshipmen paid no attention assuming that the instruction did not apply to our class. The Cadet Captain repeated the order direct to our table. 'Bandit' Crooks, who was sitting at the head of our table with his back to the Cadet Captain, turned around and, without saying a word, pointed to the blue Midshipman's patches on his collar indicating he was senior to the Cadet then continued with what he had been doing. Momentarily the Cadet Captain was nonplussed and he did not pursue the matter further but carried on with his normal routine. I suppose we should really have obeyed his order as he was in charge of the Mess, however we had not been told what was expected of us and he had not been advised as to how we should be treated. A break-down in communications.

In the corridor leading to the mess there were several large models used for instructional purposes, one of which was the bow section of a battleship complete with anchors, cables, capstans, mooring wires, etc. All the fittings right down to shackles and bottle-screws were operable so that practical demonstrations could be given on anchoring and mooring operations. A problem often arose when a ship, riding to two anchors, swung the wrong way at the turn of the tide resulting in the cables becoming crossed with possibly one or more turns around each other. The procedure to be followed in taking out the turns could be clearly demonstrated on the model – which cable to break, where to unshackle it, where and how to fit stoppers and how to run and secure the wires etc. They were beautiful examples of a model maker's craft with everything reproduced in miniature and ideal for instructional purposes.

Shore leave was restricted to some extent and we had to be back in the College fairly early in the evening. Dartmouth was a small town and there was not very much to do but on the first Saturday that we were there a local organisation held a dance to which we were invited. It was a very proper affair with plenty of 'matrons' in attendance to keep an eye on things, especially the young girls who attended to provide partners for servicemen. Some of us failed to keep an eye on the time with the result that we were late in getting back to our quarters, however a Marine sentry at a side entrance was prevailed upon to let us in and a half crown for a couple of pints helped to keep his mouth shut

Whilst getting ready to go ashore the sound of a dance band was heard coming from somewhere in the building. On investigation it was found to be coming from the 'Quarterdeck,' or main hall, where the Royal Marine band was really swinging. The floor was filled with Cadets dancing with each other, the 'ladies' being distinguished by the white handkerchiefs tied around an arm, and the Petty Officers moving amongst the couples giving the necessary instruction regarding the 'quick, quick, slow' and other steps. To us old hands who had been to sea and sampled the flesh-pots it seemed a bit 'cissie' but, to be fair, it was the only way the younger boys could learn to dance as there was no opportunity for them to attend normal dancing classes and learn to dance with girls. It was one more example of the Navy having a routine for everything; even down to making sure that young officers were taught the social graces.

The class had been sent down for instruction in boat work and we were out on the river every day. We started immediately under oars, first pulling the 27 foot whalers, then cutters and finally the big pinnaces where the oars were double banked. It was hard work and the instructors kept us at it all the time but it was out in the open, good exercise and most of us enjoyed it. For the first few days we managed to wangle brief respites when the 'heads' facilities on a tug moored near the training stretch were very much in demand. It may have been due to the change in food, but we were firmly of the opinion that something was added to the cocoa to keep the Cadets 'regular!' The sailing dinghys, whalers and cutters could be taken out by ourselves in our spare time once we had become competent to do so. The young Cadets, some only 13 or 14, spent quite a lot of their leisure time on the river sailing the dinghys and, for someone who had never sailed, I was impressed by their confidence and skill. In later years I saw the same confidence and skill in much younger children on the Brisbane River in Australia, where literally scores of youngsters would take to the water on Saturdays and Sundays in very small sail-boats, the mass of sails giving the impression of a swarm of insects moving over the water.

On Sunday mornings 'Divisions' were held on the parade ground when the Cadets and Guard were inspected by the Commandant who took the salute at the subsequent march past. I was rather surprised that we were not included in the parade but it probably was just as well as we would no doubt have been shown up by the smart turn-out and drill of the Cadets. The class was drawn up at the front of the College alongside a detachment of the Irish Guards who were present to watch the parade. The Guard was especially smart with shining rifles and bayonets, and made a brave sight marching up the curving drive-way followed by the rest of the Cadets who had marched off by divisions. The Royal Marine band played as the parade marched past the Commandant who took the salute at the College entrance.

I thoroughly enjoyed the short course at the College and the experience, if only for a short time, of being at Dartmouth. I had finally got there even if it had been achieved in a roundabout way. Although there were probably some boys who were not all that keen on joining the Navy and had been sent there by their parents because of family tradition, the vast majority were enthusiastic to become Naval Officers and to do well in the Service. It was easy to see how the young boys were moulded into the type of Officer the Navy required. They were taught that the Navy had a routine for everything, that there was only one standard and that was 'excellent' and that the highest praise given was 'well done.' An old Chief Petty Officer, who had at one time been an instructor, told me that future Admirals were often identified as the Cadets finished their training and left the College.

The class returned briefly to Greenwich before travelling by truck to Chatham. The gunnery school was a very different environment to the colleges at Greenwich and Dartmouth. The barracks were full to overflowing with men under training and we were allotted rooms in houses just completed and barely furnished, which had possibly been intended for married quarters. It was December and very cold and there was difficulty in getting sufficient coal to keep the bare rooms warm.

The guns were housed in large drill sheds which could be used for other purposes in bad weather. Instruction was given on the 12-pounder, 4.7-inch and 6-inch guns under the eagle eyes of instructors who pounced immediately on the slightest fault and kept us at it until we got it right. Those of us who had been Cadets at sea already knew a certain amount having served in the guns' crews on board, so we were not exactly green. The instructors had strong personalities which forced our attention and also enabled them to inject some humour into the proceedings without diminishing the seriousness of the point being made. On the procedure to be followed when the gun misfires: "When the gun misfires number 2 will not say .... it, but will re-cock the striker!"

Chief Petty Officer Tom Gee (we would enquire as to the health of Mrs Gee and all the wee whizzes, which he took in good part) was a pensioner Gunnery Instructor who gave lectures on such things as the 'Dumereq', a small, portable, gun control table whose dials and pointers were all rather complicated and left us all a trifle bemused. Having seen long service he was a fount of information regarding customs, traditions, procedures and routines and could spin a good yarn about his adventures and experiences. We could often divert him from the matter in hand by asking a pertinent question which would inevitably lead him to start off with, "I remember", and then continue with a story which would, more than any lecture, clearly illustrate the subject under discussion.

Each day started with Divisions on the parade ground when the training classes were inspected and reported to the Officer-in-Charge by the Class Captains before dispersing to continue their courses. The duty of Class Captain, which included marching the class to and from lectures, was rotated daily in our class so that we all took a turn, and it was during my turn that I had a spot of bother with the Officer-in-Charge of the parade. It was really all over a few inches.

After reporting the class I returned and again took up position two paces in front of the first rank. A voice rang out over the parade ground, "Officer in charge of the Midshipmen's division move closer to his division!" I turned around, marched right up to the front rank, turned again and took the regulation two paces forward in front of the class. Again the voice rang out, "Officer in charge of the Midshipmen's division come here!" Taking a deep breath I marched, as I thought, smartly across the parade ground knowing the eyes of several hundred men were following my progress, and came to a halt and saluted in front of the Officer-in-Charge who was standing on a raised platform. Looking over my head the officer gave another command, "Officer in charge of the Midshipmen's division will double when on the parade ground!" So round I went and this time doubled back to my position in front of the class, making sure that I finished up in the correct position.

Mercifully the performance was brought to a close by the order to march off and I was saved from further embarrassment. What the watching sailors made of it I do not know, they may have felt a touch of sympathy – few people went through training without receiving a rocket or being made to look foolish over something or other. Later, the Gunnery Officer met us as I was marching the class to the next period of instruction. Stopping me, he said not unkindly, "You made a bit of a fool of yourself, didn't you?" "Well, Sir, you helped me", I said, giving a weak smile. I was to meet him again under happier circumstances later in my career.

I had my first and only experience of refereeing a rugby match whilst I was at Chatham when I volunteered to officiate at a match between some young sailors and a team from the Approved School at Borstal. Boys and youths who had been convicted of various crimes and misdemeanours were sent to Approved Schools for corrective training which included being subjected to strict routine and discipline. It was often said that the regime was similar to that of a Public School. The school at Borstal was the first Approved School and thereafter other schools became known as Borstals.

I had never refereed a rugby match before and, as with most of the sports I took part in, I did not have an intimate knowledge of the finer points of the rules – having been taught to obey the referee and not to argue I was quite happy to abide by his decision. The Borstal boys were big, strong chaps and it was obvious that their punishment kept them very fit. I forget who won the match but I managed to get through it without causing too much dissent. Afterwards I was invited to have tea with the Headmaster in his home, and in future years I was sometimes able to raise a few eyebrows by remarking off-hand that I had 'been to Borstal.'

The course was due to finish about the end of December and we were still at the barracks when Christmas Day arrived. After lunch the port and cigars were passed round. The steward was going round the table with a box of cigars and when he reached me he offered the box and said, "Cigar, Sir?" I looked at him and said, "No thank you, I couldn't smoke a cigar." Quick as a flash, in broad cockney, he replied, "I can, Sir!" Reacting quickly to the implication I took two and managed to slip them to him unseen by the senior steward.

Immediately after Christmas some of us were told our future appointments and I learned that I was being sent out to HMS *Nile*, the shore base at Alexandria in Egypt, additional for appointment to a ship in the Eastern Mediterranean. I would be taking passage in the SS *Orontes*, an Orient Line passenger ship, and I would have about 10 days embarkation leave during which time I would receive orders when and where to join her.

I wanted to give Bobbie a watch for her Christmas present. I could only afford about seven pounds (a month's pay) which I had saved up so I asked grandfather where I should go to buy it as he had many useful contacts in the City. He told me to go to a certain jewellers in the Pentonville Road and to tell the proprietor that I was Bob Mason's grandson. I found the small shop without much difficulty and told the gentleman that I wanted a ladies watch at about seven pounds. He began to show me several watches, none of which immediately took my eye, and whilst we were talking I mentioned that Bob Mason had recommended the shop to me and that I was his grandson. It was rather amusing. The jeweller straightaway put the watches he had shown me to one side and produced another tray from under the counter. The tray contained a small, neat, rectangular watch which immediately caught my attention. When I pointed to the watch and asked the price the jeweller said, "For Bob Mason's grandson, seven pounds!"

Fortunately Bobbie was going on leave for New Year so we were able to arrange that she would spend it with me and my family in Edinburgh. We had a wonderful time together, an added enjoyment being that she was able to wear civvies, the first time I had seen her out of uniform. One evening I took her to a dinner dance in a hotel in Princes Street and an incident occurred which made our happiness complete. We had returned to our table after dancing when an elderly lady passing by stopped to say that we looked such a nice, happy young couple together. Bobbie was wearing a green dress and with her golden hair she looked very attractive, I felt very proud to have her on my arm.

Sadly our 10 days leave had to end and the time came for me to leave for Liverpool. The scene at the station was one which was seen in countless war films. We had arrived early to ensure that I got a seat and then we stood by the train waiting for my parents to arrive. The platform was crowded with families and friends saying good-bye to service men and women, whilst somewhere an accordion was playing romantic songs and the ever popular *We'll Meet Again*.

I stammered something about things going wrong and maybe not returning but Bobbie confidently asserted that I was the type who always returned. She was correct but little did we know that it would be 50 years before we spoke to each other again. As the train pulled out of the station my last view of her out of the carriage window was the same as when I first saw her – her golden hair standing out amongst the crowd.

Chapter 9

AROUND THE CAPE

———

It was fortunate that I had allowed myself plenty of leeway between the train's time of arrival in Liverpool and the time of reporting on board the troopship. When changing trains at Carstairs I saw my trunks taken off the train and arranged for them to be transferred to the Liverpool train, but when I went along to collect them at Liverpool there was no sign of them. It was hard not to get into a bit of a flap; I could imagine myself arriving on board with no gear and only the clothes I stood up in to take me all the way to Alexandria. I had taken great care that they were well labelled and easily identified but I breathed a great sigh of relief when they turned up on the next train. It was a narrow squeak.

The Orient Line was one of the world's top passenger lines although the fleet only comprised nine vessels whose names all began with 'O' – Orontes, Orion, Orcades, Otranto, etc. The ships were employed on the India and Australia run before being commandeered as troopships at the outbreak of war. In peacetime they would probably have carried about fifteen hundred passengers but the accommodation had been altered to carry many more and I found myself in a cabin which had been adapted to accommodate five officers, one of whom was another Mid. from the course. Pat Hamilton had been a Pangbourne Cadet and had not yet been to sea. Although we had not been companions during our training we became good friends during the voyage and whilst waiting to join our first ships. After that, as was common in war-time, we lost touch with each other.

Amongst the personnel taking passage was a contingent of Army Nursing Sisters, and the first draft of Wrens to be sent to the Middle East, about 80 in number.

The Wrens were an attractive lot, they must have been hand picked as I do not think there was a plain one amongst them. Although they were not officers they were allowed use of the boat and promenade decks for recreation and their presence certainly lightened the tedium of the voyage.

SS Orontes.
Photograph courtesy of the National Maritime Museum, Greenwich.

Also on board was an ENSA concert party going to Alexandria to entertain the troops in the desert. There were five performers in the troupe; a pianist, comedian, male and female vocalists, and a girl of the soubrette type. The pianist was Norman Hackforth who was Noel Coward's accompanist before the war and later became known as 'the voice' who asked the questions on the Twenty Questions radio show. The male singer was a tall, handsome chap and seemed the answer to a maiden's prayer until we arrived in the warm weather and he joined the officers exercising with a medicine ball. Stripped to the waist he was as thin as rail and had no shoulders to speak of, and I could not help but feel sorry for him as he was nearly knocked off his feet when the ball was thrown to him. The girl singer was named Marilyn Williams whom I saw mentioned in the Radio Times after the war. The comedian was the stand up comic who wore a thick fur coat as he told his rather blue jokes, whilst the soubrette went around with not a great deal on flirting with the officers in general. The show was called *Between Ourselves* and I heard subsequently that they did a very good job entertaining the troops in the desert. They may not have been top line artistes but their efforts were appreciated by the audience wherever they went, the servicemen realising that they were doing their bit for the war effort and were not too critical when any form of entertainment was most welcome. It was the dedication, thought and effort that was appreciated rather than reputations. One well-known London theatre personality was booed off the stage in Alexandria when he gave the impression that he was doing everyone a favour by coming out to entertain them.

The first port of call was Freetown and as we steamed into the anchorage it seemed as if I was coming home after the months I had spent there. There was considerable excitement and interest as people lined the rails and watched the natives come alongside in their dug-out canoes to sell fruit and local souvenirs. They really were dug-outs, roughly formed from a solid tree trunk and the natives handled them with great skill. They would dive from the canoes to pick up coins thrown from the ship – their preference being for silver which could be more easily seen in the water. It was amusing to see and hear their anger when they discovered the silver was a half-penny wrapped in silver paper. They had a very good choice of words in pidgin English about what they termed a 'Glasgow Shilling.' One well-known character wore a top hat and an Eton College tie which must have raised a few eyebrows amongst Old Etonians who passed through during the course of the war.

Shortly after leaving Freetown we crossed the Line and the traditional ceremonies were carried out which provided considerable excitement and entertainment for those who had never before seen them. The participants – King Neptune, the Bears, Policemen, Barber, etc. were all dressed up in traditional guise – the bears going round the ship equipped with large, dead fish with which they lashed out at all and sundry as they selected their victims. A canvas pool was rigged on the after deck for the ducking ceremony which was witnessed by the troops who crowded every vantage point and thoroughly enjoyed the proceedings.

Although we were in convoy and under threat of attack at all times from U-boats or surface raiders, in many ways the time on board was passed in much the same way as it would have been during a peace-time voyage, at least as far as we officers were concerned. Apart from having to carry life-belts at all times, no smoking on deck after dark and the presence of look-outs and guns' crews around the ship, there was no great difference to peace-time routine. Deck tennis and deck quoits could be played on the boat-deck and there were plenty of spaces and chairs on the boat and promenade decks where people could gather and pass the time together in yarning, playing games or doing crosswords. Considering that it was war-time there appeared to be little deterioration in the standard of service or the quality of the meals in the officers' dining saloon. Wine was available at dinner which consisted of four courses with a choice of dishes. There was also a bar with reasonable opening hours.

The Senior Officer taking passage in the ship was Rear-Admiral Jackson who was travelling to Turkey to take up a diplomatic appointment. The Admiral thought that two young Midshipmen should be given something to do and not allowed to waste their time on the voyage, and he arranged with the ship's Captain that we should be allowed to keep one four hour bridge watch each day with the ship's officers. So for nearly two months I kept the afternoon watch with the Second and Fourth Officers and enjoyed the experience of watch-keeping on a large ocean liner in war-time. One of my duties was to help with the signalling; bending on the flags, hoisting the signal, etc. One of our sister ships was the Commodore of the convoy and we were stationed on her port beam at the head of a column, which meant that we had to repeat all the Commodore's signals for the benefit of the ships in our column. From our bridge there was an excellent view of our sister ship's flag lockers which enabled us to see which flags were being taken out for the signal about to be sent. As the Fourth Officer read out the flags I would bend them on the signal halyard as fast as I could in order to repeat the signal in the shortest possible time. On a couple of occasions the signal was repeated before the Commodore had sent it. As a gunner's mate might put it, a case of being 'too previous.'

The Admiral liked to start off the day with a session of deck tennis before breakfast and it was not long before he asked one of us to provide the opposition. Fortunately for me it was Pat who volunteered and for the whole trip he turned out early every morning to give the Admiral his exercise. The Admiral had his own table in the lounge where he would sit studying the Turkish language and frequently we would be asked to join him at 1130 when he would ask what we would like to drink. Our answers were always the same, "Orange squash, Sir, please Sir."

On arrival in Capetown it was announced that the ship would be in port for three days and that shore leave would be granted. Along with Pat I was delighted to hear that we would have no duties to perform in port and that we would be free for the three days. Various organisations, individuals and clubs had sent invitations to the ship to be given to officers to attend functions arranged for their entertainment, or to receive hospitality in private homes. Pat and I were fortunate to be given tickets for a dance to be held at the Kelvin Country Club which turned out to be one of the top social venues in Capetown.

We set off early to have a look around the town before arriving at the Club and our wanderings took us eventually to the railway station. There we saw a large dog, a Great Dane, roaming around the station mixing with the sailors who were travelling to and from the Naval Base at Simonstown. Sometime later I found out that the dog was a well-known character named 'Nuisance' who, because of his tendency to follow sailors and be missing frequently from home, was presented to the Naval Base as a mascot. 'Nuisance' was given a Service Certificate and Conduct Sheet similar to ratings and entered as an ordinary seaman, gaining promotion or suffering demotion or other punishment in the event of being absent without leave or other misdemeanours. There were many stories told about 'Nuisance.' How he would attach himself to a group of sailors, or maybe just one individual, and accompany them on their run ashore, standing on his hind legs with his paws on the bar having a sup of beer and knocking the bread off a sandwich to get to the meat inside. Or how a sailor, with a few beers under his belt, might suddenly feel his arm gripped gently but firmly by a very large dog which put aside all thought of struggling as he was led on to the train to Simonstown. They may be apocryphal but there is no doubt he was sadly missed by the people of Capetown when he died, and by the Navy who gave him a Naval funeral complete with gun-carriage and military escort.

The Kelvin Country Club was situated amidst beautiful grounds full of tropical plants and flowers, the building and drive-way being illuminated with fairy lights which made it all appear exciting and romantic. On our arrival we were welcomed by a matronly lady who led us into the ball-room where a large group of young ladies had gathered to act as hostesses for the evening. It was a wonderful evening after the long voyage and we thoroughly enjoyed ourselves, our partners were delightful girls and full of fun.

After leaving Capetown we called at Durban but as it was only for one day there was no shore leave. The stay at Capetown had been a welcome break in the voyage and gave everybody something to talk about on the fast leg of our journey.

Several days before arrival at Suez one of the Fleet Air Arm Sub-Lieutenants had his 21st birthday and to celebrate we had a few drinks and a bottle of wine at dinner. Afterwards the party moved to the officers' lounge where we eventually gathered around the piano and persuaded Norman Hackforth to play so that we could have a sing-song. Very soon, as Robert Burns said, 'The nicht drave on wi' sangs an'clatter, an'aye the ale was growing better.' I always enjoyed a sing-song and, in my enthusiasm 'I tint my reason a' thegither' and gave a solo rendering of *Bonnie Mary of Argyll*. I had just finished when a young army officer (very regimental) made his way through the group standing around the piano and came up to me and said, very politely, "Admiral Jackson presents his compliments and suggests that it is time you went to bed." This brought me down to earth with a thud. I turned and looked towards the Admiral who was sitting at his usual table on the other side of the lounge. I caught his eye and bowed my head slightly in acknowledgement, then walked as smartly as I could (taking care not to stumble) out of the lounge and off to bed.

It seemed as if I was destined to upset Rear-Admirals and next morning I was prepared for a ticking off when Pat and myself were invited for our morning squash. However he made no reference to the previous evening's festivities and on reflection, I could see that the Admiral had just been making sure that I did not go on to make a fool of myself. When a Midshipman himself he had no doubt got up to high jinks and had been kept on the rails by advice and the odd blast from his superiors.

Orontes arrived at Suez at the beginning of March 1942 and after disembarkation we joined a troop train for the last lap of our journey to Alexandria, where we had breakfast in the Windsor Hotel on the Comiche (sea-front) before being taken to HMS *Sphinx*, a transit camp on the coast at Sidi Bish just outside the city. The officers quarters, which were in a big house near the camp site, were very well appointed, the

Mess being wood panelled, and it was quite a surprise to learn that the house had previously functioned as a high class brothel.

Next morning Pat and I reported to the Captain of the Fleet's office at HMS *Nile* to be interviewed before receiving our appointments. Whilst waiting outside who should come along but Rear-Admiral Jackson on his way to visit the Captain of the Fleet. He stopped to talk to us and asked how we were getting on and what were we doing here. When he heard we were waiting to be appointed he asked what type of ships we wanted, to which we replied, "Destroyers Sir, please Sir!"

The Admiral may have received good reports on our conduct and ability from the Captain of *Orontes* which led him to take an interest in us, as it became obvious that he had spoken about us to the Captain of the Fleet. We had no sooner entered his office when he said, "I understand you boys want to go to destroyers." He proceeded to ask about our sea-going experience and other matters, and ended up by saying that he would see what he could do about our going to small ships.

Whilst waiting to hear our fate we spent a good deal of time swimming from the sandy beaches at Sidi Bish and on several occasions had swimming parties with some of our Wren friends from *Orontes*. They were happy days, we were all young (I had just past my 19th birthday) and we were all enjoying new experiences and had much to talk about. It was sometimes difficult to believe that, not so far away in the desert, hard fighting was taking place and that some of our fellow passengers might already be in action.

After about 10 days our appointments came through; Pat was to join the light cruiser HMS *Dido* whilst I was to go to her sister ship HMS *Euryalus*. We were disappointed that we had not been given destroyers but light cruisers were the next best thing. At least I had avoided being sent to either of the battleships *Queen Elizabeth* or *Valiant* which at that moment were sitting on the bottom of Alexandria harbour, having been mined by Italian frogmen and with no hope of going to sea for some considerable time.

Chapter 10

HMS *EURYALUS* – THE BATTLE OF SIRTE

———

It was late in the afternoon when Pat and I left the transit camp to go to the base to be taken out to our ships. As we stood on the jetty waiting for our respective boats I was not aware that, when we separated and went our different ways, our paths would never cross again. Throughout my subsequent service in the Navy I never served with the same officers twice and it was only on a few occasions, either in the same flotilla or at a base, that I met up with former shipmates. As we joined our ships and took up new appointments at different times, often to a different station, and invariably lived in different parts of the country it was difficult to maintain close and lasting friendships. I suppose that this could be looked upon as a disadvantage of service life although I did not think about it at the time. It was only in later years that I came to regret not having been able to keep in touch with old shipmates with whom I had at one time been quite close, and who had shared many adventures and experiences with me. Pat eventually got his destroyer when he was transferred later to HMS *Kipling*.

I was able to have a good look at my new ship during the boat trip across the harbour to where she was moored at the buoys. *Euryalus* was one of the new Dido class light cruisers which had a main armament of ten 5.25-inch H.A./L.A. guns arranged in five twin turrets, three forward and two aft. They were the latest guns in the Navy and capable of a high rate of fire. Her fine lines and slightly raked funnels gave an immediate impression of speed and manoeuvrability and this was confirmed by her ability to steam at a speed in excess of 31 knots.

As the boat approached the quarter-deck accommodation ladder I had a few butter-flies in my stomach. This was the moment I had always dreamed about ever since I had played in Beatty's cap – joining a warship as a Midshipman at the beginning of a Naval career.

When I stepped on board and saluted the quarterdeck the Officer of the Watch, a Warrant Officer, came forward smiling as he welcomed me on board. His friendly manner immediately made me feel at home and my first impression was that I had joined a happy ship. This was confirmed when he took me down to the Ward-room where I met Commander Cook who offered me a drink and I was introduced to other officers whilst a discussion took place as to where I was to sleep, there being no gunroom. The only other Midshipman on board was a Paymaster. It was decided that I would have the First Lieutenant's sea cabin, which was just under the bridge (and only used when the ship was at sea), whilst in port and that I would 'doss down' in the wardroom or Captain's day-room when the ship was at sea. As it turned out I did not have much time off duty at sea as we were at action stations most of the time when my station was on the bridge.

Later I met the Commanding Officer, Captain Eric Bush. Captain Bush had been one of Kipling's 'Scholars,' the Cadets who left Dartmouth on the outbreak of war in 1914 and were sent direct to sea. Captain Bush joined the cruiser *Bacchante* which took part in the landings at Gallipoli in 1915, and he was in charge of the ship's picket boat towing three boatloads of ANZAC troops into the beaches in the first assault wave when he was barely 15 years old. The following year he was in the spotting top of the battleship *Revenge* at the Battle of Jutland.

A Post Captain could be an awesome figure to a very new and inexperienced Midshipman, but as he asked me about myself and showed a close and genuine interest in my background, previous sea experience, etc., his manner encouraged me to relax and feel at ease. He had a tremendous personality and I was to find that he was loved and respected by the officers and men under his command.

Shortly after I joined the ship Mrs Bush presented the Captain with a son and to celebrate the event he held a cocktail party which was attended by Rear-Admiral Vian, who was in command of our cruiser squadron, and many other Senior Officers. All the officers had gone up to the party in the Captain's day-room but I stayed behind in the wardroom as I did not think I was meant to attend, and I was a trifle hesitant about being amongst so many 'brass hats.' The Commander appeared in the wardroom and, on seeing me sitting alone, told me to get up and join the party. I went up and stood inside the door-way, taking a glass of sherry from a steward and keeping out of the way. The Admiral was standing in the middle of the room talking to Captain Bush and the other cruiser Captains and Senior Officers. Captain Bush spotted me and came over and said "Come and meet Admiral Vian, Stewart." He led me over to the group and introduced me to the Admiral saying, "This is Midshipman Stewart, Sir, who has just joined my ship." The Admiral was a tall imposing figure with bushy eyebrows and a stem countenance and, as I learned afterwards, had the reputation of being a hard man not overly popular with the sailors. However he was also an excellent seaman and tactician and they had faith in him and would follow him anywhere.

The concern shown by Captain Bush that I should meet the Admiral was an example of the close interest he took in his officers and men and gave me an appreciation of some of the qualities which had earned him so much respect and devotion. I was very fortunate to be under the command of such a fine officer in my first appointment.

My main duty was to be in charge of the officer's barge which was a fast craft with a forward cockpit, engine amidships, and a stern cabin for the officers who usually stood up facing forward and holding on to the canopy. There was usually a leading seaman in the boat for instructional purposes and no doubt also to make sure that the boat did not come to harm through youthful enthusiasm. Each morning some boats from the fleet would go inshore to refuel or pick up the mail and, as they approached the entrance to the jetty, there was sometimes quite a race to be first alongside. There was a tendency to forget the Rule of the Road as each Midshipman pressed on regardless, alarming his cox'n with the thought of having to explain to his Commander the reason the boat had been damaged. However my previous experience stood me in good stead although a motor life-boat could not compare with the barge which was much faster and more fun.

I also kept watch on the quarter-deck with the senior watch-keeping Officer when he was Officer of the Watch in harbour and sometimes I would take Colours in the morning. Colours is the ceremony of hoisting the ensign and signifies the beginning of the official day. The ceremony of Sunset in the evening when the ensign is lowered brings the day to a close. In cruisers and big ships which carried a Royal Marine band it would parade on the quarter-deck and the buglers would sound the 'still' whereupon all persons on the upper deck would face aft and stand to attention, officers saluting, as the ensign was hoisted whilst the band played the National Anthem. In smaller ships the 'still' was sounded by the quartermaster with a pipe on his bosun's call. At the end of the ceremony the order to 'carry on' was again given by bugle or pipe.

I enjoyed taking colours. The 'preparative' flag would be hoisted in the flagship, *Queen Elizabeth* and, having been acknowledged by an answering pendant, a signalman would come down from the flag deck and report, "Five minutes to eight, Sir" and bend the ensign on to the ensign-staff halyards and stand ready to hoist the ensign. At the same time the Marine band, which had formed up in the waist forward of the quarter-deck, would march aft playing a stirring tune and take up position behind me in front of the ensign staff. 'The preparative' would be lowered in the flagship, the signalman would report, "Eight o'clock Sir." the bugler would sound the 'still' and I would salute as the ensign was hoisted and the band played the National Anthem. It was also the custom to play the Egyptian National Anthem and this came to be followed by the anthems of one or more of the Allies. The bandmaster was not very happy about having to learn and play the anthems of an ever increasing list of Allies nor was I at having to stand at the salute for what seemed an interminable period whilst strange tunes were being played.

Amongst the ship's company were some boy seamen aged between 16 and 18 who had their own mess which was curtained off from the other sailors on the mess-deck and under the supervision of a Petty Officer. The First Lieutenant (a Lieutenant-Commander who was the ship's 'housekeeper' responsible for the cleanliness and maintenance of the interior of the ship) was the boys' Divisional Officer. I was invited to join in their sports and we often played water-polo alongside, the ship, the goals being suspended from booms running out from the ship's side. I sometimes wondered if they had mistaken me for the ball but all was taken and given in good spirit. We also played football and I made the big mistake of refusing the football boots from the sports locker, which had bars instead of studs, in preference to using the rugby boots I had brought out with me. On the very hard ground of the Union Stadium in Alexandria the studs put considerable pressure on the balls of my feet, causing callouses which eventually developed into corns.

Euryalus formed part of the 15th Cruiser Squadron, 'The Fighting Fifteenth' as it was destined to be known, which in November 1941 had comprised the sister ships *Naiad*, *Euryalus*, *Dido* and *Galatea* – the *Naiad* being the Flag-ship of Rear-Admiral Vian. The squadron was based at Alexandria. Another cruiser force, known as Force K, consisting of the Aurora, Penelope and two destroyers and later augmented by the *Ajax*, *Neptune* and a further two destroyers was based at Malta.

The Eighth Army opened its offensive against the Africa Corps in November 1941 and, in support of the Army, Force K and Malta based submarines and aircraft attacked the enemy's supply convoys bound for the ports of Benghazi and Tripoli. That month Force K alone sank 12 supply ships and destroyer escorts with the result that the Italian battle fleet was forced to make reluctant sorties to reinforce the convoy escorts. The Italians, however, were unwilling to seek close action and this was illustrated in December when a fast supply ship, the *Breconshire*, was being run to Malta with much needed fuel and ammunition. It had been arranged that Force K would meet the convoy at a prearranged rendezvous and take over the escort to enable the 15th Cruiser Squadron (which had been weakened by the loss of the *Galatea* a few days previously) to return to Alexandria with sufficient reserves of fuel and ammunition.

At the meeting of the two forces they were attacked by torpedo and high-level bombers and, shortly afterwards, enemy battleships were reported to the northward with a convoy. Admiral Vian sent Br*econshire*, escorted by two destroyers, to the south whilst he gathered his forces and prepared to attack the enemy.

The Italian fleet consisted of two battleships, an 8-inch cruiser squadron and destroyers, and our cruisers came under heavy and accurate fire. However the Italians turned away and retreated as Admiral Vian, using smoke to conceal the inferiority of his force, carried out feint attacks with all the fire at his disposal in an attempt to draw the enemy fleet further away from *Breconshire*. Force K was eventually detached to escort her safely to Malta whilst, under cover of darkness, The Fighting Fifteenth returned to Alexandria.

In the middle of December the fleet suffered a severe set-back when three cruisers of Force K ran into a minefield whilst steaming to intercept an important enemy convoy bound for Tripoli. The *Neptune* was sunk, the *Aurora* badly damaged and reduced to 10 knots, the *Penelope* slightly damaged and a destroyer sunk whilst trying to pick up survivors from the *Neptune*. On the same day, in Alexandria harbour, the two battleships *Queen Elizabeth* and *Valiant* were mined by Italian frogmen and put out of action for many months. This added catastrophe temporarily left command of the Central and Eastern Mediterranean to the three cruisers of The Fighting Fifteenth. There was a small force of capital ships at Gibraltar (Force H) to keep an eye on the Western Mediterranean and the Atlantic but it was withdrawn for other duties at the beginning of 1942. Admiral Vian's cruisers were the only British force from Gibraltar to the Red Sea with a heavier armament than a destroyer.

The Italians had five or six battleships, 8-inch gun cruisers and flotillas of destroyers, and one would have thought that now was the opportunity for them to establish command of the Mediterranean by coming out and forcing our ships into action. However they knew the reputation of the Royal Navy and had received a bloody nose every time they had been forced into action with our ships, with the consequence that they still did not think the odds were long enough. Before the enemy could take command of the Mediterranean, Malta had to be eliminated in order to protect the Afrika Corps supply lines, and instead of using the fleet for this purpose he decided to leave it to the Luftwaffe.

In December 1941 and throughout the ensuing months Malta came under savage bombardment through incessant air-raids. In January the advance of the Eighth Army was halted and it was forced to retreat in the face of the Afrika Corps which advanced and occupied the airfields in Cyrenaica which had been used to give air protection to our convoys supplying Malta. A small force of submarines and Fleet Air Arm torpedo-bombers continued to attack enemy supply ships, and a few Hurricane fighters continued to defend the Island, but ammunition, fuel and food supplies were running low. A small convoy managed to get through with ammunition in January but the attempt to get another small convoy through in February had to be abandoned.

Although the entry of Japan into the war had stretched resources to the limit the *Cleopatra* was sent out to reinforce Admiral Vian's squadron. Unfortunately his flagship *Naiad* was sunk by a U-boat at the beginning of March so that the squadron again consisted of only three ships with the Admiral flying his flag in *Cleopatra*.

The foregoing is a brief explanation of the situation prevailing when I joined *Euryalus* about the 17th March 1942. It had been decided that Admiral Vian should make another attempt in March and I arrived just in time to be present at the action which subsequently became known as the Battle of Sirte.

The convoy was made up of four fast merchantmen, *Breconshire* (commanded by a Captain RN) *Talabot, Clan Campbell* and the *Pampas*. The escort from Alexandria consisted of the *Cleopatra* (flagship,) *Euryalus, Dido* and ten fleet destroyers with a few small Hunt class destroyers as close escort for the convoy. The force was also strengthened by the anti-aircraft cruiser *Carlisle*, the cruiser *Penelope* and a destroyer from Malta.

The convoy sailed from Alexandria with the close escort early in the morning of March 20th and we sailed later in the day and joined up with them on the morning of the 21st. Our progress was without incident until the evening when we were sighted by enemy transport aircraft who no doubt reported our position.

The following morning *Penelope* and the destroyer from Malta had just joined up when our radar detected aircraft approaching from the north-west which turned out to be a force of Italian torpedo bombers whose subsequent attacks were poorly executed and easily dealt with, several planes being shot down. These attacks were followed by high-level bombing which again was half-hearted and inaccurate, the planes being kept at a distance by our heavy gun-fire. During the morning we were told to keep our eyes peeled as we could expect to sight the Italian Fleet; heavy ships had been seen leaving Taranto.

Like Nelson, Admiral Vian had discussed his tactics with his Captains. The plan was for the cruisers and destroyers to be organized in five divisions – *Cleopatra* and *Euryalus, Dido* and *Penelope*, and three divisions of destroyers. A smoke screen would be laid between the enemy and the convoy and attacks made with torpedoes under cover of the smoke if he tried to break through it.

HMS Euryalus.
Photograph courtesy of the Imperial War Museum (neg. A 13496).

Destroyers attacking with torpedoes

Euryalus – near miss

The cruisers were in a diamond formation on the starboard quarter of the convoy with the fleet destroyers in attendance. They were thus in a position to place themselves between the convoy and any enemy force which might appear from the northward. This threat was not long in becoming a reality.

Just after 2.00 p.m. smoke was sighted on the starboard bow and a few minutes later three ships were seen hull down on the horizon. Just as Captain Blackwood in a former *Euryalus* was the first to signal 'enemy in sight' to Nelson at Trafalgar so Captain Bush was the first to signal 'enemy in sight' to Admiral Vian.

My action station was at the forward starboard corner of the bridge near the Captain and the Navigating Officer so I had a good view of the proceedings. The Chief Yeoman of Signals had his telescope glued to the flagship ready for the Admiral's signal. No sooner had the flags appeared at the yardarm than he reported their meaning to the Captain and, as the flags came down, the order to execute. As we increased speed and took up station astern of *Cleopatra* with *Penelope* following *Dido*, the signal 'make smoke' was made from the flagship.

The weather had been deteriorating during the day and by this time a south easterly gale was blowing. The make smoke signal to the engine-room was just beside me and I played my first part in the action by pressing the button which produced clouds of black funnel smoke. As the Admiral led us towards the enemy at nearly 30 knots the thick black smoke, mixed with the white smoke from smoke floats, formed a thick screen to hide the convoy which had been ordered to steer south.

HMS Euryalus ship's company – Alexandria 1942

The three enemy ships had been recognized as two 8-inch cruisers and a 6-inch cruiser, along with some destroyers and it was not long before we were in action with the heavy ships. Because of the weather and sea conditions it was impossible to see the results of our shooting and the same must have applied to the Italians as only a few shells fell harmlessly around us. There was also some bombing from high-level bombers. The action only lasted for a very short period before the enemy broke off and retired to the north. The bombing had little effect or, us but it was a different matter for the convoy and its escort who had come under sustained attacks by waves of German dive bombers, but fortunately it had suffered no damage. These heavy attacks on the convoy were to continue throughout the day.

The Admiral led us back towards the convoy which had been ordered to steer west again on the withdrawal of the enemy cruisers. Another enemy report was received, this time it turned out to be the Italian battleship *Littorio* and four destroyers approaching from the north. Once again the convoy was ordered to turn to the southward whilst we followed *Cleopatra* as the Admiral led us round to the east laying another thick smoke screen, before turning back to the west again.

The Italians with their powerful force could have inflicted severe damage on the cruisers and the convoy but their Admiral was frightened to enter the smoke screen knowing we were waiting on the other side. Instead he tried to work his way round it to the westward and our cruisers did their best to stop him. Steaming in and out of the smoke – we knew where he was but he did not know where we would re-appear – we kept him at bay. In one of these encounters *Cleopatra* was hit on the bridge and suffered casualties but otherwise she was unaffected. Later, whilst the cruisers were searching for two enemy ships unaccounted for, some of our destroyers held off the enemy in a fierce action in which one was hit but was able to proceed.

Towards evening we were still in action in an out of the smoke. *Euryalus* did not come out of the action entirely unscathed. At one stage a smoke float became jammed in the guard rails as it was being pushed over the side and the Captain told me to go down and get it freed. The ship was leaping around at high speed in the rough seas as I edged my way along the deck to where the float was jammed in the port side guard rails abreast of the forward turrets. The sailors managed to free the float and put it overside as I arrived so that there was nothing for me to do but return to the bridge. As I reached the ladder leading up to the flag deck I could see all the signalmen were flat on the deck. As the ship heeled over to starboard I hung on to the ladder and looked round to see a deluge of water thrown up by a large shell which had just landed alongside the ship. We had come under direct fire from the *Littorio* who had seen us through a gap in the smoke screen and had straddled us with a salvo from her 15-inch guns.

The ship was engulfed in columns of water and showered in shell splinters; a large piece of 15-inch shell landing up in the Commander (E)'s cabin. Fortunately no one was injured. The Captain had altered course to change the range and the next salvo passed harmlessly overhead. *Cleopatra*, who had also been engaging the battleship, led round behind the smoke screen and the *Littorio* disappeared from sight.

Shortly after this the destroyers made a most determined attack on the Italian heavy ships. It was exhilarating and nerve-tingling to see them steaming at full speed, large battle-ensigns streaming from their mastheads and covered in spray from the seas breaking over their bows as they went through the smoke to attack with torpedoes from a range of 6000 yards. *Cleopatra* and *Euryalus* supported the attack with gunfire, dodging in and out of the smoke and, as the destroyers raced back to its safety, we continued to engage the enemy. However the torpedo attack was enough for the Italians, who turned away, broke off the action and disappeared in the gloom to the northward.

We had been in action for nearly twelve hours, from 8.00 a.m. when the air attacks started until 7.00 p.m. when the Italians broke off the action. With the coming of darkness it was unlikely that the enemy would return to risk a night action, so the merchant ships were ordered to proceed with the close escort to Malta whilst the cruisers and destroyers returned to Alexandria. Unfortunately the merchant ships were unable to arrive in the dark and when enemy air attacks were resumed on the morning of March 23rd the *Clan Campbell* was sunk and the *Breconshire* badly damaged and had to be beached. The *Pampas* and *Talabot* both entered harbour but were eventually sunk during the continuous heavy air-raids which followed during the day. Fortunately they sank in only a few feet of water and, by working night and day regardless of air-raids, much of their cargoes was saved.

Admiral Vian's objective was to get clear of 'Bomb Alley' by the next morning and, to start with, we proceeded at 22 knots. The force was steaming into the teeth of a strong easterly gale and the destroyers soon fell behind when they reduced speed because of the damage being incurred. By early morning on the 23rd we had reduced speed to 15 knots because of the weather, and further reductions were made so that the force could be concentrated to receive the air attacks that were expected. The first air attack came in the late afternoon when Ju88's and torpedo bombers made sporadic attacks which were beaten off and no ships were hit.

There was an improvement in the weather during the night and next morning speed was increased to about 25 knots. At about 8.00 a.m. on March 24th *Euryalus* was attacked by two aircraft which we thought to be Blenheims. We had been watching them closely for quite a while when suddenly they turned and headed straight for us. The Captain ordered 'hard a starboard, full speed ahead' whilst the close range weapons opened fire, which may have put the torpedo bombers off as they dropped their torpedoes too soon and the Captain was able to comb their tracks.

Our return to Alexandria was never to be forgotten. The destroyers entered first followed by *Cleopatra*, *Euryalus* and *Dido*. It seemed Alexandria had turned out to greet us with a grand chuck-up. Tugs, launches, and ships' boats led us in, their crews waving and cheering wildly as I stood beside Captain Bush who raised his cap and waved it in acknowledgement. How proud he must have felt at receiving such a welcome. My spine tingled when I heard the sound of the bands playing in the *Valiant* and *Queen Elizabeth* (our two disabled battleships) and the ringing tones of bugles sounding salutes across the harbour. Our smoke-stained funnels and upper-works, blackened gun barrels and empty cartridge cases on deck, were evidence that we had been in a hard fought action. The reception was indeed a Naval Occasion, and as I stood on the bridge and watched the scene in the harbour I felt very proud to be a member of the family that is the Royal Navy.

Later I could not help wondering how fate had made it possible for me to experience so many of the things I had read about in stories of the Navy all within a few days of joining my first ship. Ship to ship gunnery action, destroyer flotillas in torpedo attacks and ships manoeuvring in formation at high speed to name but a few. I had also witnessed the actions and conduct of the officers and men around me as they carried out their professional duties, such as the Chief Yeoman of Signals who never once referred to the fleet signal book for the meaning of a signal and whose instructions were accepted by the Captain without question. There was a lot to live up to.

Instead of going to a buoy berth we went straight alongside a jetty to begin the task of re-ammunitioning, taking on stores and refuelling so that we would be ready instantly for action. Taking on the ammunition was a big job as we had expended practically the whole outfit, and some of our gun barrels required attention as they had become worn through continual firing. Everybody turned out to lend a hand, padre, schoolmaster, doctor, paymaster, stewards all helped to get the job done so that by 3.00 a.m. on the 25th March the ship was ready for sea and we could all get our heads down.

A few nights later the ship held a dance at the *Lycee Francais*, a French school in Alexandria. The hall had a sloping floor, similar to that in a theatre or cinema, which made dancing difficult especially when going uphill away from the band. My lasting memory of the evening is of Chief and Petty Officers and other long service ratings sitting with Admiral Vian and several senior officers, drinking beer and spinning yams whilst a pool of beer formed slowly at the foot of the dance floor. It seemed a good way to celebrate a victory.

There was another notable event which took place shortly after our return and that was the visit of the Duke of Gloucester to the ship whilst he was carrying out a tour of the Middle East. Before leaving the ship the Duke took the salute at a march past by the ship's company. The Royal Marine band paraded facing the Duke who stood on a dais at the after-end of the quarter-deck, whilst the ship's company, led by the boys' division and headed by the First-Lieutenant followed by myself, marched past in single file. The ship's company then manned the port side to 'Cheer Ship' as the Duke left on completion of his visit. I will always remember his brilliant blue eyes which held my gaze for two or three seconds as I marched past.

Chapter 11

LIFE IN A MINESWEEPER

——

Although I was very happy in *Euryalus* and enjoying my work I was still very keen to serve in smaller ships where there would be the possibility of more sea-time and more responsibility. One day when I was ashore in Alexandria I happened to meet by chance a Wren Officer with whom I had travelled out in the *Orontes*. She asked me how I was getting on and what ship I was in, so I told her of my wish to go to something smaller where I might be given more responsible duties and get to sea more often. *Euryalus* had been in harbour for about three weeks and I wanted to do something more interesting than drive the motor boat and pace the quarter-deck. She must have been working in the Captain of the Fleet's office and had something to do with appointments, or else it was a remarkable coincidence, for several days later the Commander told me that I had been appointed to HMS Lord Irwin which turned out to be a minesweeping trawler based in Beirut. It might be thought that I was going from the sublime to the ridiculous but it was a different area of operations and a new experience, and I was excited at the prospect.

In a way I was sorry when it became time to leave *Euryalus*. I had started to make friends amongst the Officers and I enjoyed the happy atmosphere in the wardroom, she was in every way a happy ship. 'Toothy' Kaye, the Dental Officer, was very kind when I first joined – he had met my sister when, as a Wren, she visited the ship when it was in the Firth of Forth shortly after commissioning.

'Toothy' was involved in an amusing prank through being ill in the 'Dido's' boat one night when getting a lift back to *Euryalus*. When our Commander heard what had happened he sent for 'Toothy' and expressed his displeasure at such ungentlemanly conduct for which 'Toothy' duly apologised. The Commander suggested that 'Toothy' should also apologise to Dido's Commander for messing up his boat and tipped off the latter that 'Toothy' would be coming over. Arriving on the Dido's quarter-deck he was met by the Commander who cut short his apologies by saying that, as it was the cox'n of the boat who had the responsibility of cleaning up the mess, it was the cox'n who should receive the apology. 'Toothy' demurred about this and was not at all happy, however the Commander was insistent and the cox'n was duly summoned. 'Toothy' again made his apologies this time to the cox'n who was a Leading Seaman. After hearing what 'Toothy' had to say by way of explanation, the cox'n sucked his teeth and remarked in a broad cockney accent, "it's orlright fer ar own orficers ter be sick but we don't 'old wiv 'avin ter clean up the sick of orficers from uvver ships." It was sometime afterwards that 'Toothy' discovered that the 'cox'n 'was one of Dido's Lieutenants dressed in sailor's uniform.

Before leaving Alexandria I was able to visit 'Bandit' Crooks who was a Midshipman in the *Queen Elizabeth*. As I stepped on board I thought of my father and all the stories he had told me about his time in the 'Old Q. E.' and I was able to have a quick look at the galley which had been his domain. The Flagship carried a lot of Midshipmen and 'Bandit' pointed out the chap who had been one of the three survivors from HMS *Hood* which had been sunk by the *Bismark*. I did not speak to him and it appeared that he rarely spoke about his experience, but I was told that all he recalled was an almighty bang and the next thing he was in the water and coming to the surface in what was probably an air bubble. He certainly had a remarkable escape.

Captain Bush was very kind when I was taken to see him before I left the ship. He told me that I had conducted myself to his entire satisfaction and that he was sorry to see me go, but understood my wish for smaller ships and more sea-time. He finished up by saying that if ever we were in port together I was to come on board and see him. At the time I took this last instruction with a 'pinch of salt' but I was to be proved quite wrong.

It was quite a long journey from Alexandria to Haifa and then on to Beirut. The first part was by train changing at El Kantara on the Suez Canal to join the train for Haifa. I had very little money left by the time I had paid my mess bill and the Marine who did my cabin, etc., and I arrived at Kantara with exactly half a piastre (about a penny) to take me the rest of the journey. Fortunately for me, whilst sitting in the Arab café/canteen at Kantara I met up with an RNVR Lieutenant who was also travelling to Beirut, and he was kind enough to stake me until our arrival at Haifa.

The train left Kantara in the late afternoon and to begin with the scenery was rather monotonous, first desert then low lying scrub land where the odd cluster of Arab dwellings was the only source of interest. There was no food on the train and we had to sustain ourselves with the eggs and bread that was hawked by lots of small boys at the various stops. The following morning, after an uncomfortable night with little sleep, we were in Palestine where the view from the train was much more attractive and interesting.

When we eventually arrived in Haifa we were extremely tired, unshaven and covered in dust and looking forward to a hot bath and a decent meal. We reported to the base only to find that the paymaster was off having his siesta and that there would be a delay of a couple of hours before we could draw any money. Off we went to a hotel (the Savoy – I was to know it again 5 years later during the Palestine troubles) to get cleaned up, only to find that they would not give me a room until I had some money to pay in advance. Later on we were told that we would be travelling to Beirut by car as the railway had not yet been completed.

After two or three days in Haifa we set off on the last stage of the journey which was by far the most interesting. The road ran along the coast and offered some very fine views of the surrounding scenery as we entered Lebanon. It was an enjoyable trip and a worth while experience.

In Beirut I found that my trawler was over in Cyprus, temporarily based in Famagusta whilst sweeping the approach channel. I had to wait several days to take passage in a ship going to Famagusta so, in the meantime, I was billeted in a house and given odd jobs to do around the base. Just before I left for Cyprus I was given the task of supervising the removal of the NOIC's (Naval Officer in Charge) desk to another office. The job was carried out without any problems and I thought no more about it until, in the middle of the ocean, I found the keys of the desk (which had been locked) in my pocket. I could expect a 'big dinner' from Captain Amott when I arrived back in Beirut.

Lord Irwin was a typical coal-burning Grimsby trawler built at Fowey in 1913. The only lavatory was in a 'wee house' on the deck outside the wheel-house. The forward end of the fish hold had been converted into the messdeck for the sailors and the after end had been partitioned off to form a single cabin and a small wardroom for the two officers. Stairs led down from the wheel-house to the Skipper's cabin which was small and cramped but somehow cozy. There was a bunk with drawers underneath recessed under the stairs and, opposite, a settee covered with heavy material similar to that used in the railway carriages of the period. The settee was used for sitting at the heavy table which seemed to take up most of the deck space and there was little room for movement around it in any direction. The rest of the space was taken up by a wash-basin unit, small corner cupboard and a locker used as a wardrobe. I was very happy when I was told it would be my cabin; what a difference to sleeping in a hammock in a flat outside a gunroom, which would have been my lot on a big ship.

The ship was under the command of Skipper Cyril Sutcliffe, the First Lieutenant being Skipper Jasper Pidgeon whom I had been sent to relieve as he had been given his own Command. I always thought Jasper to be a very melodramatic name and not easily forgotten and, sure enough, it caught my eye in the papers after the war when I saw that he had won the Prunier Trophy for the biggest catch of the season.

HMS Lord Melchett, a similiar vessel to HMS Lord Irwin

The Royal Navy Patrol Service comprised the trawlers, drifters and other small craft of the fishing fleets and the majority of the officers and men at the outbreak of war were fishermen or Patrol Service reservists. The officers were given the rank of Skipper RNR or Skipper Lieutenant RNR, the 'Skipper' being dropped for the rank of Lieutenant-Commander and above.

'Suttie,' as he was known to the other Skippers, was a short sturdy Yorkshireman and, from what I could understand, had been a much respected and successful fishing Skipper in Grimsby. He could spin a good yarn and I liked to get him talking about his fishing and other experiences. I always found that one could learn a lot through listening to older and more experienced seamen, and pick up tips and advice on professional matters which might, and often did, come in handy in the future. This of course applies in any profession or trade. I came to like and respect him very much.

'Suttie's' account of how he and the *Lord Irwin* came to be out in the Middle East was something of a saga and highly amusing.

The Port Minesweeping Officer in Grimsby had called for volunteers from amongst the Skippers to take three trawlers out to the Eastern Mediterranean where they were urgently required to sweep for magnetic mines. As there were no volunteers forthcoming the PMSO sent for 'Suttie' and told him that, as a senior and respected figure in the port, if he set an example and volunteered others would follow. He was under the impression that once he had taken the ship out to Alexandria he would return to the UK. He agreed to go, and on being asked whom he would like as his First Lieutenant he named his best friend, Jasper Pidgeon. There was only one snag – Jasper did not want to go and he was most upset when he heard that he had been shanghaied.

They sailed from Greenock and for the first two weeks Jasper would not speak to his Skipper and they had reached Freetown before normal relations were resumed. From Freetown they proceeded south along the African coast stopping at various places to effect repairs; on one occasion they found themselves literally 'up the creek' with jungle on both sides of them and monkeys swinging from the trees. They took the opportunity to do a spot of trading with the natives who came out in their dug-out canoes to have a look at the unexpected visitors.

It was probably as a result of one of these visits that the crew went down with blackwater fever and malaria on the Gold Coast. At one time, when only four people on board were fit for duty, 'Suttie' went down to the engine-room and shared four hour watches stoking the boiler with the only stoker who remained fit.

The arrival of *Lord Irwin* at the Naval base at Simonstown, near Capetown, started a bit of a commotion in the dockyard. An Engineer Commander went on board and took one look at the ship and said he was amazed that she had managed to come so far. He was further dismayed when the ship's elderly Chief Engineer, sweat rag round his neck, appeared only to require some cotton waste and baling wire before continuing the voyage. Nothing would do according to the Commander (E) but a good re-fit which resulted in the ship being detained in port for the next few weeks.

It was not long before 'Suttie' and Jasper experienced the well-known hospitality afforded by the citizens of Capetown to allied service personnel on their way to the Middle and Far East. Soon after their arrival, whilst walking in Capetown, a car drew up alongside and the occupants invited them home for a meal. A friendship soon developed and for the rest of their stay they had a high old time of it with days at the races, evenings out and several days at a farm up-country. Eventually the time came to leave Simonstown and they proceeded north along the coast calling at Durban on the way. Here the same thing happened as in Simonstown and the ship was detained whilst the Naval authorities satisfied themselves that she was in a fit state to proceed. Once more the two Skippers sampled South African hospitality to the full.

It took *Lord Irwin* six months and five days to make the 11,500 mile passage to Alexandria, a voyage that should have taken no more than three months at the most. The Skipper's enquiries about passages home for Jasper and himself were met with much amusement; they were out there and they were stuck. However they had their turn to have a good laugh when, later on, the Skippers in a trawler which had newly arrived on the station announced that they expected to be going home very shortly.

Although I was pleased when I was told that I would occupy the Skipper's cabin I soon found out why 'Suttie' preferred the cabin adjoining the wardroom. Every night I was plagued by mosquitos that would foregather in the recessed bunk space, and although I rigged up a mosquito net I would still be awakened by their buzzing and bites. On putting on the light, I would see them inside the screen and on the bulkhead or bunkboard all around me. However, I never caught malaria or sand-fly fever.

Most of the crew were Patrol Service ratings and had been fishermen at some time or another. The senior rating or cox'n (Len) had been first hand or mate on trawlers and was an excellent seaman with a strong and well proportioned physique. The two stokers were Scots, the oldest, Charlie Stewart, came from Leith and was a hard-working, likeable chap who had the unfortunate tendency to take 'one too many' when he was ashore and invariably ended up in the arms of the military police. Charlie was always resigned to the punishment which followed his escapades and accepted his stoppage of leave with good grace. He would never attempt to go ashore whilst his leave was stopped, even when there was no official check on those leaving the ship which would have been the routine on a bigger ship. The junior stoker was from the Gorbals in Glasgow, about 19 or 20 years of age, and a lazy lay-about who thought nothing of having a quiet snooze on top of the coal.

Lord Irwin had been converted to sweep for magnetic mines; the mines being exploded by setting up a magnetic field behind the ship. Two buoyant electric cables, each about 3 inches in diameter, the long leg being 575 yards and the short leg 225 yards in length, were lashed together and towed astern. This was known as the 'tail.' The electrical current was supplied by a large diesel generator secured on the upper deck. When the tail was not in use it was flaked down on the deck on either side around the engine-room casing. The sweep was known as a LL sweep and the ships as LL sweepers. There were two other LL trawlers in the area and sometimes we would be in company sweeping together, at other times we would be detached to check a channel by ourselves. HMS *Cordelia* was in company when I arrived in Famagusta.

During sweeping operations my station was at the stern supervising the operation of streaming the tail after which I stayed on the bridge with the Skipper whilst the ship did its sweep up and down the channel. At the end of the day's work I returned to the stern to supervise the recovery of the tail. Streaming the tail was a fairly easy operation, the ship steaming slowly ahead helped to pull it out and it was only a question of lifting the heavy lengths flaked down on either side of the ship, walking them aft ensuring that the cable did not become snagged, and that the men were not endangered as it ran out.

Recovering the sweep was a different matter altogether and heavy work as it had to be pulled in by hand. It was done in the old sailing ship fashion with a 'chant' and a 'haul.' I stood nearest the stern with Len who would chant, "ahub, ahubinay" the latter being the signal for us all to lift and heave the heavy cable inboard. When ships were in company there was intense rivalry to be the first to recover the sweep; the record was supposed to be held by a ship in Grimsby who had recovered the sweep in 8 minutes and we were not far outside of that.

In harbour after the daily sweep all hands would sit on deck in the dog watches, yarning, drinking tea or partaking of oranges and grapefruit that the hands would find 'loafing' in the orchards when returning from a run ashore at night. There was not much to do in Famagusta and I did not go ashore very often. One night 'Suttie' took me to one of the cabarets where a dance troupe was performing. The girls were Hungarians who had been touring the Middle East when war broke out and had found themselves trapped in Cyprus where they were immediately interned. The authorities evidently thought that the girls would not pose much of a threat, and might even raise the morale of the Allies, if they carried on working and so they had been released.

The military police would sometimes stop on the jetty alongside the ship and come onboard for a yarn and a 'cuppa.' One evening I asked one of them if I could have go on his motor bike. Off I went watched by all the crew and once again I failed to slow down sufficiently when turning. This time it was not the ocean I ran into but the wall of Navy House and right under the eyes of an officer who was watching the performance from a balcony. Fortunately the bike was not damaged as the MP would have been in trouble if he had returned with a bent machine, and lucky for me he did not jump up and down too much.

On our return to Beirut I had my first experience of coaling ship, replenishing the stock of coal which fired the boiler. It was a dirty business which the Skipper left me to get on with whilst he went to visit some of his friends on other ships until the operation was completed. The ship was soon covered in coal dust (and so was I) which seemed to get into every nook and cranny and down any opening, even although I had closed or blocked off ventilators, doors and ports to accommodation and other spaces. This was made evident when, after washing down on completion and feeling quite pleased that the ship looked clean and all was well, the Skipper returned to find a lump of coal on top of his wardrobe which rather dampened my spirits.

One day when the Skipper was ashore visiting the PMSO, I was sifting through some official correspondence and came across a memorandum on ship camouflage which contained illustrations of bow waves painted on the bow to give a false impression of a ship's speed. As a U-boat had just been reported to be operating in our area I thought it would be a good idea if we had a bow wave so that in the event of being attacked our speed would be over estimated and the torpedo would pass ahead. I told the cox'n my idea to enlist his support and he was soon sitting in a carley raft, accompanied by another enthusiast, alongside the bow painting on the desired wave whilst I directed operations from the jetty. Len produced a work of art, a light blue wave with white foam at the edges, flaring up at the stem and failing away aft towards the waterline, giving the appearance of the ship steaming at twice her designed speed.

I was still on the jetty admiring the art work when the Skipper returned accompanied by some of his colleagues. I did not have a chance to ask him what he thought of my efforts at camouflage, he had already spotted it from a distance. His "What the hell is that, Mid?", told me straight away that he was not impressed by the alteration in his ship's appearance, and my attempted Explanation was quickly cut short with a "Get that damned thing off right away!" 'Suttie' took quite a ribbing from the other Skippers but later on he did give me an A for effort and enthusiasm.

One day whilst we were sweeping, two corvettes came into Beirut and tied up in our usual berth so that when we returned to harbour we had to secure alongside them. When the time came for them to leave it was arranged that we would let go our stern lines and allow them to back out of the berth, after which we could pull ourselves back alongside. However they made a bit of a mess of backing out and, having pushed our stem well off, they changed their minds and decided to go out ahead which meant we had to let go our head ropes, which had been passed to the shore, resulting in our being adrift in the harbour, and being blown by a stiff breeze down the basin on to a wharf.

Fortunately the Chief was in the engineroom at the time and had sufficient steam up to enable him to answer my urgent request to get the ship moving ahead. However there was another problem. A small convoy of merchant ships was leaving harbour whilst all this was going on and I eventually found myself caught up with them and following them out of harbour and up the channel. I had been so busy that there had been no time to call the Skipper who was having his afternoon nap, and the first he knew of it all was when he was awakened by the ship's movement and found himself at sea. I thought I might have received a ticking off for not calling him but he was quite satisfied with the way I had handled the situation and quietly turned the ship round and headed back to port. So I had taken a ship to sea for the first time.

'Suttie' would sometimes go to the races and it was at the race-course that he met a French lady whom he invited to visit his ship. She arrived on board chaperoned by an attractive Lebanese girl of about my own age who was a singer and well-known on the radio where she was looked upon as the local Vera Lynn. Nothing daunted I asked her if she would sing for us and suggested *Begin the Beguine*. What a noise. The poor girl only sang Arabic music and her attempt at western music was not very good to say the least.

The big diesel generator was serviced by a shore based electrician and whilst talking to him he asked me if I played rugby as there was a big match being held on the following Saturday and that the army officer in charge was looking for players. I was keen to have a game so I went along to see the army chap and find out what it was all about.

There was a New Zealand brigade in the area at the time and a match was being arranged between it and local British units which was to be billed as New Zealand v Great Britain. I was asked which school I had attended, my position and what team I had played for. He was English but had heard of Royal High, and when I told him I had played eight games for the 1st XV before leaving to go to sea and that my position was full-back or scrum half, he said that full-back was the remaining position to be filled and would I come up and 'punt the pill about' that evening. I went along to a sports field and spent an hour or so kicking and fielding after which I was told to be at the American University sports ground at 2 p.m. on Saturday and to bring my own kit.

The American University in Beirut had a very good reputation in the Middle East and was probably the main seat of learning in that part of the world. The campus contained many fine buildings and the sports ground was well equipped with a running track around the pitch, jumping pits at each end, a stand for spectators and changing rooms.

There was no strip for the Great Britain team so we all wore our own jerseys which provided a colourful selection of many well-known clubs. We must have looked like the 'coat of many colours' being blown in the wind as we ran about the field. In contrast, New Zealand turned out in their traditional black jerseys which made them appear as formidable as the All Blacks, and we were to find that the appearance was not deceptive when we learned that the team did contain seven or eight players who had been All Blacks.

The stand was filled to capacity and the touch line crowded with soldiers, most of them New Zealanders. I heard there were about 2000 spectators. New Zealand supplied the referee who, as it turned out, was extremely strict, blowing for the slightest infringement and causing frequent stoppages which eventually brought loud disapproval from the touch-line even when the decision went against us.

Team photographs were taken before the game and then the Kiwis performed the 'Hakka.' When I was a schoolboy I saw the All Blacks at Murrayfield during their 1935/36 tour and I never thought that I would ever have to face the fearsome challenge. I began to think a Malta convoy would be less dangerous. I also remembered coming away from Murrayfield with the lasting impression that New Zealanders had legs like tree trunks, and from what I could see they had not changed in that respect. I began to wonder what I had let myself in for.

The game had not long been started before I realised that Captain Arnott, the NOIC Beirut, was amongst the spectators in the stand and that he had recognized me (he had not forgotten about the keys of his desk). Whenever I went to catch the ball or whenever it came near me I could hear him shouting, "Come on Stewart" in encouragement which was only likely to make me more nervous knowing his eagle eye was upon me. I was the only Naval type playing and he was probably anxious that I should not let the Service down.

Our team captain was the hooker and he had the unfortunate tendency towards 'feet up' in the scrum which, from the outset, was pounced upon by the referee and resulted in our giving away many penalty kicks. The final score was something like 24 – 0 for the Kiwis – I do not recall a try being scored, all the points coming from penalties or dropped goals. It was a very good game played in a hard and competitive manner with none of the bad tempered conduct that is so often seen nowadays. The Kiwis were very good and fast and I could not help feeling at the end that it was because we seemed to get in the way, rather than through good defensive play, that they did not score a try. Then again getting in the way is what defence is all about.

One day as we steamed up the channel towards Haifa the Fighting Fifteenth were leaving harbour and were approaching on a reciprocal course, which meant that we would pass at not too great a distance from them. I was keen to pay my respects to Captain Bush and suggested to the Skipper that we should dip our ensign. I had been so used to dipping the ensign to passing warships when in the BI that I completely forgot that Naval vessels do not dip to each other. *Cleopatra* and *Dido* both passed with their noses seemingly in the air and without a movement of their ensigns, but as *Euryalus* came abeam we saw her ensign drop a couple of feet before being hauled up again. It was nice to be remembered by Captain Bush.

Because of the situation in the Western Desert in July 1942 the Navy's operational and administrative base was temporarily moved from Alexandria to Port Said. Later I was to find out than during the upheaval someone had spotted that I was serving in a trawler, and this was the reason I received orders at the beginning of August to report to the Captain of the Fleet for re-appointment.

The orders arrived at just the right moment. Steaming a few laps daily up and down an approach channel did not provide much opportunity to further my professional knowledge, although my time in *Lord Irwin* was well spent and the introduction to LL minesweeping a useful experience. I had enjoyed serving with 'Suttie' but it was time to move on.

At the Captain of the Fleet's office I was interviewed by a Lieutenant-Commander RN whose first words were, "What the devil were you doing in a trawler – how much big ship time have you got in?" I could see he was set on sending me to a ship with a gunroom so I requested, somewhat nervously, to see the Captain of the Fleet himself. I was rather surprised when my request was granted and relieved to find that it was the same officer who interviewed me when I arrived on the station. He tended to agree with the Lieutenant-Commander but when I pleaded my case he relented and said I would be appointed to the corvette HMS *Erica*.

Again I think fate took a hand as I was to have more adventures and varied experiences in *Erica* and subsequent escort vessels than I might have had in a destroyer.

Chapter 12

A Corvette in the Eastern Mediterranean

———

HMS *Erica* was a Flower class corvette, a new class of anti-submarine escort vessel which had been designed in 1939 during the expansion of the Navy. It was expected that the country would be at war by 1940 and, as the normal escort sloop could not be built fast enough to meet this deadline, a new class of coastal escort vessel which could be built within a year and which was cheap to produce was required. The design was based on a whale-catcher, the final particulars being 205 feet long, 1170 tons displacement, 16 knots, a complement of 47 officers and ratings. Over 150 vessels were built in the UK with a further 130 being built in Canada for the Royal Canadian Navy. *Erica* was completed in August 1940.

The corvettes were extremely stable but they 'rolled on wet grass' and were very wet and uncomfortable in bad weather. Although designed for coastal escort they were soon being employed in ocean escort work and this meant that the complement had to be increased drastically to avoid crew exhaustion on long passages, and modifications had to be made to ease overcrowding on the messdecks and make the ships more sea-worthy and drier in the North Atlantic. The forecastle was extended aft covering the well-deck and waists providing additional accommodation, the bridge structure and layout was altered and the ships fitted with radar. The complement was increased to about 80 officers and ratings.

Erica together with another seven corvettes was sent out to the Eastern Mediterranean shortly after being commissioned and was never modified although small alterations were made locally. Her complement had been increased to over eighty which resulted in overcrowded messdecks, a situation which could only be relieved when men were able to sling their hammocks on deck in fine weather.

HMS Erica.
Photograph courtesy of the Ulster Folk and Transport Museum.

There was a tremendous *esprit de corps* amongst those who sailed in corvettes. They were hardy little ships doing work for which they were never really designed, and their crews took pride in being able to stand up to the extremely uncomfortable conditions in which they had to operate. Although the weather in the Mediterranean could at times be very bad it was nothing compared to the conditions which prevailed in the North Atlantic, and those who were engaged in Atlantic and Russian convoy escort duty were the real heroes of corvettes. Being in corvettes was something like being in fighters in the Air Force – one went about with the top button of one's uniform undone.

I fell for *Erica* when I first saw her. She was a pretty ship painted a lighter grey than usual with everything about her looking uniform and tidy. A monkey island had been built on top of the original compass house which also contained the asdic set, and the new bridge looked very professional with wind baffles and small bridge wings, compared to some of the other corvettes whose open bridges looked rather like tea chests.

The wooden boat deck abaft the bridge was snow-white and we would often have our meals there when conditions were suitable. The ships were designed to accommodate the Captain in his own cabin on the main deck and three officers in two cabins off the small wardroom on the deck below. I was given the small cabin which had been made by partitioning off part of the wheel-house and which I considered to be the best one in the ship, if we were hit whilst I was asleep I would have a better chance than most; it was well above the water-line.

Lieutenant Adrian Seligman RNR, the Commanding Officer, had spent two years at Cambridge before suddenly leaving to sign on as steward on a coaster. He subsequently served as cook, deckhand, and ordinary seaman in other ships and made three voyages in barques in the grain trade from Australia. He held a Mate's certificate in sail which was uncommon amongst young officers at that time. In 1936 Lieutenant Seligman purchased a barquentine named the *Cap Pilar* and advertised for young men to contribute and join him in a voyage to the South Sea for a couple of years. Eventually nine or ten people joined him and the story of their adventures was contained in the book *The Voyage of the Cap Pilar* which he wrote on his return.

Before joining *Erica* Lieutenant Seligman was one of two officers who travelled to Turkey in civilian clothes to bring out a merchant ship which had been trapped in the Black Sea. The story of this daring operation was told in his book *No Stars to Guide*. After leaving *Erica* he was put in command of the Levant Schooner Squadron which was engaged in landing raiding parties on occupied Greek Islands in the Aegean, and these adventures were also recounted in a book published in later years. He was subsequently promoted to Commander and awarded the DSC.

The three officers were all RNVR and were several years older than me. Lieutenant Palmer, the First Lieutenant (Number One) had been to sea in the Twenties and held a Second Mate's certificate, but prior to the war he had sold Hudson motor cars. Guy Phipps-Walker, the Second Lieutenant and Navigator (Pilot) was a member of a well-known family of brewers, whilst George Deans, a Sub-Lieutenant, had been a banker in the Bank of New Zealand in London. After the war he became Secretary of the Royal Caledonian Schools.

I was made Officer of Quarters of the 4-inch gun on the forecastle at anti-submarine stations and put in charge of the multiple 0.5-inch machine gun mounting at A.A. stations. Like the 4-inch gun, which was 1918 vintage and only suitable for surface action, these quadruple mounted machine guns were an old type and subject to frequent stoppages. The cure for the first stoppage was to hit the gun with a mallet. I was also put in charge of the forecastle party as my station for entering and leaving harbour.

What pleased me more than anything was the Captain's decision to put me in charge of a bridge watch at sea and to act as Officer of the Day in harbour, thus freeing the First Lieutenant for other duties. I do not know if it was because I was RNR and had a couple of years sea-going experience that the Captain immediately showed trust in me, because it was highly unusual for a Midshipman to be in full charge of a watch, but I was always grateful to him for the opportunity to gain early experience of shouldering such a responsibility.

When I joined *Erica* in August 1942 most of the fleet was based in Port Said or Haifa, and we were employed in escorting convoys from Port Said to Haifa, Beirut, and Tripoli in the Lebanon, until the Eighth Army resumed its advance along the desert after the Battle of Alamein.

When engaged in escort duty we would be allocated a position relative to the convoy, keeping station on a selected ship by steaming a few knots above convoy speed and zig-zagging to confuse any lurking U-boats as to our course whilst searching for them with our detection equipment. Keeping station was not very difficult in the daytime when the convoy could be seen and the distance from it measured by the sextant and the height of a vessel's mast. At night, and especially when there was no moon, it was a different matter. *Erica* was not fitted with radar and the ships, being blacked out and showing no lights, could not be seen at any appreciable range so it was quite easy to lose station, either ahead or astern, or to wander away from the convoy if one misjudged the degree of zig-zag necessary to remain in position. It was a skill which could only be learned through on the job experience and I believe I learned more quickly by being in charge from the outset and having to make the decisions, than I would have done if I had been second Officer of the Watch as might have been expected. There were some heart-stopping moments to begin with but I used my common sense and did not hesitate to call the Captain when in doubt. All Commanding Officers had Standing Orders which contained instructions that they were to be called whenever the OOW was in doubt about any matter whatsoever, in addition to the procedures to be followed in given circumstances. As a rule they got very little rest at sea and they could take a dim view if, when they arrived on the bridge, they found that the situation could have been handled by the OOW, or it had been created by the latter's inefficiency. At the same time a rocket would be given if the Captain discovered a situation where he should have been called and the OOW had failed to do so. Officers lacking in confidence could be placed in a dilemma especially if a Captain tended to be liverish. However we had no fears on that score, and it was a weight off the mind to know that if we called our Captain, whatever the circumstances, he would deal with the matter with equanimity and understanding. We were a happy and friendly wardroom and we had a very happy ship.

On one occasion whilst escorting a group of LCT.s (landing craft tank), I was awakened in the middle of the night by the ringing of the engine-room telegraph and urgent helm orders being shouted down to the quartermaster in the wheel-house next door. Rushing up to the bridge I discovered that we were surrounded by the 'doom doom doom' sound of diesel engines signifying that the landing craft were all around us. It was a very dark night and the OOW had continued the inward leg of his zig-zag in order to sight a ship and check his position. Unfortunately, in the dark he steamed right between two ships and landed up in the middle of the convoy. Luckily he realised what had happened and quickly avoided possible collision by putting the ship on the convoy course, and then had the unenviable task of calling the Captain to extricate the ship from the convoy.

Although Port Said was much smaller than Alexandria it was still a good run ashore. There were three clubs where one could have a drink and spend an evening, the Officers Club, Maltese Club, and the Warrant Officers Club in addition to the two main hotels in one of which was a cabaret. There were the usual cafes where one could sit and watch the world go by whilst drinking Turkish coffee and eating sticky cakes or ice-cream. A ferry ran the short distance across the harbour to Port Fouad where the canal workshops and the homes of many of the European employees were situated. Just outside Port Fouad there was a private bathing beach named the *Plage D'Enfants* which all allied officers were allowed to use. It was beautifully laid out with changing rooms, restaurant and other facilities at the rear of a large sward which was dotted with palm trees and bordered the sheltered beach.

I quickly made friends with other young officers and spent most of my shore leave at the *Plage*, swimming or dancing to a portable gramophone with girls from the European community whose fathers worked for the Canal Company. One of the girls collected records and was very keen on swing music, so on my next trip, which was to Beirut, I managed to find a record of In the Mood that she was anxious to obtain and gave it to her on my return. This was the start of a very close friendship.

Elsie was the daughter of Doctor Scarpalezzo, a Greek gynaecologist who was highly respected in the European community and also by the local people for his work amongst the poor. When I met Elsie she had just celebrated her 15th birthday and was still at school although, as with most girls out there who seemed to mature more quickly, she looked much older. She was very attractive, very fair with long blonde hair. Her looks were what one might term classical Greek, compared to her sister who was a brunette. I was introduced to her parents who made me very welcome and their beautiful flat became a second home to me.

It was in Port Said that I met up again with 'Bandit' Crooks who had been in the gunroom of the *Queen Elizabeth*. This time he was serving in an ex-Dutch minesweeping trawler and he had quite a story to tell. He had been ashore in Alexandria one evening and had gone into the 'Phaleron', the only bar and cabaret that was open to both officers and other ranks. There he had met up with some other Australians and a riotous evening was had by all which ended with them shooting out some of the lights in the establishment. The Military Police duly arrived and 'Bandit' was escorted back to his ship where the news that one of the Flagship's Midshipmen had been arrested was viewed as a very serious matter. He was taken in front of the Captain who ordered him to be beaten by the Sub-Lieutenant of the gunroom – a normal punishment for a Midshipman in those days if he committed a serious misdemeanour. 'Bandit' was a big, strong chap, moreover he was Australian and there was no way he was going to bend over and let somebody give him a dozen across the backside with a cane or bayonet scabbard.

When the Sub-Lieutenant approached to carry out the punishment 'Bandit,' in his own words, threatened to flatten him. This resulted in his being sent to the

Zingarella, a Greek caique (sailing vessel with an auxiliary engine), which was famous for its adventures with the Inshore Squadron which ran supplies to the Western Desert ports, and which was instrumental in sustaining Tobruk during the long siege. Whilst in the *Zingarella* 'Bandit ' had managed to acquire a fair amount of loot – a couple of motor bikes and a selection of hand guns, Birettas and Lugers, plus an Italian Breda machine gun, something like the British Bren gun. I stayed an afternoon with him whilst they were doing a sweep of the channel and spent most of it trying out his weapons from the stem with various bottles and cans as targets. That was the last time I saw him as shortly afterwards I heard he had been killed when his motor bike crashed into a truck on the road to Ismailia. It was a sad end for a very fine chap full of energy and who enjoyed life to the full; we had had some good times together at Greenwich.

During a stay in Beirut the Captain decided we should give a cocktail party on board. Officers from various ships and the Base were invited together with other guests who included General Spears (on a Political Mission in the area) and Captain Arnott, the NOIC. No party is really complete without some feminine company and as there was a shortage of ladies, to rectify the situation, I was sent on a hazardous mission which at least was deserving of a Mention in Dispatches. My task was to visit the nearby Military Hospital and ask the Matron, in as many words but diplomatically, if she would supply some nurses for a party. That I was nervous goes without saying. I had heard of the reputation enjoyed by hospital Matrons, especially in Military Hospitals where they were extremely strict and took a poor view of junior officers who appeared to have designs upon their nurses.

I was more confident when I entered the Matron's office and found a very pleasant lady who looked remarkably like my mother. I introduced myself (calling her Ma'am) and said the Captain presented his compliments and would be very pleased if she and some of her nurses would care to visit the ship and attend a cocktail party on board. Matron asked me several questions about the ship, the Captain and who would be attending, no doubt to satisfy herself that it was an official do and not just an excuse for the officers to have some women on board. The Captain had asked me to try and get a certain number to attend and it was a bit difficult to make the request without sounding as though I was placing an order. However I think Matron had a certain sympathy for me in my mission. She did not think that she would be able to manage, but she was sure the required number could be found who would like to attend. I went back to the ship rather pleased with myself at having contributed towards the party by organizing the 'popsies.'

The two boats were put into the water to give a clear deck space the width of the ship and an awning was rigged overhead. A temporary gangway was rigged from the boat deck to the jetty to allow visitors straight access on to the deck. This gangway was to be the cause of an embarrassing mishap to one of the guests at the end of the party.

The nurses and other guests duly arrived and the party was soon going with a swing. This was due in no small measure to the efficiency and devotion to duty of the stewards and others who kept the glasses well topped up. By the end of the day it could be seen that they too had enjoyed themselves.

Unfortunately it had started to rain and by the time the guests began to leave a large pool had formed at the foot of the gangway. I was standing at the head of the gangway, seeing the guests 'over the side' when Captain Arnott, the NOIC, and his lady companion were preparing to leave. The Captain went down the gangway followed by the lady who held on to the man-ropes of the gangway to steady herself. The gangway was a temporary affair and the man-rope stanchions had not been intended to take any appreciable weight. Just as she was a couple of feet from the bottom of the gangway the lady put too much weight on the man-rope, the stanchion gave way and she landed up sitting on her bottom in the pool of water. It was so funny that I started laughing before I quickly collected myself and hurried down to help her in her distress. Captain Arnott, who had been in the act of getting into his car out of the rain, appeared to be more embarrassed than sympathetic as he urged her to get up and into the car which she did without any fuss. I learned many years later that they married and went out to live in Kenya after the war.

I met several of the other corvette Commanding Officers one evening when our wardroom visited a ship where the Captain was being relieved. He was an RNR Lieutenant named Potts who was leaving to take up a shore appointment. Before the war he had been in command of the Bibby liner *Somersetshire* (now a hospital ship) and he was upset at being given a staff appointment, and in addition, he was worried about what his company would think about it. He eventually made representations to the powers that be and was allowed to return to his company. There was another officer present whom I had heard about before the war. Lieutenant-Commander Martyn Sherwood RN had written a book called *The Voyage of the Tai-Mo-Shan*; the story of how he and five other officers on the China Station had a yacht built in a Chinese yard and had sailed it home to Dartmouth where it was eventually sold. It was interesting to meet someone I had heard about, and to find out he was just as I imagined he would be when I had been reading his book. One other officer was Commander Courage RN a member of the brewing family. He was a big, bluff and imposing man, every inch the popular conception of a Naval Officer. Some ten years later, when I was serving behind the bar in the family hotel in Perthshire, I recognized him immediately when he came in on his way up to the family shooting lodge in a nearby glen. I believe he was related to Piers Courage, the racing car driver who was subsequently killed.

It was also in Beirut that I found Fluffy, a little mongel puppy. Number One, Pilot and myself were having a meal in an open-air restaurant; I remember it was the first time I had Vienna Schnitzel, a particular favourite of the Pilot's who insisted that the recognized drink to accompany the dish was vodka. I enjoyed the veal but I thought the vodka was pretty wild stuff.

The puppy appeared and started playing around underneath our table. Her coat was brown and white and very soft and curly, just like a ball of wool and I took to her straight away. Although we already had a dog on board I decided I wanted to take the puppy back with me so, when the waiter did not appear to have any interest in it, as we left I picked her up quietly and hurried out of the restaurant. On board it was discovered that Fluffy (I had already given her a name) had fleas so I gave her to the cox'n to do the necessary. When faced with an unusual situation one always sent for the cox'n (the senior rating in the ship). The puppy was placed in a bucket of water and the fleas picked off with tweezers as they ran up on to her head.

I had my last meeting with Captain Bush of *Euryalus* at a tea dance in the Officers Club in Port Said. I was with a group of people in the far corner of the room when I saw him walk in accompanied by Lieutenant Don, the Navigating Officer. They were both in 'fine trim' which I later found was possibly due to Captain Bush having been awarded a bar to his D.S.O. Although he had told me to come and see him if ever we were in port together as he was with other officers I decided to adopt a low profile. He soon let me know, that he had spotted me when I heard my name being called across the room. When I crossed over to where he was standing his first words were to ask me why I had not come over to say hullo. As I spluttered an excuse he quickly moved on to ask how I was getting on, what had I been doing, what was I doing now and when was I going to be promoted to Sub-Lieutenant. He really had meant what he had said when I left *Euryalus*.

Captain Bush's last appointment in the service was Commanding Officer of HMS *Ganges* the shore training establishment for boy entrants, and when he retired from the Navy he became Secretary of the Sea Cadets organization. Both of these appointments were evidence of the close interest he took in the training and welfare of young people. Although I only served under his command for a short period he left a deep impression on me and I have always thought of him as being the finest example of a Royal Navy officer.

After the Battle of Alam Halfa at the beginning of September 1942 the build up began for the planned offensive by the Eighth Army and we began to spend more time in Alexandria. When the army attacked our role would be in the Inshore Squadron escorting the ships which would keep the Army supplied as it advanced along the desert.

Chapter 13

THE END OF A PRETTY SHIP

––––

The Eighth Army started its advance along the desert at the beginning of November 1943 after the Battle of Alamein and by the 13th Tobruk had been cleared of the enemy and re-occupied. *Erica* left Alexandria a few days later escorting the first convoy which entered Tobruk on the 19th November.

The town of Tobruk was situated on the western side of a large natural harbour approached through a narrow entrance from seaward. As we entered the harbour it was easy to see why we had not been able to use the port as soon as it had been occupied. The whole anchorage was covered with the masts, funnels and sections of superstructure of the ships and craft of both sides which had been sunk during two years of fighting. Stranded wrecks were strewn all round the shoreline, the largest being an Italian passenger ship, *Georgio*, which, in addition to carrying troops, was said to have been used as a brothel by the German and Italian garrison. Many of the wrecks were the result of recent attacks by the Desert Air Force and it took the Naval Base party, which had entered with the army as soon as Tobruk had been captured, six days to clear the obstructions sufficiently for us to enter, and to enable the supply ships to start unloading. There were about 100 wrecks in the harbour, and we were able to secure alongside one of them, the *Chakla* a British India ship, which was sitting on the bottom of the harbour with only her forecastle and a bit of superstructure above the water.

I went ashore with the Captain in search of some loot. Specifically, machine-guns and a motor-bike. There were large stocks of Italian Breda machine-gun ammunition in Alexandria which had been captured during the first desert campaign against the

Italians, and we hoped to lay our hands on a couple of these guns to supplement our armament. We started searching the dug-outs and defensive posts which had been established along the shore between the town and the harbour entrance. The state of these dug-outs was evidence of the hurried departure of the occupants, in some cases they did not have time to finish the meal which was still on the table. They were in a pretty filthy state, probably Italian troops as the meal was spaghetti.

In the ruins of the town we stopped to talk to an army officer who had been trying to locate the old billet he had used during previous visits. He was most upset that it had been demolished and he was now having to look for somewhere else to stay, he did not know who to blame, the Jerries or our own, forces. Whilst we were chatting a Colonel drove up in his jeep, stopped beside us and asked the Captain what we were doing and where we were off to. When he heard the purpose of our visit ashore, he very kindly offered the use of his jeep and told the driver to take us to the railhead where we might find what we were looking for.

As we drew further away from the town and into the desert signs of the recent fighting became more apparent. Wrecked vehicles and equipment lay by the roadside and in the desert beyond. We were keen to get a motor-bike and whenever we saw one we stopped to examine it to see if it was in working order. It was only afterwards that we realised how careless and irresponsible we had been, in our enthusiasm we had not stopped to consider that the bikes may have been booby-trapped. We did not collect a motor-bike on the way to the railhead as it was hoped that the next bike would be better than the last one, and we would pick up the best of the bunch on the way back. There was one with a little two wheeled trailer which would have been ideal for collecting stores back in Alexandria. Sad to say, through being too particular, we left it too late and discovered on our return journey that all the machines that might have been of use had already been lifted by the more experienced soldiers.

As we neared the railhead I began to get my first impression of a battle-field. There was a crashed German Heinkel 111 bomber partially burned out; the clocks from these aircraft were said to be prized items. Tin hats, 'red devil' hand grenades and all sorts of items of equipment littered the ground. There were two large box-cars at the railhead and, again, we gave no thought that there might be mines or booby-traps as we crossed the virgin sand and entered the cars.

The first car was full of underwear, string type singlets and pants made from what appeared to be an *ersatz* material. This was not of much use to us so we moved on to the second car which turned out to be more promising as it was full of crates and boxes. I found a long, thin, case made of polished wood and opened it to find a baize lined interior containing a Spandau machine-gun for a Heinkel bomber. I could not help but wonder at the German standard of production in war-time, the wooden case was like a presentation item. The gun was just what we had been looking for and the next thing was to find ammunition for it but this turned out to be more difficult than expected. It was belt-fed ammunition and we never did manage to find any, either in Tobruk or Alexandria, so the gun finished up as a prized souvenir hanging on the bulkhead of my little cabin.

Whilst ashore in Tobruk I also managed to collect a German helmet, an Italian rifle that had a folding bayonet and was much smaller and lighter than the British rifle, and several items of German insignia which later had mounted on a wooden shield by a carpenter in the dockyard in Alexandria. However I lost them all three months later when *Erica* was sunk. In the end our expedition did not achieve its objective and was not very successful, but it was an adventurous sortie and an exciting and interesting experience.

Benghazi had been captured whilst we were at Tobruk and it now became the main supply base for the army during the advance westward. We therefore started running the convoys direct to Benghazi, although the enemy was digging in and stopped his retreat at El Agheila only 50 miles away.

On the 19th December, just after the army resumed its advance, we left Benghazi escorting a convoy which included a large Dutch freighter. We had sailed in the late afternoon and had only been a few hours at sea when Benghazi came under a heavy air attack. It was a clear night with a half moon and we could see the heavy barrage being put up by the town's air defences. We heard later that the German pilots had been heard to say on the radio that the 'flak' was too heavy and that they should go for the convoy instead.

The first indication that we were under attack was the roar of a diving plane and the eruption ahead of us as the bombs exploded. We were dismayed to see that the Senior Officer of the Escort, *Snapdragon*, had been hit and was sinking rapidly. We steered towards her to lend assistance and look for survivors. I had been sent down from the bridge to assist the First Lieutenant and I suggested that I should take away a boat to help in looking for, and picking up, any survivors. The ship could not remain stopped for too long in case there were still enemy aircraft around. The boat was lowered quickly and with four seaman at the oars we pulled towards the shouts we could hear coming from the men in the water. It was no easy task pulling the boat in the moderate sea that was running and the crew did a wonderful job, putting their backs into it to get to the men struggling in the oil covered water. *Snapdragon* was our 'chummy ship' and we all had friends on board.

Whilst we were pulling away from *Erica* a stick of bombs exploded about 30 feet off her starboard quarter and that she was missed was due to the Captain suddenly giving the order, "Hard-a-starboard, full ahead." He said later that he had a psychic flash which told him that he had to alter course NOW as though the voice of God had spoken to him. No one had heard or seen the aircraft coming, it must have been diving at the speed of sound, but as it roared away it was seen to be a Ju88. There was no doubt that the Captain's premonition had saved his ship; if he had not acted when he did *Erica* would have suffered the same fate as *Snapdragon*.

Although there was a moon it was still hard to see men in the water at any distance and I had to be guided by their shouts as I approached them. The men were covered in thick fuel oil and once alongside it was extremely difficult to pull them into the boat, and very soon the boat itself was covered in oil which made matters worse. We picked up about 10 men and returned to the ship which had stopped not far away and was getting men inboard. I put my survivors on board and set out again to see if I could find any more. We picked up another three and, whilst doing so, we could hear someone shouting in the distance but as we pulled in his direction the calls for help suddenly stopped, and though we searched there was no sign of him. If only we could have been a little bit quicker.

Approaching the ship for the second time I was hailed and directed towards a big spar in the water about twenty feet from the ship. As I drew alongside the spar I saw two men clinging to it, one supporting the other. I received the shock of my life when I recognized Lieutenant Seligman and found that he was supporting Commander Sims, the Commanding Officer of *Snapdragon*, who was in a very bad way.

Commander Sims was a big man and very heavy and it was a hard job to get him into the boat, but with the Captain urging us on we soon had both men inboard and I was able to take the boat and the rest of the survivors alongside the ship. Once on board I left the boat to be hoisted and helped to carry the Commander to the Captain's cabin. There the Captain, still soaked and covered in oil, carried out immediate artificial respiration in an effort to get the water and oil out of Commander Sims and to bring him round, he was breathing but only just.

In all *Erica* picked up about 60 survivors and then proceeded at full speed to Benghazi to land them for urgent medical attention. Later we heard that the Commander had been operated on in Benghazi and was found to have severe internal injuries. He was sent to Cairo by air but died in the aircraft. As soon as the survivors had been landed *Erica* set off to rejoin the convoy.

I soon learned from the other officers how the Captain had come to be in the water. He had spotted the Commander and had realized immediately that he was injured and in need of prompt assistance if he was to be saved. Leaving Pilot in charge on the bridge the Captain, without a moments hesitation, had dived into the sea to support and assist his Senior Officer until other help could arrive.

The Captain's action was the subject of quiet discussion amongst the officers. It was a brave thing that he had done and only to be expected of him, but we were worried in case he might have landed himself in trouble through his action in leaving the ship in such a manner. Technically, it might be said that the Captain left his ship in the face of the enemy, at the least he might be held to have acted irresponsibly in suddenly leaving a subordinate officer in charge during a difficult operation, and at a time when a situation could have developed which required him to take immediate action.

I was given the task of typing the Report of Proceedings which was sent in at the end of each convoy or other operation and in it the Captain made no mention of his part in the rescue of Commander Sims. He did, however, report the activities of myself and the boat's crew and asked for my actions to be noted. I had been 'mentioned in dispatches!' There may have been a special form that had to be submitted as I did not hear any more about it and did not receive an official award, always assuming that I had deserved it in the first place.

Shortly after our return to Alexandria Lieutenant Seligman was relieved and appointed in command of the Levant Schooner Flotilla. We were very sorry to see him go as we had been a happy wardroom, and his enthusiasm and leadership had resulted in *Erica* being an efficient and happy ship. To me, Lieutenant Seligman had an adventurous character made evident by his experience in sail, his round the world voyage in the *Cap Pilar,* bringing out the tanker from the Black Sea and our run ashore in Tobruk. It may sound fanciful but with his dark hair and tanned handsome features I sometimes thought that all he required was a gold ring in his ear to look like some 17th century pirate, and that in an earlier age he would have been in command of a privateer, or one of Nelson's frigate captains. His new appointment to the Levant Flotilla, which was to take raiding parties into the Aegean and Dodecanese, was entirely in keeping with his adventurous character. I was very grateful for his interest and encouragement and I always remember him with the greatest respect and affection.

Many years later, on the 19th December, the anniversary of the loss of *Snapdragon*, I received a telephone call from Ken Scarfe who had been a Sub-Lieutenant in the ship. He had been given my number when discussing the incident with Commander Seligman when they met whilst attending one of his lectures at a yacht club. I remembered his name and meeting him when our ships had hoisted the 'gin pennant!' Ken, who had his leg broken, had been one of the chaps we had hauled into the boat, although I did not recognize him at the time, and he said he had just telephoned to say, "Thank you for saving my life."

Our new Commanding Officer was Lieutenant-Commander Hayes RN, who we later heard had undergone some unnerving experiences and had two ships sunk under him. I suppose that it was due to his being RN and used to the peace-time routine for Midshipmen that he showed surprise at, and disapproved of, my being in charge of a watch at sea, and I was very disappointed when he put the First Lieutenant back on watch with me. However I could see his point of view. If anything went wrong he could not be found lacking in judgement, or to have been irresponsible, in allowing a Midshipman to be in charge of the watch. As it turned out Number One left me to get on with things very much as before, and merely kept an eye on what was going on, whilst he attended to other matters.

Shortly after our new Captain joined the ship we took another convoy to Benghazi. Half way between Alexandria and Tobruk two ships were torpedoed almost simultaneously whilst Number One and myself were on watch during the forenoon. It was put down to torpedoes as there was no known minefield in the area, and it was highly unlikely that two ships would have struck floating mines at exactly the same time.

Erica was on the seaward side, the likely area from where the attack was made, so we turned away quickly from the convoy and proceeded to do a search for a possible submarine. After a fruitless sweep of the area we returned to find that one ship had sunk and the other was still afloat but down by the head, having been hit in the bow, and with some smoke coming from her stem.

The damaged ship was named *Corona* and from her survivors we learned that she had Norwegian officers and a Chinese crew. As she was still afloat there was a possibility that she might be salvaged so the crew were asked to return to their ship but this they refused to do, probably because she was carrying ammunition and they had seen smoke coming from her stem. The Captain decided to take the *Corona* in tow and called for volunteers to form a boarding party. By some strange coincidence we had been given the towing wire of the Hunt class destroyer *Eridge* before leaving Alexandria, which was extremely fortunate as our own wires were of insufficient strength.

I expected the First Lieutenant to be in charge of the boarding party and told him that I would go as well, however he came back to say that the Captain required him on board to take charge of the towing arrangements and that I was to take charge of the boarding party. There was very little sea or swell and the conditions quite favourable when *Erica*, with plenty of fenders out, was taken gently alongside *Corona's* port side to allow the boarding party to scamble on board.

The first job that had to be done was to find out the extent of the damage, whether she was still making water and if, in fact, she would stay afloat. She had been hit in the bows, right in the chain locker, and I could see lengths of anchor cable trailing in the water. The forward bulkhead of No.1 hold appeared to have been opened as some cargo, boxes of oranges, could be seen floating around the bow. The ship was down by the head and listing to starboard but soundings in the other holds indicated that they were not making water. Down in the engine-room I found about two feet of water in the starboard side. I asked the Stoker Petty Officer if there was any hope of getting the engine going but it appeared there was a problem with an air pump that had been damaged and he was not very hopeful. He thought that if we attempted to raise steam there might be a big bang so there was nothing else for it but a tow.

Down aft the smoke was found to be coming from a rope which had somehow been set on fire. The rope was cut adrift and a signal made to *Erica*, "Fire extinguished." Back came the reply, "Well done!"

The deck plating on the forecastle had been badly buckled by the explosion and the rivets holding down the windlass, bitts and other deck fittings had been badly sprung, so I had a job in deciding where to secure the towing wire. As we heaved the heavy wire on board by hand I decided that, instead of putting the end on a set of bitts, I would take two turns around the base of the windlass before backing the end on to the bitts. If that did not hold nothing else would.

Erica took the strain, the wire held and very slowly *Corona* started to move through the water bound for the nearest port which was Tobruk. The men were divided into two watches and posted as look-outs and guns' crews and one was stationed on the forecastle to keep an eye on the towing wire. The signalman, Schofield, and I stayed on the bridge and commandeered the Master's cabin for the odd forty winks. It was the first time I had seen a four poster bed in a ship.

In the cabin I found a Plath sextant (German made and considered to be the Rolls Royce of that instrument), Zeiss binoculars, and a Luger automatic pistol all of which I was very tempted to appropriate. However I realised that these were the possessions of a fellow seaman and as such to be respected, and anyway the Master would no doubt be on board as soon as the ship arrived in port and there would be a an almighty row if he found them to be missing. I did not take them and passed the word to the sailors not to touch any of the personal possessions they found in the officers' cabins and the crew's quarters. There was plenty of food but we quickly ran out of cigarettes and I had to break into the bond to get some to share out amongst the men. I also took the opportunity to get a bottle of gin to give the lads a tot after their hard work.

One of the first things I had done on boarding was to rig up a plumb line in the wheelhouse to keep a check on the vessel's list. As we moved slowly towards port the plumb line mark moved gradually to the right, imperceptibly at first but by the time we were nearing Tobruk the ship was listing well over and I was being asked by the Captain if I thought that she would stay afloat. I was beginning to be concerned myself but it was a difficult question to answer. If I said I did not think she would last and abandoned her and she subsequently did not sink, I would look a bit foolish and appear to lack judgement. If I said she would last the distance and stay afloat only to find her suddenly turning over, my crew would be in danger of going down with her. What had to be remembered was the importance of the cargo so I told the Captain we would make it and kept my fingers crossed.

Off Tobruk two trawlers came alongside the *Corona's* starboard side to hold her up and take her into harbour whilst *Erica* cast off the tow. A launch came out from Tobruk with an RNR Lieutenant who was coming to pilot the ship into harbour. Accompanying him in the launch was the Naval Officer in Charge, Tobruk, whom I recognized to be Commander Alexander who was in charge of the naval contingent on board *Kenya* when we were on the Dakar Expedition in 1940. As I watched them from the bridge he looked up and, recognizing me, shouted, "Hullo Stewart, what are you doing there?" I replied, "I am in the Navy now, Sir" to which he answered, "Well done!" I was quite relieved when I saw the Commander as I knew I would have a friend at court should there be any trouble with the Master of the *Corona* when he returned to his ship once we were in port.

The Lieutenant came up to the bridge and told me to go on to the forecastle and be prepared to let go the anchors. I tried to explain that everything was shot away forward and what was left of the anchor cables was trailing in the sea but I was just told to "get up there." The *Corona* was run ashore and beached at the south end of the harbour and, needless to say, there was no attempt made to let go the anchors.

Erica had followed us into harbour and soon a boat arrived alongside, with the *Corona's* Master on board, to take us back to the ship. Whilst I was mustering the boarding party the Master went off to inspect his ship and eventually returned full of complaints. I had to hide my indignation when he appeared to suggest that my sailors might have taken items from the cabins and I felt like telling him he should have stayed on board his ship. However that would have been impertinent, in any case it was against all my training to speak back to a senior officer. Instead I invited him to search the boarding party who were lined up on deck behind me. Fortunately, as it turned out, he declined the invitation.

Back on board *Erica* I went up to the bridge to report to the Captain who asked me what I had brought him from the *Corona*. "Nothing, Sir", I replied, rather surprised at his question. "What!", he exclaimed, "Did you not bring me a case of gin?" I must have sounded somewhat self-righteous as I answered," No, Sir, we did not touch anything." "Come here", he said as he led me to the after end of the bridge. "Look!" He pointed to the boarding party who were gathered on deck below, opening up their lifebelts which had concealed various small items; I never did find out everything they managed to win. Sometime later I learned that a side of beef was also brought on board. The Captain was disappointed at not getting his gin and may have thought me naive when I told him about the sextant and the binoculars, but he was very pleased with our performance and that was the main thing.

One member of the ship's company must have had a premonition that our next trip was to be our last and that was Bob, the ship's dog. He had failed to return on board the night before we were due to sail and there was no sign of him in the morning. Although the Captain delayed sailing as long as possible in the hope that he would turn up, we eventually had to leave without him. As the ship was leaving harbour the Leading Telegraphist said to me, "Something is going to happen this trip, Sir, it is the first time that Bob has missed the ship."

We arrived safely at Benghazi where we heard that a naval tug, HMS *St. Issey*, had been sunk off the coast to the north-east. It was thought to have been sunk by a U-boat and it was decided to route our return convoy between the coast and a minefield which was located in that area to give the convoy protection against possible attack if the U-boat was still around.

I had had a good wash down after lunch and then dressed before laying down for an afternoon's rest, but I forgot to put the chamois leather belt, which held my caul, gold watch, rabbit's foot and the letter my father gave me when I first went to sea, back on around my waist.

I was awakened by the clamour of the alarm bells and shot out of my bunk to take up my action station at the 4-inch gun. The ship had obtained an asdic contact and was even then making an attack, and soon the sea behind us erupted as a five charge pattern of depth charges exploded. We slowed down and turned around to point at the target and regain contact but the force of the explosion had knocked the asdics off the board. As we waited for the power to be restored I thought I would take the opportunity to go down from the gun to the deck below to answer a call of nature. I left the gun platform and had taken one step down the ladder from the forecastle when my conscience pricked and I realized I was leaving my place of duty. I turned around and took the six paces back and had just stepped on to the gun platform when there was an almighty explosion, I saw a sheet of flame and went up in the air and landed on my back on the gun-deck.

At first it was thought that the ship had been torpedoed but it later transpired that we had hit a mine. When power was restored to the asdics the operator had obtained one echo but before he could obtain another to identify the contact the ship had gone up. We had been hit in the area underneath the wardroom, in the fuel tanks between the boiler-room and the 4-inch magazine. Two men were killed in the boiler-room but, fortunately the magazine party, who should have been below, were on deck watching the attack and so they were lucky to escape. For myself, if I had carried on down to the deck below I might have been seriously injured and I often wondered what made me change my mind and turn back. Was it something similar to Lieutenant Seligman's experience in the *Snapdragon* incident? I do not know. What I do know is that since that day I have said my prayers every night.

Erica settled quickly by the head and we could feel her going for within ten minutes the water was just under the level of the forecastle deck. A Fairmile launch, which was one of the escorts, eventually arrived alongside and started taking survivors on board. Some chaps had been blown into the water and were picked up by another escort. Down at the depth charge racks two sailors were calmly but quickly removing the primers to make sure the charges did not go off when the ship went under. Whilst I was down there I found Fluffy who, fortunately, had been on deck instead of down below in the wardroom flat. Several men had been injured quite badly including Pilot who had injured his back and could hardly walk. He was on the bridge wearing sandals with no heels and the doctors later reckoned that the effect of the explosion had gone up his legs and cracked his spine like a whip. He was in plaster from chin to waist for a considerable time.

I went back to the forecastle and I was able to step on board the motor launch. The First Lieutenant more or less had to drag the Captain from his bridge; he had been standing facing aft, saluting the ensign and no doubt in a state of shock at losing his ship and wanting to go down with her. We all felt very sorry for him; he had been invalided with shock for a time previously and he had tried so hard to prove himself to be effective once again.

Erica sank in about fifteen minutes. When all the people remaining were on board the launch pulled away and we watched our ship go down. She went like a lady; no fuss. Still upright and at a shallow angle she slid slowly under until, at the last moment, she cocked her stem up in a cheeky farewell as she finally disappeared from sight. I was very sad to see her go, she was such a pretty ship and she had been a very happy one. It may be difficult for a landsman to understand but to a sailor a ship is more than just a ship whilst he is serving in her, it is also his home. To a Captain she takes first place in his life whilst she is under his command. I lost my home on the 9th February 1943.

In the motor launch the Lieutenant RNVR in command passed round the rum before transferring some of us to the *Southern Isles*, a South African Navy ship which was one of the escorts. Before we left the motor launch the Lieutenant asked our Number One to sign for the rum that had been issued which was rather an unusual request to make to a group of survivors. However in those days rum was the most important store item in the Navy and had to be strictly accounted for. It was said that it was better to lose a 15-inch gun than a gallon of rum. Having used up all his supply the Lieutenant was no doubt anxious to have proof of where it had gone to satisfy the supply people in Tobruk where he was based. We thought he was being a bit of an old woman.

Several days later we arrived back in Alexandria where we were taken to HMS Nile, the shore base. In the wardroom, where we were taken for a drink whilst arrangements were made for our disposal, the Base staff must have thought us an odd group with me dressed in blue uniform trousers and roll-neck sweater and holding Fluffy in my arms. I was issued with khaki battle-dress and given a piece of paper bearing my name, rank, and official stamp in place of my lost identity card.

We officers were sent to the Villa Rosa, a large house in a residential area which was used as an Officers' Rest House. Whilst enjoying survivors leave I was already looking forward to my next appointment and wondering what further adventures lay ahead.

Chapter 14

GENERAL POST

––––

Whilst waiting for a new uniform to be made I took the opportunity to obtain a price list from Gieves to help me to compile the claim to replace my kit. I had had a very good outfit and by the time I had finished the sum came to about £160. Needless to say I only bought what was necessary and the balance became the start of my savings.

It was a pleasant stay at the Villa Rosa which was managed by an attractive French lady whom everybody called Madam. She was a jolly and friendly person who took an instant fancy to Fluffy and I had quite a job in keeping my little dog. *Erica's* officers went their separate ways. Lieutenant Palmer was given command of the Naval tug HMS *St. Monance*, Sub-Lieutenant Deans went to another ship and Guy Phipps-Walker, the Pilot, was in hospital. I believe it was sometime before the Captain returned to duty. He was very distressed about the loss of his ship – Pilot had reminded him about the presence of the minefield and had advised against entering it, but the Captain thought that the contact might have been a submarine posing a threat to the convoy.

At the end of February I was appointed to HMS *Antwerp*, a cross-channel passenger ship which, together with her sister ship, *Malines*, had been taken into naval service at the outbreak of the war. She was classed as an anti-aircraft control ship and not at all my cup of tea. Fortunately I only served on board for a couple of weeks or so, and maybe Fluffy had something to do with my short stay.

When I boarded the ship I arrived on deck with Fluffy in my arms and I had put her down before I noticed that *Antwerp* already had two dogs, wire-haired terriers, which were running around the deck area. When they saw Fluffy they stopped playing and came over and started to sniff around her in the usual fashion. She put up with it for a minute or so and then, all of a sudden, there was a flurry of dogs and the next thing Fluffy was chasing the two terriers around their own ship. The Commander, who was on deck at the time and saw the whole performance, was not amused and told me to keep my dog under control and that she was not to be allowed to run around the ship. So during the time I remained in the ship Fluffy had to stay in my cabin, which was on the boat deck, and go for her walks on the end of a piece of string.

Fluffy on board HMS Croome

Antwerp had one article in the officers' mess which was a bit of a novelty. It was a large round dining table capable of seating 10 or 12 people. The centre piece of the table was a beautifully finished revolving wooden buffet which held the condiments, sauces and other bits and pieces. One had only to give it a twirl to obtain the desired item. I had learned early on in my career that conversation at breakfast was not always welcomed, especially by senior officers, but I thought that this was carrying things too far, one did not even need to break the silence by asking for the salt.

I was promoted to Sub-Lieutenant on my 20th birthday March 3rd 1943.

Towards the end of the month I escaped from *Antwerp* when I was sent to HMS *Croome*, a Hunt class destroyer, to take the place of an officer who had been taken ill.

She was preparing to sail as part of the escort for a convoy which was being run to Malta and, again, I arrived just in time to go on the operation.

Tripoli had been captured at the end of January and, with the desert airfields once again in our possession, the RAF was able to provide the convoy with the air cover which had been needed so desperately on previous occasions. Although we suffered several attacks from torpedo and high level bombers there were no casualties and the convoy got through safely. There was no sign of the Italian battle fleet.

The siege of Malta had been lifted the previous November when the convoy and escorts entered harbour to a tumultuous welcome from the inhabitants. We also went into the harbour and received a similar reception. Crowds of people cheering and waving lined the breakwaters, battlements, and streets around the harbour area, presenting a never to be forgotten sight. Everywhere there was evidence of the destruction and damage caused by the tremendous hammering Valetta and the dockyard had taken from the incessant air raids. I wondered how the population and garrison had managed to hold out for so long, but only those who had lived through it would know.

Fluffy was being looked after by the rating who acted as ship's postman – Able Seaman Bell who had been in the *Exeter* at the Battle of the River Plate – and she had spent most of the trip with him at his action station on 'A' gun. Postie had become quite attached to Fluffy and made sure the doggie had a very good run ashore when he went to the mail office.

On return to Alexandria I was appointed to HMS *Delphinium* another Flower class corvette. I found out that *Delphinium* already had a dog (another fox terrier – or at least most of it was) so, to avoid any more problems, I asked Postie if he would keep Fluffy if the Captain allowed me to leave her in *Croome*, and this he was happy to do.

The Commanding Officer of *Delphinium*, Commander Vivian Funge-Smith RNR had recently joined the ship as Senior Officer of the escort group having received promotion and been awarded the DSO after sinking a U-boat when in command of the corvette *Aubretia*. Before the war he served as Chief Officer in B.P. oil tankers. The First Lieutenant and Roger Deacon, the navigator, were RNVR Lieutenants and Sub-Lieutenant Church RNVR joined the ship about the same time as me.

Before deciding on the watchkeeping arrangements the Captain questioned Church and myself regarding our previous experience. Church had been with the MNBDO (Mobile Naval Base Defence Organisation) and had had very little sea-time until he managed to get on board a destroyer where the Captain gave him a restricted Watchkeeping Certificate (destroyers and below) after only three months experience as 2nd OOW Commander Funge-Smith did not appear to set much store by the Certificate, or consider that Church had sufficient experience, as I was given a watch whilst Church, who was senior to me, was put on watch with the First Lieutenant. I was also put in charge of the ship's office and given the job of Captain's Secretary, a job which everybody disliked, including me.

Although the Captain was RNR, in common with many officers from the big shipping companies, he was a strict disciplinarian and he insisted upon, and made sure he obtained, a high standard of efficiency from his officers. Everything had to be just right, second best was not good enough and the slightest neglect of duty, whether unintentional or unavoidable, was jumped on from a great height.

For the first couple of months life was a bit difficult whilst we adjusted to his ways and I seemed to get the worst of it. Each morning I had to take him the official mail, which was often quite heavy as he was Senior Officer of a Group. He would go through it with me and dictate or outline the replies, or action to be taken concerning other matters which might involve one of the other officers. If they were slow in responding it was up to me to expedite matters; if they dragged their feet I was the one who received the rocket.

I had not done much typing and I had to learn the hard way. The Captain would not allow erasures or corrections in a letter and if even a comma was misplaced it had to be typed again. I would sit in the small office, which was made more cramped by the installation of the radar set, with a wastepaper basket beside me for the letters which had to be discarded because of typing errors. Sometimes I almost felt like weeping when, after taking great care to get it right, I would make a slip towards the end and have to do it all over again. However the training had a point – if you do not want to suffer the punishment (spend all your time in the ship's office) do not commit the crime (get it right first time). The training he gave me stood me in good stead later in my career when as Master in the Merchant Navy I had to deal with all the ship's business and correspondence myself.

I sometimes thought that he was harder on me than on the other officers but I think that this may have been because I was a professional and he knew I was going to make a career at sea. When he made me Navigating Officer (the work I was really interested in) the Captain gave me the same strict training and supervision. When he was satisfied with my performance and I had gained his trust, he never interfered and accepted my word without question. Although he was strict he was also friendly and approachable and we had a happy ship.

Our Escort Group consisted of an odd collection of ships. The *Saktouris* and *Apostolis* were former British corvettes which had been handed over to the Greek Navy. There were two South African whalers, HMSAS *Southern Maid* and *Protea* and the trawler HMS *Wolborough* which was one of the latest to be built before the war (the skipper had his own bathroom!) and quite big and capable of a good speed. At different times other ships would join us for a short while and one or more of our own ships might be detached for one reason or another, so we did not always know which ships would be with us at any specific time.

The first convoy had entered Tripoli at the beginning of February and the port had become the advance supply base for the Eighth Army. When I joined *Delphinium* the Army was about to break through the Mareth Line and advance into Tunisia to link up with the First Army, which had landed in North Africa, and entrap the enemy with his back to the sea at Cape Bon. A plan had been drawn up to counter any attempt that the enemy might make to evacuate his troops in a Dunkirk type operation. It was called Operation Retribution and we were one of the many ships, with red lead painted on the superstructure for easy identification by our own aircraft, which waited off the coast hoping for a 'turkey shoot.' But the enemy decided to surrender instead on 12th May 1943 and we did not get our revenge.

Shortly after the enemy surrender in North Africa a convoy left Gibraltar bound for Alexandria and arrived at that port at the end of May, thus opening up the Mediterranean from West to East for the first time in over two and a half years. From then on *Delphinium* was engaged in escorting convoys from Port Said and Alexandria right through to Gibraltar, and return convoys to Egypt.

When the orders for the invasion of Sicily were received it was found that *Delphinium* would be the Senior Officer of an enlarged group escorting the convoy of oil tankers which would refuel the fleet supporting the landings.

The invasion was planned for the 10th July and a few days beforehand we sailed from Alexandria with our convoy to rendezvous with the Fleet on the morning of D-day. *Delphinium* was in her usual position in the screen two thousand yards ahead of the Commodore's ship.

I was on watch as we approached the rendezvous in the early morning and at first light an impressive sight came into view. The horizon ahead was filled with ships, dim shapes to begin with but, as the sun arose and we drew nearer, we could see the powerful fleet which had been assembled. It was a magnificent sight. Battleships and cruisers surrounded by a protective screen of fleet destroyers steaming towards us in a massive array.

The convoy steamed at slow speed whilst the destroyers refuelled in succession. Whilst this was going on the heavy ships steamed up and down in our vicinity, as though carrying out fleet manoeuvres, which allowed a close up view of the ships. There was one unforgettable moment when the Nelson passed very close to a South African whaler which appeared minute against the massive bulk of the battleship. The ship's wag voiced our sentiments when he sucked his teeth and remarked, "and that is supposed to protect THAT?"

During the passage from Alexandria I had badly scraped my leg whilst rushing up a ladder. I did not pay much attention to it but by the time we entered Valetta harbour in Malta after the invasion I had a large swelling in my groin and had difficulty in walking. I also felt rather ill. The Captain had given me the job of checking on various matters concerning the ships in the group such as refuelling, defects, stores, etc., and when I mentioned that I was feeling ill his answer was to enquire how the refuelling was progressing, and to let him know when it was completed. The First Lieutenant hailed a passing landing craft to take me to a doctor. Fortunately it had a nursing sister on board who found my temperature to be 103°F and she had me in the boat and away from the ship before the Captain could be informed. I hardly had time to take a change of clothes or any personal belongings. I was taken to the Military Hospital at Imtarfa in the centre of the Island where, in addition to a poisoned leg, it was found that I had sand-fly fever.

I did not remember much about the first couple of days in hospital. There were still sporadic air raids on the island and I woke up one night to find some of the other patients under their beds but I was out like a light for most of the time. After about 10 days in hospital I was discharged, and then I had the problem of finding my way back to Alexandria to rejoin *Delphinium*.

Whilst awaiting passage I had to find somewhere to stay so this meant a visit to the accommodation officer who was an RNVR Lieutenant named Duncan. He told me that there was hardly a bed to be found anywhere, even the rooms in the Union and other clubs, which had been filled with camp beds and turned into dormitories, were packed solid. When it transpired that we had both been to the same school he offered me a spare bed in his flat, which solved my immediate problem.

Every day I went along to the transportation section to see if there was any news of a passage. There were other people in the same fix but all the harassed staff could say was, "Go away and await further orders." There was nothing much to do in Valetta, many of the streets were still partially closed by the huge blocks of stone from bombed buildings which made moving around a problem. There was one cinema still operating, the Manoel Theatre, said to be the oldest theatre in Europe. It was showing the film Mrs Miniver and, to pass the time I went to see it five nights in succession.

After a week I began to feel unwell again and developed a high temperature which resulted in another stay in hospital. This time they thought that I had had malaria although the length of time I had been at sea before I became ill appeared to discount the possibility. In the ward I came into contact with my first American. He was the only one in the ward and he was regularly visited by a very attractive 'popsie' which made us all very envious, especially when she supplied him with American cigarettes. We could only get Victory V cigarettes which were made in India and had an unpleasant taste and smell, and the Yank's failure to pass his around did not add to his popularity. When I was discharged from hospital I only had to spend a couple of nights on a camp bed in the Union Club before I was told to report to the RAF at Luqa for a flight back to Cairo.

I had never been up in an aircraft and it was with some concern that I viewed the rather battered looking DC3 which we were to board. Most of the passengers were officers and we sat down along each side of the aircraft with bags of mail and other items stowed down the middle. I was seated beside another Sub-Lieutenant near the entrance to the cockpit, which was covered by a black curtain, and adjacent to the starboard wing where I could see the engine over my shoulder. After the aircraft took off I looked out of the window and saw a trickle of oil running down the wing from the engine. My imagination came into play and I visualised a spark from the engine igniting the oil. I pointed this out to the chap sitting beside me and, acting on the old maxim, 'When in doubt tell somebody' I suggested that he should go and tell the pilot. Off he went only to return a couple of minutes later, his face red with embarrassment. As he sat down he muttered that the oil was nothing to worry about which was a comfort, although it looked as though he had had his head bitten off by the pilot.

The aircraft landed at El Adem, the airfield just outside Tobruk, where we disembarked for some refreshments. On leaving the canteen I saw a remarkable sight, the aircraft appeared to be sitting in a gigantic lake and it was a moment or two before I realised it was a mirage. Arriving in Cairo I was sent straight to Alexandria where I reported to the base only to find that *Delphinium* was at sea, and to be given a rather unusual assignment.

When France capitulated in 1940 a squadron of French warships, cruisers and destroyers, which refused to fight on with the Free French, was interned in Alexandria. The ships were moored in the centre of the harbour, the breech blocks of the guns were removed and they were only allowed sufficient oil and provisions for their daily requirements. To guard against the possibility of the ships attempting to leave port or cause disruption in the harbour, they were kept under close observation from a small cabin cruiser moored nearby. The observation post, which had a direct telephone line to the Duty Staff Officer in HMS Nile, was manned by an officer and two or three Royal Marines whose duty was to watch for any unusual movement of personnel between the ships, any increase in ship-to-ship communication, the movement of fuel lighters or any occurrence which appeared at all suspicious. It was a trifle boring but there was plenty of opportunity to have a good yarn. The Marines had taken part in the unsuccessful raid on Tobruk the previous year when the *Zulu* and *Sikh* were sunk, and they were convinced that the failure was due to the enemy receiving prior warning from spies in Alexandria or Port Said. It seems that the planned raid was common knowledge as a Wren told one of them that she would not be seeing him for a while as "He was off to Tobruk in a couple of days."

From the cabin cruiser I was shanghaied once again, this time to an Australian sloop HMAS *Cessnock* to replace an officer who had been hospitalised. I began to wonder if I would ever get back to my own ship. I was beginning to miss my kit as I only had two or three sets of whites and I felt 'jury rigged ' most of the time. Officers had to supply their own sheets, pillow cases, etc. and I was having to rely on the good-will of other people.

I was in *Cessnock* for nearly a month during which time we escorted a convoy through to Gibraltar and a return convoy to Port Said. I enjoyed serving with the Aussies. I met quite a few in Beirut and I had a soft spot for them. I always remember one of them saying to me, "We may call you Pommie bastards but God help anybody else who does." I had heard the usual comments about their lack of discipline and disrespect for authority but I saw no evidence of this whilst I was with them. In fact quite the opposite. There was a Midshipman on board who had displeased the First Lieutenant for some reason or another and he had received six across the backside with a bayonet scabbard. The Midshipman did not think that this was legal and asked the Cox'n for a copy of KR & AI (*King's Regulations and Admiralty Instructions*, the Navy's bible) to check up on the subject. The cox'n reported his request to the First Lieutenant and the Mid received another six for discussing the matter with the Cox'n.

One of the officers' stewards was a chap in his late forties, and whilst talking to him I found out that he had been in the Navy in the last war and that he had served in the *Queen Elizabeth*. He remembered hearing that a chef was coming to replace the Admiral's cook, who was named Richards, and was quite surprised when I told him that person had been my father.

The officer I was replacing was due to return to the ship in Port Said but a few days before our arrival another officer became ill and, at the same time, instructions were received to land certain confidential books at Port Said and the ship was to proceed to Colombo. The sick officer would need to be landed when we arrived at Port Said and by this time the Captain had decided that he was not going to sail short-handed and wanted to keep me on board. I was in a bit of a flap as the last thing I wanted to do was to leave *Delphinium* and go all the way out to the Far East.

A few hours before the *Cessnock* was due to sail for Colombo the Captain's plans were thwarted, and I breathed a sigh of relief, when he received the signal, "Sub-Lieutenant Stewart is not repeat not to leave the station."

Chapter 15

MEDITERRANEAN CONVOYS

———

I had been away from *Delphinium* for over two and a half months and when I returned on board I found that the number of ships in the convoys we were escorting had greatly increased. With the Mediterranean being opened, ships from India, Australia and the East Coast of Africa no longer had to pass round the Cape of Good Hope but could take the short route home through the Suez Canal and then on to Gibraltar.

In some ways it was rather similar to a bus service picking up and putting off passengers along the way. After leaving Port Said ships bound for ports such as Tripoli, Malta, Taranto, Augusta, Tunis, Bizerta and Algiers would leave the convoy at suitable points and others would join for the onward passage to Gibraltar. This meant that we were often handling a total of approximately seventy ships. The same procedure applied on the return passage to Alexandria and Port Said.

The biggest problem arose when ships were leaving and joining the convoy. There were extensive minefields around the Tunisian coast and between Sardinia and North Africa and, after the North African campaign, a channel 200 miles long had been swept through these minefields to open the Mediterranean from West to East. It was the biggest minesweeping operation in history. The channel was not very wide and, in order to pass through safely, the formation of the convoy had to be altered and the ships formed into two long columns with the leavers taking station at the rear. The convoy would enter the channel at a point East of Cape Bon and as it passed Tunis and Bizerta the planned procedure was for leavers to be detached to enter port independently whilst the joiners took their places at the rear of the columns.

In theory this was a fairly straight forward operation but in practice it never turned out that way. Instead of waiting until the convoy was past and the leavers were clear, some joiners would inevitably come out too soon and get in the way of the leading ships of the convoy and, being out of position, they would hamper the vessels that were being detached.

Shortly after I had returned to *Delphinium* the Captain gave me a Full Watchkeeping Certificate which allowed me to keep watch on any class of warship, and it was also required for accelerated promotion to Lieutenant. He also made me Navigating Officer, the job I had always wanted to do. As Pilot I was responsible for keeping the convoy lists – particulars of the ships, destinations, position in the convoy, etc. and so I was always on the bridge when ships were joining and leaving.

I was always apprehensive as we approached Bizerta at the head of the convoy, usually about midnight, when I was on watch and had to suffer the Captain's frustrations as he tried to sort out the various ships and get them into their proper positions. Many of the ships were American Liberty Ships, big, bulky and difficult to manoeuvre especially when in ballast, and due to the rapid expansion of the American merchant fleet many of the officers were relatively inexperienced. Going from ship to ship we would pass instructions over the loud-hailer, and the Captain often had difficulty in keeping his cool when the people on board seemed a bit obtuse or subsequently did the wrong thing. On one occasion he threw down his binoculars and stumped off down below in a fury leaving me all alone and surrounded by ships. Having cooled down he returned a few minutes later and said, "All right, Pilot, we'll try again." Senior Officers of the Escort got less rest than anyone else, they not only had their own ships to worry about but also the other ships in the Group, not to mention the safety of the convoy. It was no wonder he blew up now and again but, although it could be uncomfortable at the time, it was soon passed over and forgotten about.

During a passage the Captain would sometimes need to discuss various matters with the Commodore of the convoy or give instructions to the Masters of joiners and leavers. Instead of sending messages by signal lamp we would frequently go alongside the ship in question so that the Captain could speak with the Commodore or Master over the loud-hailer, or a message could be passed by line. I enjoyed these occasions when I was on watch. At first the Captain conned the ship alongside and then handed over to me to keep her in position whilst he spoke over the loud-hailer. Eventually he allowed me to do the whole job, keeping an eye on me as I manoeuvred *Delphinium* through the columns of ships and alongside the ship he wished to talk to.

The Commodore's ship of one convoy to Gibraltar happened to be the *Modassa*, sister ship of *Mulbera*, my first ship. Whilst we were alongside I noticed her Chief Steward on deck and recognized him as having been Second Steward on *Mulbera*. We exchanged waves and at the same time I remarked to the Captain that I would like to taste a BI curry once again. The Master of *Modassa* was a white haired gentleman, probably back from retirement, and he smiled and waved when the Captain told him that he had one of his 'young gentlemen' on board who was longing for a BI curry. This exchange was heard by many of the passengers, some of them women and children, who lined the rails to have a look at us and wave to the sailors. We returned to our station ahead of the convoy and about two hours later, just before lunch, a signal was received from the Commodore which simply read, "Your lunch is ready."

The invitation could not be refused and we turned around and headed for *Modassa*. Once alongside a line was fired across to bring on board the basket containing the lunch the Chief Steward had prepared for us. On the way back to our station the basket was opened and it was discovered that he had really done us proud. There was a lovely curry complete with all the trimmings, poppadam, Bombay duck, dried fried onions, raisins, currants, chutney, luncheon rolls and napkins. Our cook was a bit put out when he was told we would not be requiring lunch.

In appreciation of the lunch we had received *Modassa* was given a surprise the next time we had occasion to go alongside. The Master was informed over the loud-hailer that we had on board a very important and distinguished person whose presence was a matter of great secrecy, however he wished to take this opportunity to say a few words to the people on board *Modassa* who were now returning home.

Able Seaman Gocking, concealed in the wheelhouse and primed with a large whisky and a cigar, then began his very good impression of Winston Churchill, the Prime Minister. It was funny to watch the various expressions on the faces of the people on board the *Modassa* as they heard the seemingly familiar voice come over the loud-hailer. Amazement changing to doubt and then disbelief when they heard the phrase, "Our gallant-allies, the Royal Marines,"as Gocking misquoted one of Churchill's well-known lines.

It was a short but pleasant interlude, the sort of incident which, during the war, helped the break the monotony, ease the tension and give everybody a good laugh. The lunch and the speech would give the passengers something to talk about and a story to tell their friends when they arrived home.

It was in *Delphinium* that I had experience of another mutiny and this time it was the Greek Navy. Returning to harbour with out Group, we had just secured to our buoy (K buoy) in Alexandria harbour when the Captain received a message that the Greek corvette *Saktouris* would be berthing alongside *Delphinium* at K buoy, and that he was to report to the Commodore (Destroyers) in the Depot Ship without delay. When he returned on board the Captain had all the officers and petty officers muster in his cabin and told us that the Greek Fleet had mutinied and had refused to go to sea. The Communist committees had taken over the ships and the officers were unable to do anything about the situation and had lost control. He told us that we might have to board *Saktouris*, an action which would probably be resisted, in the meantime there was to be no communication with personnel. This was a bit awkward as the officers of both ships had visited each other for drinks on several occasions.

All shore leave was stopped and boarding parties organized so that there was always one mustered in readiness on the blind side of the ship out of sight of *Saktouris*. Sub-Lieutenant Davenport and myself were sent ashore for instruction in handling the Lanchester sub-machine gun, an early British type of automatic weapon which was not very much of a success. For a couple of days we stood by wondering what was going to happen. There was no rowdiness or disorder in the Greek ship, only what appeared to be religious services which involved much chanting and walking round the ship in procession carrying candles.

Eventually orders were received that the group was to go to sea to search for a submarine which had sunk a Red Cross ship taking supplies to Greece and it was hoped that this operation would encourage the Greek seamen to return to duty. This they refused to do whereupon a British Rear-Admiral came to *Delphinium* to interview the Commanding Officer of *Saktouris*.

Once again I had a first class view of the proceedings. I was Officer of the Day and after meeting the Admiral at the gangway I escorted him to the Captain's cabin, where the Commanding Officer of *Saktouris* was waiting, and then stood in attendance outside the doorway which was kept open. The British officer started off by stressing that the *Saktouris* was urgently required for the proposed operation and emphasised that the Red Cross ship had been carrying relief supplies for his countrymen. In the strongest terms he told the Greek officer to go on board and take charge of his ship and get it to sea.

With tears in his eyes the Captain of *Saktouris* pleaded that he had tried to do this but the crew was under the influence of the committees and there was nothing he could do about it. At this the Rear-Admiral lost his patience altogether. He said, "Then what you should do, Sir, is take your revolver and go on the forecastle of your ship and blow your brains out. You are a coward, Sir, a coward."

The Group put to sea without the Greek corvettes and proceeded to the area to search for the submarine. I had to keep a plot of the operation which consisted of a series of square searches over a wide area. It was very detailed showing the track, in different colours, of each vessel and the Captain was very pleased with it.

When we returned to harbour he was not in a very good humour when he arrived on board after making his report to the Staff Officer of Operations. Although he did not say as much we got the distinct impression that the whole business had been a wild goose chase and had been devised solely to get the Greek ships to sea. When I asked him what the Staff had thought of the plot he said nobody had bothered to unroll it let alone look at it; the plot had been tossed aside and ignored.

The mutiny was over by the time we returned. A trawler had gone alongside the Apostolis at night and a party of loyal Greeks led by Commander Papadiamantopolous, who had a British DSO, successfully boarded the vessel. Unfortunately in the initial melee the Commander was killed.

After Italy surrendered the main danger to our convoys were air attacks off the Algerian coast from enemy bases in Northern Italy and the South of France, and the ever present threat from U-boats. The air attacks regularly occurred near Cape Tenez and were invariably delivered at dusk by torpedo bombers. Often flares would be dropped to illuminate the convoy to make an easier target and it became the usual practice to make smoke and attempt to hide the convoy behind the smoke screen. This could be quite effective but it could also raise other problems. Some American ships were often trigger happy with little fire control and, in the smoke, would fire indiscriminately, which endangered other ships in the convoy. Enemy pilots, attempting to sight the convoy, could get too close in the smoke and fail to see a ship before it was too late to avoid a collision. The enemy aircraft would certainly be lost but so would a valuable ship and its cargo.

On one occasion we all got rather a fright in *Delphinium*. Suddenly a plane roared out of the smoke ahead of us, low over the water, its engines straining at full power as the pilot endeavoured to gain height to avoid hitting our mast. He must have got as big a fright as we did. It was a Heinkel 111 bomber and it flew so close as it flashed past on a level with our bridge that we caught a glimpse of the occupants in the transparent nose. That was the end of the action for the evening, I think they were all pleased to go home.

Hardly a day or night went past without obtaining an asdic or radar contact indicating a possible submarine, either submerged or on the surface. Each one had to be investigated, sniffing around trying to identify the echo. Invariably the underwater target would turn out to be fish or a thermal layer or the echo would simply disappear and be lost. Most of the times we would go to action stations hoping that this time it would be a submarine, but although we had several possible contacts and dropped many depth charges we never had any luck.

One particularly dark night I was on watch with the cox'n, the ship being in her usual position two thousand yards ahead of the convoy. Standing by the compass my feet felt a very slight tremor which could only have lasted for a second. I was well used to ship vibration and normally would not have given it another thought. However some sixth sense made me turn round and I thought I saw a glow, it was only momentary, in the direction of the convoy. I sounded the alarm bells and had the ship turned round and heading for the convoy by the time the Captain came on the bridge.

We went down through the convoy and after passing the rear ships the faint twinkle of lights could be seen in the water ahead. As we drew nearer men could be seen clinging to a life-raft, we stopped alongside and pulled them on board. There were only six of them, one was the Second Officer and they appeared to be the only survivors from a ship that had been at the rear of the convoy.

Alexandria was always known as a good run ashore with many bars and night clubs such as the Monsigneur and Femina, and restaurants and cafes like Pastroudis which was very popular for afternoon tea and sticky cakes. Several good cinemas offered a choice of recent films which was my main choice of entertainment when I went ashore. There were also clubs that one could go to. The Union Club, the E.F.I. Club and the Alexandria Sporting Club were open to officers of the three Services, and the Naval Warrant Officers Club made commissioned officers honorary members in certain circumstances, usually to allow junior officers to attend the weekly dance when selected local girls were present to provide partners. I met a girl whose father had been an officer in the Polish cavalry during the First War, after which he landed up in Egypt and was then head waiter in Pastroudis. It was quite amusing, and not unusual, to see a fairly senior officer, invariably army, sitting with a young woman whose mother, stout and dressed in black, was in attendance seated at another table nearby.

I celebrated my 21st birthday in Alexandria although celebrated is hardly the word to use. The ship was unexpectedly sent out to do exercises, anti-aircraft firing, etc., but due to bad weather there was so much delay and hanging about that, when the exercises were finally cancelled, we returned to harbour feeling tired and jaded. The other officers did not feel like going ashore and only wanted to have a quiet night, but I felt I had to mark the occasion somehow and went ashore by myself. I decided to go and see the *Merry Widow* which was being performed by an ENSA touring company at the Alhambra theatre. I had never seen an operetta so it would be a bit of a treat.

It was not to be my day. My seat was situated right behind a pillar and I could only see half of the stage at a time. I spent the entire evening with the pillar between my legs and dodging my head from side round it to see what was going on. Whenever I hear the well-known song from the show *Velia* I remember my 21st and the night behind the pillar.

One day the Captain returned on board rather pleased with himself and announced that he had managed to get hold of a 'skimming dish' through a friend in the dockyard and that we would be landing one of our oar-propelled boats. A skimming dish was a very small motor boat, about eight or ten feet in length, and only capable of accommodating four people under the small canopy at the stem. The cox'n's cockpit was close up to the bow immediately in front of the engine compartment. The boat was extremely fast and manoeuvrable, skimming over the water with the bow out of the water and spraying on either side. They were mainly used by officers and the normal practice was to stand up, hold on to the canopy and enjoy an exhilarating ride, bouncing over the waves with the wind blowing in one's face. They were usually only carried in the bigger ships and the 'old man' had been very lucky to get one and, what is more, had been allowed to keep it.

When the boat was delivered it was in a bit of a mess so I was made boat officer with instructions to do it up. It was a new toy and we set about turning it into a craft that would be a credit to the ship. During the next trip the boat was thoroughly overhauled, the wood work was rubbed down and several coats applied to the varnished areas. A thick rope was given a canvas covering, painted white and fitted round the boat as a rubbing strake and the First Lieutenant made curtains for the small windows in the canopy, teasing out the bottom of the canvas to make them look 'tiddley.'

All that remained was to decide what colour the boat should be painted. I told the Captain that there was a really nice shade of green in the paint locker which would finish the job and make the boat look really smart. He was quite pleased with this and he told me to go ahead and use it.

Arriving back in Alexandria all hands were on deck to watch the Captain set off in his new boat to go to the Depot ship to make his report to Commodore (Destroyers.) We used binoculars to watch his progress through the harbour and noticed that as he passed ships enroute there was a bit of a scurry on their quarterdecks, and what amounted to confusion and a mini panic on the quarterdeck of the Depot ship as he arrived alongside.

He had hardly been on board the Depot ship for five minutes before we saw the boat heading back towards us. The Captain came or board, his face red with embarrassment, and stumped off to his cabin without saying a word. I soon found out what had gone wrong when he sent for me a few minutes later. As soon as I entered his cabin he said, "Get that bloody boat painted grey, Pilot, don't you know that green is the Commander-in-Chief's colour?"

I had completely forgotten (and so had the Captain) that Flag Officers' barges were painted different colours (green, blue, red, black) to make them more easily recognizable when they were afloat. Ships were always advised by signal beforehand when the C-in-C was going to be afloat and whether the affirmative or negative was applicable. If the affirmative pendant was being displayed on the barge it meant that full ceremonial was to be carried out. In a battleship this could mean parading a guard and band. A negative pendant meant that there was to be no fuss. A Duty Officer would salute and have the still piped as the barge passed by.

We could imagine the flap that our Captain had caused as he sped across the harbour in his tiddley craft. Sighting the green boat Duty Officers would immediately think that the C-in-C was afloat and, as there had been no previous signal to the effect, they would not know whether affirmative or negative applied, or if their particular ship was about to receive an unexpected visit from 'Himself.' The scurrying and unusual activity we had observed were signs of the hurried preparations being made, and it was not hard to imagine the Commanding Officers demanding to know why they had not been informed earlier, and interrogating their Yeoman of Signals as to why he had not received the signal that the C-in-C would be afloat.

When he arrived on board the Depot Ship the Captain had received quite a rocket for creating such a flap. He was a very efficient officer who was not slow to speak his mind when he disagreed with the staff, which did not add to his popularity, and they took this opportunity to put him in his place.

We had upset the staff on another occasion. On checking the records it had been found that *Delphinium* had steamed so many thousand miles (I think it was. 150,000) since she commissioned and the Captain decided that this should be made known to the authorities. At the very least we hoped for a, "Well done!" It was just after Admiral Cunningham made his famous signal to the Admiralty after the surrender of the Italian Fleet, "I have the honour to report that the Italian Fleet now lies at anchor under the guns of Malta.", and the Captain phrased his signal in similar fashion.

The signal was addressed to the C-in-C Mediterranean and repeated to the Commodore (Destroyers), Rear Admiral (Alexandria) and the Admiralty, and read, "I have the honour to report that HMS *Delphinium* now lies at K buoy under the guns of Ras-el-Tin having steamed 150,000 miles."

It was sent to the Depot Ship for onward transmission to the addressees. We heard later that when it was received the Commodore (D) exploded and said, "Good God! The man can't be drunk at this time in the morning?", and stopped the signal from going any further. He evidently had a different sense of humour!

In the summer of 1944 Elsie left school and, as a reward for doing so well in her examinations, her parents brought her through to Alexandria for a short holiday whilst *Delphinium* was in port for ten days boiler cleaning period. I had received word that I was to be relieved and go home from Gibraltar on our next trip so this would probably be the last time we would see each other.

During the ten days we had a wonderful time and thoroughly enjoyed ourselves. I was invited to a dinner party at the L'Auberge, a hotel on the Corniche, given by Dr. and Mrs. Scarpalezzo for some of their friends. The main attraction in the cabaret was a 12 piece band composed of Chinamen playing mandolins, their big number being *Deep in the Heart of Texas*.

The Alexandria Sporting Club was a very big complex. In addition to horse racing there were rugby and soccer pitches, tennis courts and a large swimming pool. Adjoining the large club-house and restaurant were wide terraces where one could sit and enjoy the surroundings whilst having tea or drinks which were also served at the pool. One day I took Elsie to the Club to go swimming and, as she was not a member and would not otherwise be allowed entry, I took the chance and tried to pass her off as being a Wren. I did not think we were going to make it when, at the entrance, she was asked to show her identity card. Elsie satisfied the official by calmly remarking, in the most natural manner and without a trace of accent, "I quite forgot to bring it with me."

On our final outing to the cinema Dr. Scarpaiezzo paid me the compliment of allowing us to go unchaperoned. Although our friendship was platonic we had grown fond of each other during our many happy times together in the past two years, and we both felt sad that we would probably never meet again. However we promised to write to each other which we did, until we lost touch when Elsie married and went to live in Hong Kong.

Just over twenty years later whilst passing through Port Said on the way to the Persian Gulf, I asked the port doctor if Dr. Scarpalezzo was still in Port Said. When he told me that the Doctor had returned to Athens and that his wife still corresponded with Mrs Scarpalezzo, I asked if she would kindly convey my respects and kindest regards the next time she wrote to Mrs Scarpalezzo, and to say I had never forgotten their kindness. When my ship arrived in the Persian Gulf I received a letter from Elsie who had returned to Athens from Hong Kong. Some ten years after that my ship was in the shipyard at Piraeus undergoing repairs. Whilst waiting to make a telephone call I was idly leafing through a local telephone directory and found a section in English at the rear of the book. There I found Elsie's name and number. That evening, after thirty years, we once again sat together drinking coffee and eating sticky cakes as we did in our golden days, and for three hours told each other how life had treated us in the intervening years. We remained pen-pals and some years later we met again in London when I was introduced to her daughter and her family. From Gibraltar I took passage home in HMS *Flint Castle* a new class of corvette which was bigger and rectified the shortcomings which had been found in the Flower Class. *Flint Castle* was fitted with all the latest radar, anti-submarine and depth charge equipment and I could not help thinking how lucky the officers were to have a gyro compass, instead of having to use the magnetic compass with all the inconvenience of variation and deviation. To me it was rather like driving in a Rolls Royce after being used to a Baby Austin. I was also impressed by the arrangements that were made beforehand to get part of the ship's company away on leave as soon as the ship arrived alongside at Liverpool. The turnaround period in port before the next convoy was usually so short that every minute counted. Travel warrants, ration cards, etc. were issued to the men due for leave the day before arrival so that they could proceed ashore as soon as the ship had berthed.

The family received a pleasant surprise when I telephoned from the jetty to say that I would be home the next day after being away for nearly three years. Like many others I had only been at home for approximately three months all told, since I went to sea four and a half years previously.

Sadly there was nobody waiting for me on my return. Whilst I was away I had unexpectedly received a letter from Bobbie to say that she had married a Canadian Air Force officer. She had written several letters to let me know what was going on but they had gone astray, which was not unusual in war-time. At the time I was upset as I was extremely fond of her, but I realised I was very young and that it was unrealistic to expect that such a lovely girl would not be pursued and won over by an older chap. Bobbie was my 'first love' and I never forgot her and through the years I often wondered where she was, how she was getting on and if she was happy.

Just before Christmas 1991, and again through the telephone directory, I spoke to Isobel in Canada – nearly fifty years after we said goodbye. A couple of years later, when she visited 'the auld country' with her husband Bob, we really did *Meet Again*.

I had a quiet leave mainly visiting friends and relatives. At the end of three weeks I was pleased when I received an appointment to HMS *Tavy* with instructions to join her on lst September 1944 in Glasgow.

Chapter 16

ARCTIC CONVOY

HMS *Tavy* was a River class frigate, a new class of ocean escort vessel which was larger, faster, and more heavily armed than the corvettes. The ship was commanded by Commander G. Thring who was Senior Officer of the 20th Escort Group which was mainly composed of Colony class frigates. These ships were built in America and were named after British colonies. They were not so well fitted out as British ships which still had wood furniture in the cabins and chartroom and the traditional settees, easy chairs, and club fender round the fireplace in the wardroom to give some comfort and a homely touch. The American ships were extremely bare and functional, all internal fittings being made of metal. Their one redeeming feature was the equipment which provided an endless supply of coffee in the ward-room.

The ship was in dockyard hands undergoing a refit when I joined and I was sent straightway on a radar course to receive instruction on a new set that was being fitted. Whilst I was there I saw the radar panel being assembled for the new battleship HMS *Vanguard* that was being built at John Brown's yard on the Clyde. It was a massive installation compared to the compact units which eventually came into service.

After I had completed the radar course I went down to the Royal Compass Observatory near Slough to do a course on the gyro compass. It was a very pleasant interlude. The Observatory was a large country house complete with moat and situated in extensive grounds quite close to Datchett, a small typically English village which had four or five pubs around the village green. I had never sailed with a gyro compass so I found the course interesting and informative, a great deal of time being spent in stripping down, reassembling and balancing the compass which at that time required more adjustment and maintenance than later models.

When passing through London at the end of the course I was able to meet up with my sister, Chris, who was stationed at Cowes where she was a Signals Officer in Force J, Admiral Vian's command at the Normandy invasion. She had been at Cowes since receiving her commission and, by an unhappy coincidence, the first message she had to handle on taking over her first watch as an officer was the one reporting the loss of the *Erica*. She had to keep the news to herself and could not tell our parents until it was announced officially. However the senior Signals Officer made some urgent enquiries and had assured her that I was on the list of survivors.

Tavy carried several more officers than a corvette. Because she was the Senior Officer of the Group she carried the specialist navigating and anti-submarine officers and a specialist Sub-Lieutenant responsible for HF/DF (High Frequency Direction Finding) operations, which enabled the monitoring of U-boat radio transmissions so that their positions could be ascertained by radio bearings. She also carried a doctor and a Warrant Engineer Officer in addition to the First Lieutenant and four Sub-Lieutenants who were the watchkeeping officers. In all a total of eleven officers.

HMS Tavy

Depth charge deck

Watch relief

As the Group navigating officer was on board there was no requirement for one of the ship's officers to be navigator but I understudied him to learn more, and in case he was detached from the ship for any reason. I was made victualling officer responsible for ordering stores and provisions and I was also given the job of radar officer.

My action station was Officer of Quarters of A gun and I was put in charge of the Hedgehog ahead throwing weapon which I had never seen before. When attacking with depth charges the asdic set could not keep contact when the submarine was overrun during the final phase of the attack. This meant that during the crucial moments before the depth charges were dropped, the escort Captain had no information about the submarine's evasive movements. The Hedgehog was a multiple spigot mortar which fired 24 bombs in an elliptical pattern ahead of the ship, so that an escort could attack whilst still holding contact on asdic with the submerged submarine. The bombs were contact fused and filled with 32lbs of a new explosive enabling a hit from one bomb to cripple a submarine. The bomb had to hit to explode since its small casing could not accommodate hydrostatic firing gear, so it lacked the main advantage of the depth charge and never replaced it. It had one unique advantage in that an explosion usually signified the destruction of a submarine except in shallow water when it might explode on hitting the bottom.

The 20th Escort Group was based at Lisahally on the River Foyle near Londonderry and on completion of the repair period we proceeded there to join up with the rest of the Group. Exercises were carried out during the passage when I had the opportunity to learn the drill for firing the Hedgehog. The mortars were mounted on the fore deck immediately forward of the superstructure on either side of which were large ready-use ammunition lockers. There was a small shelter in the superstructure under A gun for the firing control. A pattern of bombs was always kept loaded on the spiggots. On the nose of each bomb there was an impeller which was rotated on entering the water thus priming the bomb. As a safety measure the impeller was locked by a pin and covered by a cap both of which had to be removed before firing. In bad weather with the ship leaping about, and seas and spray coming over the f'c'sle, it was a difficult and sometimes hazardous job to remove the pins and caps before firing, and to remove the heavy bombs from the lockers when re-loading the spiggots. It was most frustrating when an asdic contact turned out to be a false alarm and the pins and caps had to be re-inserted and replaced in similar conditions, especially in the dark.

At Lisahally the buzz went around the ship that the Group would be going on the Russian run to Murmansk, and the rumour became even stronger as we prepared to sail to Loch Ewe on the west coast of Scotland which was the assembly point for convoys to Russia. The rumour was confirmed when a load of bales was delivered to the ship a couple of hours before sailing. They were later found to contain Arctic clothing and the late delivery was no doubt for security reasons. There was no time to open the bales to check the contents so I signed the receipt notes to that effect which did not please the Wren driver. When the bales were opened I found the classic situation – we had all the anorak tops and another ship had received all the trousers.

There were many other items all of the best quality. White seal-skin mitts which were worn over blanket liners, long thick oilskin 'Bull's-wool' lined coats, Jaeger cardigans and sweaters, long-john underwear, leather sea-boots and balaclava helmets. The anorak with its fur trimmed hood was worn over a thick blanket liner and, together with the trousers which were made of the same thin material, was extremely effective in keeping one warm in the freezing conditions that were experienced later during the passage north.

The convoy sailed from Loch Ewe in November 1944 supported by the cruiser *Kent*, the Woolworth aircraft carrier *Nairana* and several fleet destroyers with an inner screen of escort vessels. Our role in the operation was to act as a Support Group, steaming in line abreast and zigzagging several miles ahead of the convoy with the object of locating any U-boats which might be lying in wait, and sinking them or keeping them under until the convoy had passed. If one of the close escorts obtained a contact, one of our Group would be detached to take over the hunt to enable the close escort to return to her station, and thus prevent a gap appearing in the screen.

The passage to Kola Inlet, the entrance to Murmansk, was approximately 2,500 miles and for the first few days everything was quiet. Then we ran into bad weather and at the same time the gyro compass became defective when I was on watch. It was a most important piece of equipment as, apart from being required for navigational purposes, repeaters were part of the asdic, radar and HF/DF installations to provide the accurate bearings required in their operations. It was bitterly cold and I was pleased when the Captain told me to go down and find out what was wrong. It would be warm in the gyro room and I could have a smoke. The rating who normally looked after the compass had already found the cause of the trouble by the time I arrived.

The compass was stopped whilst the defect was rectified and, when the time came to re-start it, I was thankful that I had attended the course. When a compass was started it could take some time for it to settle on true north during which time it would hunt from side to side of the bearing. The settling down process was made more difficult by the ship's sometimes violent movement in the rough seas, but we were able to expedite matters by carrying out some procedures which I had learned on the course. After about three hours I was able to return to the bridge and report (with my fingers crossed) that the compass was working again and could be relied upon. Fortunately we had no more problems with it.

During the passage the officers were in two watches for most of the time, four hours on and four hours off. As senior watchkeeper I had the junior Sub-Lieutenant on watch with me whilst Alan Hirst and Guy Jessop, the other Sub-Lieutenants, were on watch together. The two Lieutenants, Adam Guthrie the A/S Officer (Ping), and Tony Shepherd the Pilot were also on watch and watch. As staff officers they were able to handle routine operational matters and allow the Captain to get as much rest as possible. They had suggested this arrangement as they were concerned about his health after four hard years in command of destroyers and escort groups. Commander Thring was highly respected and much loved by us all, he was a first class example of an officer and a gentleman and we all pulled together to lighten his load and to give him no cause for concern that his high standards would not be maintained.

As the convoy progressed further to the northward the days became shorter until there were only a few hours of daylight. The long hours of darkness gave us protection from the constant air attacks from the enemy bases in Norway which were a feature of the summer convoys, but even in the limited daylight hours a reconnaisance aircraft would circle the convoy and report its position, course and speed of advance. We came under air attack several times during daylight and also at night when torpedo bombers attacked by the light of flares. There were many asdic contacts reported by the escorts, and attacks made on targets that were doubtful but which had to be positively classified just in case.

As the convoy approached the Arctic Circle I found the Arctic clothing which had been issued extremely effective in keeping out the bitter cold wind which swirled around the open bridge. The merchant ships had wheelhouses which gave protection to personnel not required to go out on the bridge wings but warships all had open bridges with no protection from the elements. The leather sea-boots on top of a couple of pairs of thick stockings kept the feet fairly warm but they were very heavy and there was always the thought that they would drag one under in the water and make it impossible to swim. At that time if one had to go in the water the main fear was drowning, and there was concern about having too many clothes on which would hamper movement in the water. In later years it was proved that most men died from hypothermia, especially in the Atlantic and Northern waters, and rather than take clothes off before going into the water more clothes should be put on to retain body heat. For the same reason energy (heat) should not be wasted by attempting to swim and the life-jacket should be relied upon to keep afloat. However it was reckoned that a man could only last three or four minutes in the water before succumbing to the extreme conditions and, in any case, the naval lifebelts were ineffective in supporting the body and keeping the head out of the water.

In *Tavy* I had my first experience of dehydrated food – vegetables and meat – and of bread rationing. We were allowed three slices of bread per day. The potatoes did not have much of a flavour and were rather salty, and in the end I found the best way to eat dehydrated food was to cover it with HP sauce. In subsequent years it became a practice to issue dehydrated items once a month to give the cooks experience in preparing them.

Because the war was in its final stages the enemy attacks had not been as fierce or as continuous as those experienced by the earlier convoys and we arrived at Kola Inlet at the beginning of December without suffering any loss. The merchant ships proceeded to Murmansk whilst the escorts berthed and refuelled at Polyarno.

A pilot came on board to take the ship into harbour. He was a man in his late twenties, strong features with close cropped blonde hair; one might say a typical Russian. The ship had to anchor in deep water so the anchor was walked out instead of being let go at a run. When the pilot decided that the ship was anchored practically all the anchor cable was out and little left in the chain locker. We were all in the ward-room when the Officer of the Watch sent down an urgent message that the ship was drifting and had dragged her anchor. It transpired that the anchor was not even on the bottom, and when it came to weighing it the weight of all the cable was too much for the windlass to heave up. In order to ease the weight on the windlass the ship had to be steamed in close to shore until the anchor and some of the cable were on the sea bottom. This turned out to be a risky business and by the time it was over the Captain did not have a high opinion of Russian pilots. We took good care not to mention the species in his presence.

The pilot was quite a nice chap and 'Doc' Walbaum, the Surgeon Lieutenant, was given the job of looking after him and entertaining him whilst he was on board. Apart from his professional duties, which fortunately were usually fairly light and consisted of looking after minor ailments, Doc also looked after the mess and wine accounts and did most of the de-cyphering of secret signal traffic. Entertaining visitors until the appropriate officer or host was available was just another of his odd jobs. Because of this he had developed a fairly good capacity for the grape but he met his match with the Russian pilot. This chap was used to vodka which he indicated was much stronger than our whisky which he consumed as though it was lemonade. Doc could not keep up with him and had to retire. He was another one who could be upset by the mention of Russian pilots.

The pilot did give us cause for sober reflection when apologies were made for a rather plain lunch that was being served – dehydrated meat and vegetables and apples and custard – which was put down to food rationing. "Ah", he said, "you British do not know what is hunger." He then cut a slice of bread in half and half filled two glasses with water. "My fiancee in Leningrad has that for breakfast," he said pushing forward a half slice of bread and a glass of water. "The other half slice and water is her supper."

Alongside the oiling jetty the Russians appeared to be rather a subdued lot and there were not many welcoming smiles in evidence. However our sailors soon found that British cigarettes were highly valued by the Russians who had to make do with a cardboard tube with a little tobacco at the end of it. Some of the Russians had small red metal stars which could be worn in the lapel and these were offered in exchange for cigarettes. One or two sailors also managed to exchange cigarettes for knives which had a red star on the handle. All this bartering was done in a cloak and dagger atmosphere as the Russians could get into serious trouble if they were reported for accepting cigarettes.

Tavy was subsequently berthed alongside some other frigates and destroyers at a jetty which was at the end of a long narrow inlet near the small town. Some of us went ashore to stretch our legs and have a look around during the short period of daylight. There were a couple of large wooden buildings, one was the Red Star Club or canteen for their servicemen and the other appeared to be the only store or shop serving the community. There seemed to be only one street which was lined by wooden houses, and banked by deep snow which was piled down each side of the road. The town was situated slightly above the harbour and one could see for miles across the surrounding countryside. The view was totally depressing, as far as could be seen there was nothing but snow-covered tundra which looked bleak and bare and most inhospitable. Just miles and miles of sweet damn all. How anyone could live in such a place I could not imagine and it did much to explain the dejected and subdued look of the inhabitants.

There were some children playing by the roadside and some of our sailors offered them chocolate and sweets and tried to make friends with them in the traditional way of British sailors. A Russian went up to the sailors and indicated that the parents would get into trouble if their children were found to have accepted sweets and that they should not be offered. The Russian authorities were very suspicious and security conscious. No newspapers or other reading material could be taken ashore, there was a strict curfew at night for the local inhabitants, and the women guards at the entrance to the jetty would shoot on sight if at all doubtful of the identity of anyone approaching.

On the evening before we were due to sail the Senior Officer of the destroyers, Captain (D), invited Commander Thring and some of the other COs to dine with him onboard HMS *Caesar*. In *Tavy* we had had a few visitors after dinner and a bit of a party was developing when someone suggested that we should all go over and visit *Caesar's* wardroom. Our sudden arrival at the end of the dinner party caught the *Caesar's* officers unawares but very soon a sing-song was in full swing around the piano. Captain (D) was very keen on Gilbert and Sullivan and he played the piano and led us through the popular choruses, performing a duet with the Captain of one of our frigates, the *Bahamas*. He was a Lieutenant-Commander RNR with experience in towing which, unbeknown to us at the time, was shortly to be of crucial importance.

On the return voyage we ran into trouble in heavy weather just after rounding the North Cape. It was just before midnight when the clamour of the alarm bells roused all hands to action stations. It was a wild night, the ship was rolling and pitching in the rough seas and I had to concentrate to keep my feet as I edged my way along the starboard side of the slippery upper deck to my station at the Hedgehog. Out of the corner of my eye I thought I saw a large, dark mass pass close down our starboard side, I only had a momentary glimpse before it was swallowed up in the dark.

Word was soon passed that the destroyer *Cassandra*, a sister ship of the *Caesar*, had either struck a mine or had been torpedoed. She had been hit just forward of the bridge and had broken in two, the after section had remained afloat and the bow section had sunk. It must have been the bow section that I saw just before it sank.

The following day the weather moderated sufficiently for the *Bahamas* to take the *Cassandra* in tow during the short period of daylight, and *Tavy, Tortola, Somaliland* and *Monnow* were ordered to carry out an anti-submarine patrol around the two ships and escort them back to Kola Inlet. The weather soon deteriorated again and for the first two or three days progress was very slow. The tow's speed of advance was only three or four knots, and we were all worried about the close proximity of the enemy held coastline and the possibility of air attack.

My sister had meanwhile been promoted to Second Officer and had been transferred to Lyness at Scapa Flow. Being a Signals Officer she was one of the first to learn about *Cassandra* and that *Tavy* was escorting her back to Russia. The position of the tow and escort was plotted on the large map in the Operations Room and indicated by a marker. Later on Chris told me that each time she went on duty she looked at the map to see how we were getting on, and how she became anxious when we appeared to be stopped and making little progress. As the weather improved the tow made better speed and we eventually rounded the North Cape and, after six days, brought *Cassandra* safely to port.

Many years later I met a supervisor on the tanker jetty in Botany Bay, Australia, who had been a stoker in *Cassandra* that night off the North Cape. He was lucky enough to have been on watch in the boiler-room when the ship was hit.

After refuelling, *Tavy* and the remainder of the Group sailed immediately on the return passage home. There was no hope of catching up with the convoy which by this time was too far ahead, and as we steamed at full speed there was concern that we might encounter some German destroyers which were based in ports on the west coast of Norway. An operation had been planned to take place during the passage of the return convoy when these destroyers were to be enticed out of port to be engaged by our cruisers and destroyers. There was always the possibility that things might go wrong and that the enemy might miss the bait and find us instead. There was much discussion as to how four 19 knot frigates would take on two or three 30 knot heavily armed Narvik class destroyers!

It was an uneventful passage until we were nearing the north coast of Ireland on our way to Loch Foyle. An approaching destroyer turned out to be the *Caesar* and, as she passed, Captain (D) sent a signal, "How is *Cassandra*?" to which Commander Thring replied, "*Cassandra* well your operatic lover took the weight."

At Lisahally the warm clothing had to be returned to the base as it was only on loan. There had not been a great deal of time for an accurate check to be made when the clothing had been delivered and the mix-up in the delivery of the bales had not helped matters. The clothing was all gathered in and checked against the delivery note when quite a few items were found to be missing. There were Some very good woollen cardigans which had been issued to the Petty Officers who said they had lost them and were quite happy to pay for them. This idea was soon knocked on the head and, eventually, they were returned. However several other items could not be traced and I wrote a rather sharp covering letter to Captain (S), the Base Supply Officer, pointing out that it had not been possible to check the clothing when it was received due to the hurried and late delivery, and suggesting that there may have been an error in the stores department. I explained the situation to the Captain when I gave him the letter for his signature and it was a measure of the trust he placed in all his officers that he signed it without further comment.

The letter was sent off and I thought no more about it until later that evening the Stores Petty Officer reported that he had found more clothing. They were some items which had not been issued and had been stowed away and forgotten about. This put the cat amongst the pidgeons as far as my letter was concerned, the facts and figures were wrong and I had to get it back quickly before Captain (S) saw it.

First thing next morning I telephoned the Base and asked to speak to his secretary who turned out to be a Wren Third Officer. I introduced myself and as I explained my predicament her only response was a curt "Yes?" as I finished each point in my story. This did not provide me with much hope as she did not seem at all sympathetic, so I finished up by saying, "If you want to save the career of a promising young officer please send the letter back unopened." She replied, "We'll see", and hung up. I was not very confident about the outcome of my call but I had misjudged her as the letter arrived unopened the following morning. I eventually met Third Officer Dilly Little on VE night at a party in the Wren Officers' mess.

Chapter 17

THE LAST LAP TO VE DAY

————

From January 1945 until VE day the Group was employed in escorting troop convoys to the Mediterranean and hunting U-boats in the Channel. The Group remained at Gibraltar whilst the troop-ships carried on eastward, and subsequently joined the escort of homeward bound convoys as they passed Gibraltar.

On the first passage to Gibraltar Commander Thring decided that, during the turn around period in port, the maximum amount of time would be given over to sport and recreation, and that it would be a good idea to organize a concert party and put on a show. Huff-Duff (H.F/DF Officer) was put in charge of the arrangements and all ships in the Group were asked for volunteers. By the time we arrived at Gibraltar he had things so organized that rehearsals started very soon after we arrived. The Group berthed at the South Mole where there was a building with a large hall which was turned into a theatre for the occasion – the lighting, etc. being set up by the ships' electricians.

The Captain roped in the wardroom officers for his own act in which he played the part of a surgeon carrying out an operation, during which he produced various items of ship's equipment from the body with an amusing comment on each one. Some of us acted as patients, lying on camp beds and calling for the nurse to bring bed pans. When 'she' eventually arrived we would announce, "too late!"

The show was a big success and ran for two nights after which a shorter version was put on for the army in one of the garrison canteens.

Gibraltar was well supplied with bars and cabarets but there was not much night life after 9.30 p.m. when they all had to close, although there was one establishment which had a room upstairs where the cabaret continued for those in the know until 11.30 p.m. Most of the artistes were Spanish from La Linia across the border and had to return each evening. The Rock Hotel, an imposing building overlooking the harbour, was one of the best hotels in the Mediterranean and an evening there was a pleasant change from the NOP (Naval Officers' Pavilion) a small club-house with a bar near the dockyard and a favourite meeting place and watering hole for officers going ashore.

We had some good nights at The Rock. On one occasion, on the night before we were due to sail, Guy Jessop decided that he wanted to take some flowers from the dining room back to the ship and the head waiter eventually allowed him to collect a bunch of large white lilys. As we were leaving, Guy weaved his way up to the elderly officer who was to be Commodore of the convoy and invited him to, "Smell the pretty flowers, Sir." The old boy humoured Guy and bent down to have a sniff. Unfortunately Guy had filled a flower with some brown sauce and the Commodore received a nosefull. But he took it in good part, no doubt remembering his own youthful escapades.

In the submarine situation report that was broadcast each evening by the Admiralty, it was invariably stated that one U-boat was thought to be patrolling the entrance to the Strait of Gibraltar. During one of our visits the Group was given the task of carrying out a thorough sweep of the Strait and the approaches in order to try and locate this U-boat, and put an end to it for once and for all. We thought we had found it one very dark night when, after a depth charge attack on an asdic contact, starshell and rockets were fired to illuminate a radar contact which was thought to be the enemy surfacing. But both contacts turned out to be false echoes.

I had an idea that a U-boat might shelter in the bay of a small town, Larache, in Spanish Morocco where it could lie on the bottom during daylight and re-charge batteries at night, between making forays into the Strait. A proposition was put to Commander Thring that the motor boat, armed with a couple of depth charges, and an armed party should be sent in to investigate the anchorage. As one of my duties was boarding officer should we ever force a U-boat to the surface, I was given charge of the proposed expedition. We were all organized and ready to go when the Captain decided to inform the Admiral at Gibraltar of his intentions, only to receive a reply to the effect that the operation was not approved. It was a big disappointment but there was reasoning behind the Admiral's decision. We would be entering Spanish territorial waters and, although a U-boat would be acting illegally by sheltering in the bay, any incident could result in diplomatic problems for our Government.

By this stage in the war there were many wrecks on the bottom of the English Channel and its approaches. It was thought that U-boats had devised a new tactic of lying on the bottom close to them, in the hope of being mistaken for wrecks by the ships that were hunting them, and this meant that each asdic contact had to be very closely examined. Whilst the appearance of oil after a depth charge attack usually indicated the presence of a submarine, in shallow water it could also be released from a wreck which had been disturbed by the explosion. The usual procedure was to steam slowly over the contact in an endeavour to get an outline an the echo-sounder trace. We obtained the shapes of hull, masts and funnels but never had the luck to find a U-boat.

Time in port at Lisahally was usually taken up with training. The A/S officer and operators attended the submarine attack table, depth charge crews the depth charge driller, A.A. guns crews the dome teacher, and signalmen, coders and telegraphists attended the signal school.

Commanding Officers and their Navigators took part in convoy escort exercises. In these games the Officers were given small cubicles representing their ships and supplied with a chart, plotting materials and signal pad and each ship allocated a position in the convoy screen. In accordance with a timed schedule which had been drawn up previously the ships were advised of incidents and operational matters affecting them, e.g. "You have obtained an asdic contact.", "A ship has been sunk on your starboard side." or, "You have an engine defect." The ship in question then had to make the necessary signals to the Escort Commander showing the action being taken, and all ships had to respond to the signals received from him. The information and signals were passed to the ships by Wrens. Having been closely involved in many exercises they had learned a great deal about convoy escort operations and what was expected of the Captains in various situations. They were therefore very helpful at times with a quiet word of advice, "You will leave a gap in the screen, Sir", when a Captain was about to take the wrong action, and for which he might receive a reprimand.

I had been temporarily transferred to HMS *Pitcairn*, one of our Colony class frigates, at the beginning of May 1945 to take the place of an officer who had been hospitalised. The ship was doing trials off Largs in the Firth of Forth on VE day when orders were received to return to Lisahally. At lunch there was a general air of excitement and a feeling of relief that the war was over, which led to much good humoured banter and yarn spinning amongst the officers. As I left the table I jokingly remarked that when any of them had been fourteen days adrift in an open boat they could then tell me about their war experiences.

We had just secured in our berth when the order was received to "Splice the Main Brace." In the sailing ship Navy the main brace was one of the strongest and most important ropes in the ship, and splicing it was a heavy job of work which was sometimes rewarded by an extra issue of rum. It subsequently became the custom for the Monarch to order an extra ration of rum to be issued whenever there was a great occasion to be celebrated, such as a notable victory, a Fleet Review or State ceremony. The signal "Splice the Main Brace" could only be originated by the Monarch and it was the only occasion when officers received an issue of rum. Navy rum was much stronger than the rum sold onshore and could bring tears to the eyes of anybody not used to it. I had not tasted it again since the *Erica* went down and it brought tears to my eyes on this occasion, but it was a good way to start the victory celebrations.

In the evening we attended a party in the Wren Officers' mess and during the course of the evening I happened to be standing by the fireplace when someone said, "Come and meet the man who was fourteen days in an open boat." A cluster of Wrens gathered round asking questions so, to keep the fun going, I started to spin a line about my supposed ordeal, knocking down seagulls with an oar for food, etc. Whilst this was going on I noticed that my glass on the mantelpiece was being topped up by an attractive Wren with auburn hair. When I finished my yarn we started chatting and who should she be but the Wren Officer who had saved my bacon in the Arctic clothing affair. I was able to thank Dilly properly by giving her dinner in the Officers' Club and we became good friends. On two or three occasions we made the popular trip across the border to the Loch Swilly Hotel for a meal of fresh salmon and a walk in the country.

Many of the U-boats at sea at the end of the war were met and escorted into Lisahally by the ships which had hunted them for so long. Most of them were covered by thick strips of rubber which were intended to insulate the steel hull from asdic transmissions, and make it more difficult to obtain good solid echoes to identify the target. The U-boats hulls showed evidence of long periods at sea and, with their glistening green rubber coating, still looked evil and menacing as they lay side by side in their trots. One could not help but think of the death and destruction they had caused during the past five years, of the hundreds of ships that had been sunk, and the thousands of merchant seamen who had given their lives in keeping the convoys sailing in the face of their constant attacks. There was also the constant vigilance of the convoy escorts, the hard conditions experienced by the crews of the small ships in the hazardous waters of the North Atlantic and Artic Oceans and the many well-known ships that did not return to harbour. Their presence in our harbour and under our guns was the conclusive evidence that we had finally beaten them and swept them from the seas.

Commander Thring was relieved shortly after VE day and we were all very sorry to see him go but he deserved a long leave and a good rest. He had very kindly recommended me for accelerated promotion to Lieutenant and I had been promoted in March 1945, six months ahead of the normal time. I met him again when he was Commander in charge of the Drafting Office in Chatham Barracks and again in Malta in 1949 when, as Captain, he was Chief of Staff to the Rear Admiral (Destroyers) Commander Thring was subsequently promoted to Rear-Admiral and was serving as Flag Officer Malaya when I called at Port Swettenham in 1957.

The officers of the 20th Escort Group gave him a good send off at a farewell party in the Officers' Club in Londonderry. At the end of the evening we lined the entrance to the Club and piped him out of the door and over the side into a dinghy which was mounted on a wheeled cradle. The Officers then tailed on to the drag lines and pulled the dinghy down the drive to the taxi which was waiting at the entrance to the grounds.

In June 1945 I was relieved from *Tavy* and after a period of leave I received an appointment to HMS *Cockatrice*, an Algerine class Fleet Minesweeper based at Harwich. Once again I was lucky. I was going to a class of ship that was new to me, and where I would get further experience in another area of naval operations.

Chapter 18

PEACETIME MINESWEEPING

––––

The Algerine class Fleet Minesweepers were laid down and built between 1940 and 1944 and were designed to combat the changes in mine warfare which had become apparent during the early months of the war, and for which the existing minesweepers were quite inadequate. Mines were being laid by the enemy in much deeper waters and the swept area was being considerably extended, making it essential to have larger and more sea-worthy vessels, so the Algerines were often referred to as Ocean Minesweepers. It was also found that different types of mines were being encountered, acoustic and magnetic, which meant that more equipment had to be carried. The ships were also designed to have the dual role of minesweeper and anti-submarine escort vessel.

The ships were equipped with the normal wire sweeping gear for moored mines (Oropesa), the LL electric cable sweep for magnetic mines and an oscillator installed in the ship's fore-peak for the acoustic mines. The electric cable was stowed on a large drum behind, and geared to, the minesweeping winch which made its recovery a much more simple operation than the hard work of heaving it in by hand which was the practice in trawlers.

For their role as escort vessels the ships were fitted with asdic and equipped with four depth charge throwers, two sets of rails and 92 depth charges. The main armament was a 4-inch Q.F. gun fitted on a high angle mounting which also made it suitable for anti-aircraft defence which was provided by four twin 20mm Oerlikon guns. The ships were bigger than a corvette and smaller than a frigate having a length of 225 feet, a speed of 16.5 knots (twin screws) and a complement of 104 but more were often carried. They were, therefore, good general purpose ships and some were employed on Russian convoys for part of the journey to Murmansk.

The class had a reputation amongst the crews as being splendid sea-going ships able to cope with bad weather, and with a number of comforts not found in vessels of a similar size. One particular benefit to the seamen ratings was the upper messdeck (minesweeping messdeck) for eating purposes and which was used by all hands when the lower messdecks were closed off during minesweeping. This gave much more space to the seamen and petty officers, and because of the extended upper deck reaching almost as far as the minesweeping deck, the minesweeping party had plenty of shelter in bad weather.

I joined HMS *Cockatrice* on 11th July 1945 at Harwich where the 18th Minesweeping Flotilla was based. Since April the Flotilla had been engaged in sweeping a channel from the Humber to the Heligoland Bight, and opening up the ports of Hamburg and Cuxhaven and the clearance of Rotterdam.

Lieutenant-Commander D.A.R.M. Ramsay RN (he was called 'Dad') was a big, bluff chap who had the distinction of being one of the few naval officers (if not the only one) at sea to have an artificial leg. He had lost a leg whilst serving as First Lieutenant of the cruiser HMS *Spartan* when the ship was hit during the landing at Anzio in the Italian campaign. Whilst he was convalescing a good friend who was commanding a destroyer allowed him to sail with the ship, and subsequently provided a certificate to say that 'Dad' had performed satisfactorily, and that his disability had not proved to be any drawback in his ability to move about the ship. The medical board was ready to pronounce him unfit for active service but when he produced the certificate it had no other option but to pass him fit for sea. It was rather weird to see his leg hanging up beside his bunk. At times he made rather a joke of it – on one occasion he was walking down Piccadilly when the foot came off, and we were in fits of laughter as he described the amazement and horror of the passers-by as he calmly bent down and re-attached what they must have thought to be his own foot.

Charles Kavanagh, the First Lieutenant, had also been severely injured when his destroyer had blown up some two years previously. He suffered many broken bones and it was eighteen months before he was again fit for duty. When minesweeping the First Lieutenant was in charge of operations on the sweep deck aft. I was Second Lieutenant and Navigating Officer. There were three watchkeeping officers and two engineer officers; the 'Chief' was an RNVR Lieutenant who had been in the MN at some period before the war. There were two RNVR Midshipmen, one was Mike Anderson whose father was Lieutenant-General Sir John Anderson commander of the 1st Army in the North African campaign. When he was demobbed from the Navy Mike joined his father's old regiment, the Seaforth Highlanders, and he was serving with them when he was killed during the guerilla war in Malaya. The other Midshipman, Bob Currie, became my good friend and he was best man at my wedding. After the war Bob became a teacher and was awarded the MBE whilst serving as

Director of Primary Education for Edinburgh and East Lothian. Sadly he died at a relatively early age.

Again I had been fortunate to join what was to turn out to be a cheery wardroom and a happy and efficient ship.

Minesweeping was a hazardous operation. The ships in a minesweeping flotilla had to work as a team and maintain a very high standard of efficiency, both with regard to handling and setting the sweeps and keeping in exact station when steaming in sweeping formation, in order to provide the maximum protection for each other. Poor station-keeping could result in holidays or unswept areas being left in the field, or ships steaming through unswept waters and not protected by the sweep of the ship ahead.

Officers of HMS Cockatrice 1946

Harwich harbour on VJ night 1945

The Oropesa sweep was the normal method of sweeping moored mines. It involved towing a serrated wire fitted with steel cutters which entrapped and cut the mine mooring, allowing the mine to float to the surface where it could be destroyed by gunfire. The end of the sweep wire was attached to a torpedo-shaped float. A steel frame, known as the kite, attached to the sweep wire and lowered from the stern, was designed to keep the sweep at the required depth and towed at a specific angle from the ship. A similar piece of equipment, known as the otter, was attached to the float (the Oropesa) and designed to keep it running true, parallel to the ship and at the proper angle. Sweeping on one side only was known as single Oropesa, with sweeps out on both sides it was known as double Oropesa. Most of our sweeping was done in single Oropesa. The Oropesa Sweep was named after the trawler in which the technique was developed during World War 1.

Two main formations were used during mine clearance. G formation for the initial search sweep and A formation as a check sweep on completion of G after mines had been cut.

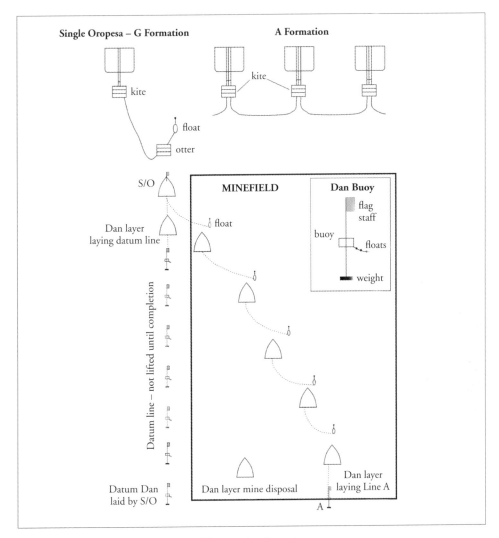

Minesweeping formations

When sweeping in G formation with the sweeps out on the starboard side the flotilla would steam behind the Senior Officer, each ship keeping the one ahead approximately 23 degrees on the port bow at a distance of approximately 700 yards whilst keeping the next ahead's float approximately 12 degrees on the starboard bow to ensure that the ship was always in swept water. In A formation the ships were joined together by their sweep wires kept at the required depth by their kites, and steamed in line abreast thus being able to cover a wider area on each lap. However, as each ship was exposed this was essentially a checking formation, and if mines were cut again the usual procedure was to revert to G and re-sweep the area.

There were three danlayers in the Flotilla, small Admiralty Isles class trawlers, which were used to lay the dan buoys marking the area swept during each lap, and to sink any mines that were cut, before they drifted into unswept water.

The clearance operation of a known minefield started with the Senior Officer laying a datum dan at a corner of the field. He then steamed on a stem bearing of the buoy along the edge of the field, keeping a few cables outside, followed by a danlayer laying dans at one mile intervals up to the next corner. This line of dans was known as the Datum Line. The Flotilla then formed up in G formation and the SO would run the Datum Line keeping his ship as close to the line of dan buoys as possible whilst a second danlayer, inside the float of the last sweeper, laid A line opposite the Datum Line to indicate the limit of the lap. On the next lap one danlayer would follow the SO as he ran line A and pick up the dans once the second danlayer (behind the float of the last sweeper) had laid the dan in Line B. The third danlayer would follow up ready to deal with any mines which might be cut. The sequence then continued; one laying, one picking up and one following up. The Datum Line was left in place until the clearance was completed.

On some occasions more mines were cut than the danlayer could deal with and we were often detailed to give a hand in sinking them before they drifted away or into unswept water. It was pleasant to sit on top of my chart table canopy with a rifle and a box of ammunition, and pot away at the evil objects floating with only the top part of the casing and the horns showing on the surface of the water. Mike Anderson was the expert. He had been a member of the Glenalmond School shooting team, a school renowned for shooting and which regularly won the Public Schools Shooting Championship. He never missed, with every round he fired there was a thud as the bullet struck home. The idea was to fill the mine with holes so that it filled with water and sank, but if a horn was hit the mine exploded so we could not afford to get too close to them. If a mine was taking too long to sink the 20mm Oerlikons might be used but this was expensive with regard to ammunition expenditure and was only adopted as a last resort.

In G formation, at the end of a lap, each ship would alter course directly astern of the next ahead on leaving the field and recover its sweep. The sweep was streamed from the opposite side whilst the Flotilla circled round taking up formation prior to entering the next lap.

Minesweeping involved a great deal of manoeuvring in close formation, often for long periods at a time. A very high standard of ship-handling was required of the Commanding Officer, and Officers of the Watch had to pay strict attention to their station-keeping which required a high level of concentration.

When preparing to sweep in A formation the Flotilla first formed line ahead behind the Senior Officer. Each ship then streamed a grass line (light rope) with a float on the end of it which was picked up with a grapnel by the next astern and connected to his sweep wire. The grass line was then heaved in and the sweep wire made fast. As each ship's sweep was secured it would move out and take up station in line abreast abeam of the Senior Officer with the ships being about 100 feet apart. If the Senior Officer was already on course to enter the lap the ships would then open out to sweeping distance, all the time maintaining the line of bearing. Sometimes a turn of 90 degrees would have to be made for the Senior Officer to come on course for the first lap. On these occasions the Flotilla would wheel round with each ship adjusting speed to maintain the line of bearing. In a flotilla of eight ships the inside ship would steam slowly at a speed of 6 knots whilst the outside ship, having the furthest to go, might have to steam at 12 knots or more to maintain station. When the wheel was completed the ships moved out to sweeping distance. At the end of the lap the ships would close in again on the Senior Officer and the Flotilla would make two 90 degree turns, this time keeping station on the 2nd SO who would be the other outside ship and who would be running the next lap.

Being a new boy to Fleet Minesweepers I was very impressed when I first saw these manoeuvres being executed, especially when I saw an apple being thrown from bridge to bridge during a wheel in close formation.

In my previous position as Navigating Officer I had been engaged mainly in ocean navigation but now I was operating in coastal waters with buoyed channels subject to strong tides and currents, and from ports and anchorages with difficult navigational features. There was more pilotage involved (direction in confined waters) which made my work much more interesting and I was able to gain a lot of experience.

Leaving or entering port or an anchorage I conned the ship to the Captain's orders, advising him of the courses to be steered between the buoys, any navigational hazards and other pertinent information. All this was entered in a note-book before-hand so that I did not have to be constantly referring to the chart. The Flotilla always left and entered port in formation so that, in addition to keeping in proper station, I had to keep a careful check on our position in case we were being led into danger. Once clear of the channel the Officer of the Watch took over the station-keeping whilst I kept the ship's position on the chart. This meant fixing the position every five minutes or so, a Captain always wanted to see the ship on the chart, which may appear to have been an unnecessarily short interval, but in waters affected by strong tides or currents any tendency to be set off the desired track had to be noted quickly.

During sweeping operations I was on the bridge from the time the Flotilla left port or weighed anchor in the morning until it anchored at the end of the day's work. The Captain also had a long day being on the bridge all the time, as did the First Lieutenant on the sweep deck. The other officers were in three watches, four hours on and eight hours off. Sweeping was carried out from dawn to sunset which in the summer-time could mean a very long day indeed. If the anchorage was some distance from the sweeping area it meant weighing anchor in the dark so that we arrived at the field in time to put the sweeps out at dawn, and not returning to the anchorage until well after sunset.

For the second half of 1945 the Flotilla carried out sweeping operations in the North Sea off the Norfolk coast, and at the eastern end of the Channel where a safe channel was swept along the Dutch and Belgian coasts. For the last operation the Flotilla returned each night to anchor in the Downs.

Whilst sweeping my principle task was to keep an accurate plot of the ship's track during each lap. If out of sight of land or there were no prominent features available from which to obtain fixes, a 1 metre range-finder, slung round the neck, was used to obtain the distance off as we passed each buoy laid on the previous lap. On completion of each day's work a tracing was made showing the area swept to date and the position and number of mines cut by each ship. A copy of this was posted on the ship's notice board.

The Flotilla Navigating Officer (a specialist) was responsible for the accuracy of the sweeping operations and for ensuring that the mined area had been completely covered and that no holidays had been left unswept. A detailed report and plot of the operation had to be submitted to the International Mine Clearance Board who then decided whether the area was safe for navigation.

The Captain took all his meals on the bridge and I should really have done likewise, but I detested half-cold food and so I became expert at dashing down at the end of a lap and wolfing my meals in 10 minutes or so. Although I did not realise it at the time this practice was to have a detrimental effect on my digestive system.

At Harwich the Flotilla berthed at Parkeston Quay which was the terminal for the ferries running to the Hook of Holland. For runs ashore people went to Dovercourt, a small seaside resort adjoining Harwich, where the Dovercourt Hotel was the local for most officers. The Cliff Hotel had been commandeered to accommodate the Wrens (the Wrennery) but there was still a good bar in the basement. I first heard the minesweeping songs, *Sweeping, Sweeping, Sweeping* and *When They Sound the Last In Sweeps,* during a ride in a truck taking libertymen back to Parkstone Quay. The first was sung to the hymn tune, *Holy Holy Holy* and the latter to the waltz, *When they Sound the Last All Clear."*

I had joined *Cockatrice* in time for VJ day in August 1945 but I do not recall a great deal about the celebrations except that a truck load of Wrens arrived on the jetty and some came on board (most irregular) to join the wardroom party. Along with many other ships in the harbour we also fired off every rocket and pyrotechnic in the ship (this took some accounting for afterwards) which resulted in a spectacular firework display.

Parkstone Quay was just across the harbour from Shotley where the Boys Training Establishment, HMS *Ganges* was located. AB Hyde-Lay, my yeoman who helped with chart correcting had been to Oundle, a well-known Public School, and he was a very good rugby player. We were able to organize a team and play a couple of matches with a team from *Ganges*. Although they were termed boys they were big, fit lads able to cope with their older and, to some extent, unfit opponents.

On one occasion when I was in Ipswich I met two army Captains who were stationed at an experimental unit nearby, one was in the Tank Corps and the other in the Royal Engineers. They were both jolly types and, I think, a trifle 'round the bend' which may have been due to their work. They were engaged in experiments with land mines, the Engineer assembled and laid the mines after which his friend drove over them in a flail, or other type of tank, to see how effective they were. I was invited to have lunch in their mess, which was in a farm-house adjoining the experimental area, and afterwards I was given the opportunity to ride in a tank and find out a little of what it was like to be a member of a tank crew.

The experimental area was extremely sandy and covered by steep hummocks which provided a very bumpy ride, jarring every bone in my body. When I eventually emerged I was aching all over and my blue uniform was khaki-coloured, covered in sand that had penetrated the tank. I had seen tanks in Tobruk and this experience gave me a little sample of the conditions their crews fought under.

Whilst sweeping off Yarmouth we had a slight accident which resulted in the ship having to go up the River Orwell to Ipswich for repairs. The first night in port, when I was duty officer, some of the officers decided to visit the local theatre and as I could not go with them I jokingly remarked that they should bring the chorus back after the show. I received a big surprise when they took me at my word and arrived on board with six or eight members of the chorus accompanied by the ballet mistress as chaperone. The girls were pretty hungry after their performance but the steward was very good in turning out to whip up sandwiches and coffee. They were all quite young, between 16 and 20, and the ballet mistress was the only one to have anything stronger than a soft drink. She told us something about the life the girls led whilst they were touring; the strict discipline she imposed on them, the physical fitness required of a dancer and the hard work involved in rehearsals. The ballet mistress must have been over 40 years of age but she could still do her high kicks as she demonstrated whilst holding on to the ward room stanchion.

The young ladies had never been on board a warship before so we invited them to come on board for tea a couple of days later when they were able to see over the ship. They appeared to thoroughly enjoy themselves and the little bit of fuss that was made over them. Being young, and it being their first visit, it would be an unusual and exciting experience.

One day I was called to the Captain's cabin on some matter or other and when I entered I found that he had two guests, a Lieutenant-Commander and a lady. As the Captain proceeded to introduce me as 'Prince Henry' (he either called me Pilot or Prince Henry, after the Portuguese Prince Henry the Navigator) the lady exclaimed, "Timothy!", which was the nickname I had sometimes been given in the *Orontes* when on passage to the Middle East in 1942. She was the Wren Officer whom I knew in the *Orontes* and who had arranged for me to go to a small ship when I was serving in *Euryalus*. I in turn recognized her husband, the Gunnery Officer who had given

me such a hard time at Chatham. Lieutenant-Commander Cavendish had been
Gunnery Officer in the Dido in the Fighting Fifteenth Cruiser Squadron and had
met his wife in Alexandria. It was a small world.

At the beginning of 1946 we spent some time in and around Chatham before
going over to sweep the minefields off the South Coast of Ireland. It was in the Sun
Hotel that I met up with 'Stumpy' Mason, one of our quartet at Greenwich, whom I
had not seen or heard of since we finished our training. I told him the sad news about
' Bandit ' Crooks and it seemed that we were the only two left as 'Shag' Lacey had
been killed whilst fishing with hand-grenades in Bougie, North Africa. The boat he
was fishing from was over a wreck containing ammunition and the whole lot went up.
I had seen people using hand-grenades to stun fish from the jetty in Beirut and it was
just the sort of mad-cap caper that 'Shag' would have got up to.

Arrangements had been made with the Irish Government for the Flotilla to
use Queenstown, near Cork, as its base during its next task which was the clearance
of the minefields around the south coast of Ireland. When Ireland was partitioned
Queenstown was retained as a treaty port and continued to be a Naval base until
1938 when these rights were withdrawn by the Irish Government. This meant that
Britain was deprived of an important base which would have been of great value in
convoy operations, and in the fight against the U-boats when war broke out in 1939.
Many ships and the lives of hundreds of seamen could have been saved if Britain had
been allowed to use the port, and a great deal of bitterness still remained at the Irish
Government's refusal to grant this facility. The 18th M.S.F. would be the first Royal
Navy ships to visit the port since 1938 and we could not help wondering what sort of
welcome we would receive.

To prepare the way for our arrival the Senior Officer went on ahead of the
Flotilla and made contact with the local dignitaries and official bodies – the
Archbishop, the Mayor, the Chief of Police and local councillors. It was rumoured
that he had changed his religion to Roman Catholic to ensure a friendly reception. A
local lawyer was engaged to handle any problems which might arise involving Flotilla
personnel. He subsequently turned out to be quite a character who was extremely
helpful and adept at negotiating with the law when the odd sailor landed in trouble
which, happily, was not very often.

For some reason or other *Cockatrice* had to call into Plymouth when the Flotilla
sailed for Ireland at the beginning of March 1946 and it was several days later that we
joined the rest of the ships in Bantry Bay on the west coast. On the morning we left
Plymouth the visibility was very poor and after the Eddystone Lighthouse it became a
real pea souper; I could not see the jackstaff at the bow of the ship, let alone any land
to fix the ship's position. The bad visibility meant that we had to steam at reduced
speed which made the ship more subject to the strong tides and currents encountered
during the three hundred miles passage. However I was able to practice a navigational
technique I had never used before, running a line of soundings.

On the chart the contours showing changes in depth were shown at 10 fathom intervals. The exact time the ship crossed each line of soundings (the depth being adjusted for rise/fall of tide) was noted on the echo sounder trace and the distances travelled in the intervals between crossing each line (according to engine speed adjusted for propeller slip) were laid out at the edge of a strip of paper and marked at the appropriate intervals. The paper was then laid alongside the course line that was laid down on the chart and the marks lined up to coincide with the depth contours. In this way it was possible to ascertain if the ship was making good, or being set off, the course line and if the designated speed was being maintained.

The visibility was still zero as we approached the Irish coast and the time fast approaching when, according to my reckoning, we would have to alter course directly towards the land for our approach to Bantry Bay. Although we were too far away to obtain a good position by radar we could hear, faintly, the ships in the Flotilla talking to each other on R/T. I had had a difference of opinion with 'Dad' over the pilot arrangements when leaving Chatham and our relationship had been rather cool for a week or so. Normally we got on very well together and he had never questioned my decisions. When the ship arrived at the alteration I told him to alter course 90 degrees to starboard for the run into Bantry Bay. The Captain had good reason for feeling anxious when he said, "Are you sure, Pilot?" When approaching land in bad visibility it was sound practice and good seamanship to stand off and wait until the ship's position was confirmed. If my navigation was out and the ship ran into danger he would be in trouble. At the same time the ship was required to join the Flotilla as soon as possible. Being reasonably sure of my calculations I confidently replied, "Yes Sir."

As the ship wheeled round to the new course I looked down and saw that quite a few of the ship's company were on deck, alternately peering into the wet fog and glancing up at the bridge, which seemed to convey to me that they hoped I knew what I was doing. Speed had been reduced and, as we crept slowly towards the land, the fog began to lift and the visibility gradually improved until the land ahead could be identified. There, just off the port bow, was Beare Island, a small island just inside the Bay. We had hit the target right on the nose. I was quite pleased with myself and the occasion was made complete when 'Dad' turned and said a sincere, "Well done, Prince Henry!" We were friends again.

The extensive mined area around the South coast of Ireland was British and the Flotilla's work was made somewhat easier, although no less hazardous, by having available detailed charts of the minefield. The sweeping operation started about the middle of March and the intention was to spend 10 days sweeping, anchoring in a convenient bay at night, and then four days in port at Queenstown. However frequent spells of bad weather caused interruptions to this programme and it would be a case of one day sweeping and then having to wait a couple of days for the gales to subside. But in spite of weather problems the Flotilla made steady progress with the clearance operation and in the three months up to the end of June nearly 400 mines were swept.

We did not have long to wait to sample the Irish hospitality. Two days after our arrival a retired naval officer, Commander Crosbie, and his family held a dance in their large and attractive home to which they invited several officers from each ship in the Flotilla. This time it was not the colleens who attracted our attention but the sumptuous buffet that was laid out before us. We had forgotten that such food existed after six years of war. Cold meats of every variety, fresh salmon, salads, trifles and jellies and lashings of fresh cream and cakes. The Commander had also provided a very good bar from which drinks were dispensed liberally. It was an excellent way to start off our stay in Ireland.

A good meal was usually our first objective when we went to Cork. The Oyster Bar, a well-known restaurant, became our favourite eating place after the first visit when it was a treat to sit down and go through the menu after years of rationing. The locals were a good crowd and made us welcome, it was not unusual for one of them to come rolling up and say, 'Ave a drink, Soir, I was in the Iniskillins meself.' As there was no clothes rationing in Ireland I took the opportunity to fit myself out with a sports jacket and flannels, my first civilian clothes in six years.

In Queenstown there was a very good golf club which invited the officers to become honorary members. The club-house was in the ruins of an old castle known as Pennyfarthing Castle. Local legend had it that the castle got its name because the woman that built it made a profit of a pennyfarthing after the castle had been completed. She decided to build the castle after her husband went off to the Crusades, and during the building she charged the workmen for their food, clothing and shelter to such an extent that she made a profit on the venture. She operated a medieval company store.

There was also a very good local rugby club and a match was soon arranged with the Flotilla and I was fortunate to be picked for the team. After the match both teams trooped off to the local pub and as we walked along we seemed to be passing nothing but small cottages with not a pub or hotel in sight. We were all surprised when we were led into a small cottage which turned out to be the local. There was hardly room for us all but that only served to make the occasion more jolly and friendly. The pub certainly had character. It seemed that in Ireland you could have a pub in your front room.

Every April it was the local custom to hold a parade through the streets of Queenstown to mark and celebrate the uprising which took place in 1916 and which was a factor in the establishing of the Irish Free State. The Flotilla happened to be in port on the day of the parade and, as the route followed the road alongside our berths, all leave was cancelled and we had to stay on board and keep a low profile until the marchers had passed by. It was the first time the parade had followed that route and it may have been because of our presence that the die-hard IRA supporters had chosen it in order to flaunt their independence.

The Flotilla was due to return to the UK for a short spell in June and before we left a dance was held to return, in some small way, the hospitality we had received from the friends we had made onshore. People also started to stock up with the items which were in short supply at home such as silk stockings, linen and also certain commodities in the food line such as hams, tinned meats, coffee and sugar.

Demobilisation had started just after the war had ended and some of us were due to be demobbed when we returned to the UK. I had very mixed feelings about being demobbed. On the one hand I was caught up in the general excitement at the prospect of being demobbed (another new experience) and on the other hand I was sad at having to leave the Service I had tried so hard to enter. I had been hoping to be able to remain in the Navy but as yet I had not heard of any schemes whereby Reserve Officers could apply for a permanent or short service commission. I did not want to return to the Merchant Navy after experiencing the life in the Royal Navy and I had never given a second thought to anything other than going to sea.

The Flotilla returned to Plymouth where I left the ship to proceed on demob leave. Before going alongside in the dockyard the ship anchored for the night in a small bay, and those of us going on leave were able to pass through a gate which was not covered by a Customs Officer. We had declared some of our goods to the officers who had boarded the ship on arrival at the anchorage, but there was always the possibility that we might have been searched going out of the dockyard.

And so ended six adventurous years during which time I served in nine different types of ship and performed a variety of interesting and responsible duties. I had been fortunate to be involved in many of the different types of Naval operations, occasions and activities, that I had read about in my *Wonder Book* and other books about the Navy and seafaring, from surface action involving big guns and destroyer attacks to convoy escort and minesweeping, and from boat work in open waters to boarding, towing and mutiny. All my boyhood wishes had been fulfilled except one, I had yet to drive a picket boat with a brass funnel!

Chapter 19

A Shore Appointment

———

When I returned home it was not to Edinburgh but to the Perthshire village of Comrie where my father had bought the Royal Hotel. I had only lived in Edinburgh for about 18 months whilst I was at school and not long enough to form any real attachment to the city so I had no regrets about leaving it.

Before the war Comrie had been a popular spot for holidays. The nine hole golf course and the tennis courts provided for young and old, there was fishing in the three rivers which joined at the village and there were many attractive walks in the surrounding countryside. There were quite a lot of young people in the village, many of my own age who had recently been demobbed, and it was not long before I was making friends at the tennis courts and golf course. In common with every other community in the country the village held a Welcome Home celebration for all returning Service personnel. It took the form of a sit-down meal in the Public Hall followed by a dance, and a gift of five pounds. Father was asked to do the catering which he subsequently provided as his donation to the Welcome Home Fund. It was a very generous contribution, but it was typical of him as was his evident embarrassment when this was pointed out. He jokingly said to me afterwards that most of the five pounds probably ended up over the bar in the Royal.

I had a happy and carefree holiday for two months playing golf, tennis and cricket and going to dances in the Public Hall and other places round about. It was a complete change to the stresses and strains of the past six years and I thoroughly enjoyed myself.

All good things have to come to an end and I had to decide what I was going to do with my life. I was not keen to return to the Merchant Navy but as I had sufficient sea-time to sit the examination for a Certificate of Competency as First Mate I thought it advisable to obtain this qualification. I still wanted to rejoin the Navy which I felt sure would be requiring officers to replace those being demobbed from ships still in commission. A Board of Trade Certificate of Competency would give me an edge over other applicants, and it would be a qualification which would enable me to get a job at sea at any time in the future if I ever found myself out of work, or if I failed to settle down on shore.

At the beginning of September 1946 I enrolled at Leith Nautical College for the three months course for Second Mate's Certificate which I was advised to take before going on for First Mate as I had little experience of the Merchant Navy. I soon found that I had a considerable amount of catching up to do and that I would have to get down to some work. Although the Royal and Merchant Navies were both sea-going professions their roles were totally different and apart from basic navigation, seamanship and signalling, the professional knowledge required by deck officers in both Services differed considerably. I would have to learn about cargo stowage, stability, merchant ship construction, knowledge of principles and other matters, and show the mathematical proofs of the calculations used in navigation. Then there were the dreaded 'Articles', The International Rules and Regulations governing the Rule of the Road at Sea, the position, type and colour of lights and shapes to be carried by different types of vessel, and the signals to be sounded or displayed by these vessels in various situations. There were thirty-one Articles, some of which were lengthy, and they had to be repeated word for word without even substituting a will for a shall. The pass mark of 75% overall required for the Board of Trade examinations was amongst the highest of any of the professional bodies.

I very soon got into a routine. Arriving in Edinburgh on Monday morning I went straight to the School and returned to my digs at 5p.m. I studied for five hours in the evenings and returned home on Friday. Over the weekend I practised reciting the Articles.

At that time there were many navigation schools and examination centres in the country, the main ones being London, Cardiff, Southampton, Liverpool, Glasgow and Leith. There were no common examination papers set for the different certificates and it was the practice for one examination centre to set the papers for another centre. Liverpool set the papers for Leith. At the end of each examination the examinees reported the contents of the paper to the school lecturers who kept a record of the questions which had been asked. As the people who set the papers tended to repeat the same questions at regular intervals, by referring to their records, the lecturers were able to have a pretty good idea of the questions that were likely to come up when an examination was due. I was very lucky when the lecturer, two days before my examination, gave me two questions to do as homework both of which appeared in the examination paper.

The examination was in three parts, written, orals and signals and a failure in one part meant that the whole examination had to be taken again. A failure inevitably meant that a further six months sea-time had to be completed before re-sitting the examination. My main worry was the orals as I only had fifteen months experience of merchant ships and only four months of that was involved in carrying cargo. But again I was lucky. Very few merchant ships were fitted with radar and the examiner knew very little about the equipment, the way it was operated or how it was used for navigation and in traffic. When he found out that I had been in the Navy he asked about radar and I spent the rest of the examination period telling him all about it. I got away with a few questions on the sextant and the Rule of the Road. Fortunately I passed.

As soon as I received the Certificate of Competency I wrote to the Admiralty to find out if there was any way in which I could rejoin the Service. I received an almost immediate reply indicating that I could apply for an Extended Service Commission which might lead to a Permanent Commission, depending on future manning requirements. I sent in an application and after a successful interview I was granted a Commission as Lieutenant RN with seniority September 1945. My original seniority had been March 1945, the loss being the time between the end of my demob leave and the application to rejoin.

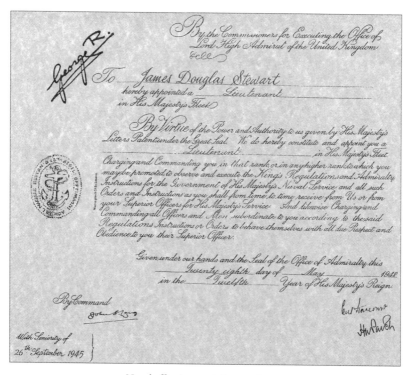

Naval officer's commission parchment

When my appointment arrived from the Admiralty I was extremely disappointed to find that instead of going to a sea-going ship I was being sent to a Shore Establishment, the RN Camp at Bedhampton near Portsmouth. A shore job was the one thing that I did not want but at least I was back in the Service and one never knew what further adventures lay ahead.

Belmont Camp was located on the main road leading into Havant and about 6 miles from Portsmouth. The camp, which covered a large area and contained Nissen huts, had been built during the war to house the overflow from the Barracks in Portsmouth. When I arrived in March 1947 the accommodation problem had eased considerably and the only personnel in the camp were a few petty officers waiting to go on pension and a few ratings awaiting demob. The camp still had a full complement of staff personnel and, on the face of it, was rather overmanned.

The Commanding Officer, Commander Ransome RN, was a gunnery specialist who had been an acting Captain in command of a destroyer flotilla at the end of the war. He was a fine officer but I think he was due to be retired, as rumour had it that he had been inclined to be too outspoken in his opinions in the past, and this had spoiled his chances of further promotion. He was fond of golf and invited me on several occasions to play at the Havant Golf Club.

Lieutenant-Commander Sam Williams RN, the First Lieutenant, was a well-known and popular character in Naval circles in Portsmouth. At that time he was the senior Boatswain in the Navy and was awaiting appointment as the Commanding Officer of HMS *Victory*, Nelson's Flagship, in Portsmouth Dockyard. Command of the *Victory* was traditionally given to the senior Boatswain for the fast two years of his service before retirement. Sam had joined the Navy as a boy seaman and, at the age of 16, he had been in the starboard 6-inch battery of the battleship *Malaya* at the Battle of Jutland. During his subsequent 30 years service he had been everywhere and had done everything from chasing pirates on the China Coast to surveying in the Red Sea and along the Arabian Coast where the charts still indicated that the natives were unfriendly.

Sam took command of the *Victory* before I left Portsmouth and on several occasions I went on board and had tea with him in his cabin on the starboard side of the poop under the quarterdeck. I enjoyed walking round the decks and giving free rein to my imagination. I had read the stories of naval life and the battles of the eighteenth and early nineteenth centuries and I could picture various scenes taking place. It was hard to believe that 800 men had lived and fought in the confined spaces. Looking at the massive masts and yards and the maze of running rigging I could visualise the men climbing aloft to shorten sail in a Channel gale, possibly whilst blockading a French port, and I wondered how the pressed men (who had probably never been to sea before) must have felt as they were driven aloft in stormy conditions. Down on the gun decks I imagined the scenes as the guns' crews fought their guns firing three rounds in two minutes. The Navy's efficiency and ultimate reputation of being the best in the world, was achieved by the continuous and relentless sail drill and gun drill which was carried out all the time the ships were at sea.

The rest of the officer complement comprised three Lieutenants, a dentist and a doctor who were also responsible for another camp which became HMS *Phoenix*, the Damage Control and Fire Fighting School. Doc Pugh's father was a Surgeon Captain at the RN Hospital, Haslar, and I discovered many years later that Doc himself had reached that rank when I found that he had looked after one of my officers at the RN Hospital, Plymouth, after he had been repatriated from Penang with severe injuries to both legs.

As there were few people in the camp there was relatively little for us to do. I was responsible for the administration and welfare of the men in my division, and for the fire fighting equipment which consisted mainly of a trailer pump and other bits and pieces. The area at the rear of the camp had become a bit of a wilderness inhabited by many cats which had become wild living in the tall grass growing between the empty huts. On one occasion the RSPCA were called in to try and solve the problem.

Gardening had become an occupation to pass the time and many chaps had plots where they grew vegetables and flowers. A corner of the camp was given over to hens and ducks which were in the charge of Petty Officer Callaghan who fussed over them like a farmer. Callaghan was another character with a fund of yarns. He was taken prisoner at the fall of Singapore and for some reason was put into the condemned cell at Changi prison. He was over 6 feet tall, big and strong and when the Japs came to take him out of the cell for punishment he put up such a fight that he earned their respect and they finally left him alone. Later he was eventually sent to Japan. He told me that if I ever went to Changi I would see his name carved on the wall of the condemned cell. I never visited the prison, but whenever my ship passed it on the way round the Island to discharge oil to the new power station near the old Naval Base, I always thought of Petty Officer Callaghan and his scrap at the door of the condemned cell.

I had plenty of opportunity for sport whilst I was at the camp. A Commander who had a big house nearby had turned one of his buildings into a squash court and we had permission to use it whenever we wanted to. The camp had a recreation area where we were able to have several games of cricket during the long, hot summer and there was tennis and swimming at Southsea. I had arrived too late for the rugby season but at the beginning of September I joined the United Services Rugby Club and eventually became Captain of the 3rd XV. United Services was drawn from the Army, Navy and Air Force personnel serving in the Portsmouth area and the 1st XV had fixtures with the top clubs in the country. Other Military and Naval establishments had their own teams, such as the Royal Marines at Eastney Barracks and the RN Barracks in Portsmouth, so that between the established rugby clubs and Service establishments we had a wide variety of fixtures.

The Osborne, a pub in Osborne Road, Southsea was a popular meeting place for young officers on Saturday nights, especially the rugby crowd. One evening my girl friend, Megan, was speaking to one of her friends and I thought I recognised her companion. He turned out to be a chap from Royal High whom I had known quite well as we had played in the same rugby team. Wilder had gone on to study medicine and, having just completed his training, he had joined the Navy and been appointed to the RN Barracks in Portsmouth. Doc told me an amusing yarn about his arrival at the Barracks. When he reported to the Surgeon Captain he was asked what school he had attended in Edinburgh and when he replied, "Royal High", the Surgeon Captain said, "Good, it is about time the Barracks had some decent rugby players." It seems he was a former pupil. Doc was a hard playing wing forward well used to chucking bodies about, but his style of play did not go down well with a referee. In his first match he had been warned three times about rough play and told that, "We don't play rugby like that down here." We had some good times together before I left Portsmouth. When he was seconded to the Marine Commandos I met him again in Palestine, and in Malta where the Commando was stationed after our forces left Palestine.

Ivy Benson's All Girl Dance Band had been entertaining the troops in the Far East and passed through Malta on the way home. The band put on a show at the Barracks where the Marines were based and Doc invited me to dinner at the mess and to see the show. After the performance there was a party in the Sergeants' Mess and I was able to meet some of the members of the band. The band had been in Bristol when HMS *Tavy* was commissioned and it had been invited to the commissioning party. Some of the girls still remembered the occasion.

During the summer King George, Queen Elizabeth and the Princesses returned to Portsmouth in HMS *Vanguard* after their tour of South Africa, and the whole of Portsmouth turned out to welcome them home. Out at the camp we managed to keep out of sight, and avoided being roped in to form part of the vast contingent of sailors and other Servicemen who were required for duty in Guards of Honour, and to line the streets and the dockyard area. Not having any official duties we were able to get into the dockyard and find a position where we could see the Royal Family come ashore, and obtain a good view of them as they passed by in their car. On the way to the dockyard there seemed to be bands and marching men everywhere. The Guard from the RN Barracks, which was to form the Guard of Honour when the King came ashore, looked supremely smart and made a fine sight as, with bayonets and the chromium plated metal-work of the rifles gleaming in the sunshine and led by the Bluejacket Band, it marched through the Barracks archway to the Officers quarters to collect the Colours.

In the dockyard I had a good position near the archway leading to Farewell Jetty where the *Vanguard* was berthed. I had never seen the Royal Family and I had a very good view of them as the car slowly made its way along the route lined by the cheering crowd. It was a happy experience to be there to welcome them home.

On August Bank Holiday I spent an enjoyable day swimming at Hayling Island but the following day I learned of a tragedy involving a petty officer in my division. I was called to the guard-room at the camp entrance where his wife was waiting to see me. She had come to report that her husband had been found dead the previous evening, he had committed suicide by putting his head in the gas oven. She seemed very self-possessed as she told me the sad news, there were no tears or obvious signs of shock or distress and I found out later that she was probably at the root of the matter. It was the classic case of the lodger and the neglected husband.

The petty officer, who was a quiet and very likeable man waiting to take his pension after 22 years, for some time had been returning home to find the house empty, no meal prepared and no word of where his wife had gone or when she would be returning. On August Bank Holiday, when he arrived home and again found the house empty and himself alone he must have decided to put an end to it all. The senior NCOs were very upset at his death and they had no hesitation in blaming his wife for her part in the matter, making strong representations that she should not receive any award from King George's Fund for Sailors.

A Naval funeral was another new experience. The funeral arrangements were organized by the Barracks. The band, gun-carriage and crew and saluting party were drawn up near the small chapel at the entrance to the cemetery where the body was resting. As his wife came out of the chapel she at last shed a tear, the first sign of emotion she had displayed since the start of the whole affair. The coffin was placed on the gun-carriage, the sailors picked up the drag-ropes and, headed by the band playing the *Funeral March*, the procession slowly marched through the cemetery to the grave. It was a most moving experience. I found the sound of the gun-carriage wheels crunching in the gravel added a further poignancy to the melancholy music.

After the burial service a volley was fired over the grave and the bugler sounded the Last Post. We formed up to march off but this time we set off at the quick march, the band playing a rousing tune which was in sharp contrast to the sombre air it had been playing only a short time before. To an onlooker it may have seemed callous and insensitive but Servicemen, by the very nature of their calling, have little time for lamentation.

My appointment at the camp was what was known as a 'quiet number,' that is, not much work to do and a relaxed routine. It gave me the opportunity to make a circle of friends and to attend various functions and have something of a social life. When an American Squadron visited Portsmouth the officers at the Barracks held a Ball in their honour to which I was invited. I became friendly with an Ensign who was attached to the American Embassy in London and needless to say he spent most of the evening dancing with my partner. I met him a couple of times in London when he repaid my hospitality by taking me to the Embassy, an exclusive nightclub for members only. Floyd had a friend who knew the manager who arranged for us to be admitted.

After six months in the camp I found myself wanting to get back to sea. A quiet number ashore may be alright for a married man but I wanted to make progress in my career and I was not going to make much headway growing cabbages and feeding chickens, although I had been taking the opportunity to do some studying towards the First Mate's Certificate of Competency. Ships were still being laid up in reserve and I knew that sea-going appointments were hard to come by.

However, I obtained permission to go to the Admiralty to see the appointments people. I was interviewed by a Commander who started off by asking what he could do for me. Without any preamble I said, "I want to go to sea, Sir." His fist crashed down on the table as he glared at me and said, "Good God, boy, don't we all?" He then asked about my present appointment and what I was doing there, and smiled sympathetically when I told him I was in a camp growing cabbages. I got the reply that I was more or less expecting, he would see what he could do but was making no promises.

About ten days later I received a bit of a shock when the Yeoman of Signals told me, unofficially, that I had been given a Command. I thought he was pulling my leg, but later on, when I received the official appointment I was delighted to find that he had been speaking the truth. I had been appointed to HMS *Stag* (Haifa) additional for HMMFV 132 In Command. The appointments Commander must have known his man as I could not have asked for anything more suitable. The appointment was on a foreign station, I would receive hard-lying and command allowances totalling seven shillings a day and, to warrant a commissioned officer, the MFV, although only a small craft, would probably be carrying out duties associated with the Palestine Patrol. This would offer the opportunity to gain experience in a new area of operations.

I had ten days embarkation leave before taking passage to Malta in the aircraft carrier HMS *Illustrious* which was ferrying personnel to and from the Far East. We sailed from Portsmouth on the day that the Queen and the Duke of Edinburgh were married in November 1947.

Taking passage in *Illustrious* added one more class to the types of ships I had sailed in, I only needed a couple more to complete the list. I had to share a cabin with two officers who were also taking passage. It was an inside cabin, i.e. not adjacent to the ship's side, which gave me a slight feeling of claustrophobia. A visit to the flight deck produced the opposite effect. Having been used to the confined deck area of a small ship with superstructure which offered some shelter from the elements, and with bulwarks or guard-rails, I felt rather unsafe on the vast exposed flight deck, especially when I ventured near the edge and found that there was nothing to prevent me from going over the side. I took my daily stroll on the quarterdeck at the stern underneath the flight deck, and spent the rest of the six day voyage in the wardroom or my cabin.

After a few days at St. Paul's Bay rest house in Malta I took passage to Haifa in the Bird class sloop HMS *Magpie* where she was to relieve another ship on the

Palestine Patrol. *Magpie* eventually became the Duke of Edinburgh's first Command and my tenth class of Naval vessel.

As we drew near to Haifa I was quite excited at the prospect of joining my ship, wondering what she would look like and what sort of work I would be engaged in. It is every seaman's ambition to command his own vessel and his first Command, regardless of type or size of vessel, is a memorable event in his career. Although my MFV was just a small craft she was in Commission and wore a commissioning pendant (for which reason I was paid command allowance) and I was entitled, as Commanding Officer, to be piped when boarding another HM ship. A small matter maybe but it meant a lot.

Chapter 20

FIRST COMMAND

——

HMMFV 132 was an Admiralty Type Motor Fishing Vessel of 50 tons displacement, length 70 feet, speed 9 knots and a nominal complement of six. The craft were of wood construction, usually oak or teak. Over 400 of this class of MFV were built and their design enabled them to be used in a variety of roles, the fish hold being adapted as necessary for the job in hand. They were used in harbour duties taking stores and libertymen to and from ships in the fleet anchorages, as despatch vessels and in contraband control, and as patrol craft in which case there was an increase in the complement, to mention a few of their activities.

When I joined the 132 I found that the officer I was relieving had managed to carry out quite a few unofficial A & As (Alterations and Additions) which enhanced her appearance and the living conditions to such an extent that she appeared to be quite the little yacht. The derrick had been taken off and put on shore to provide an uncluttered foredeck, the coal burning stove in the crew messdeck had been taken out and a small galley, lined with mono-metal sheeting behind the bottled gas rings, fitted in the bow. The wash-hand basin in the small toilet leading off the CO's cabin was supplied with water from a tank fitted on top of the deck house. Immediately behind the deck house four slim, aluminium painted stanchions had been erected to support a neat snow-white awning rigged over the skylight of the after accommodation. On the bulkheads opposite the ladders leading down to the engine-room and petty officers' accommodation aft large sheets of brass had been fitted to protect the paintwork from dirty hands, and brass handrails had been fitted around the deck house and at the entrance to the wheelhouse.

I was told that most of the extra equipment and fittings had been won from the dockyard stores when no one was looking and one day, shortly after I assumed Command, I returned to find a large domestic electric fan sitting on the table in my cabin. When I made enquiries as to its provenance one of the crew said that he had been up at the Naval Stores and had found it loafing!

There were two other MFVs and our main role was to patrol the sea anchorage and protect the ships at anchor from possible attack by terrorist frogmen attaching limpet mines to their hulls. During the hours of darkness small explosive charges were dropped in the sea near the ships in order to deter any attackers and force them to the surface. One had to take care not to drop the charges too close to the ships at anchor as the noise of the explosions resounded through their hulls which did not go down at all well with the people on board who were trying to sleep. Many years later, during the Vietnam war, I was to get a taste of my own medicine when patrol craft dropped similar charges in the river whilst my ship was discharging petroleum products at Saigon.

HMMFV 132

HMMFV 132 – Ship's Company

Illegal immigrant vessel aground at Haifa 1947

Royal Navy diver in sub-acqua equipment – Haifa 1947

We worked in a three day cycle, 24 hours on patrol, 24 hours standby and 24 hours maintenance. Originally the craft were only intended to be used for patrol duties and when the King's Harbour Master (KHM), a Lieutenant-Commander, had endeavoured to use them as maids of all work the COs had appealed to The Commodore, Palestine, the Senior Naval Officer, against this practice. Fortunately they found an ally in the Commodore. As a Sub-Lieutenant his first command had been a steam drifter (a fishing vessel) commandeered by the Navy in World War 1, and he appreciated the feelings of the MFV officers and would not allow the craft to be used for any other purpose. However, when the Commodore was relieved, his successor, Commodore Peachey, was not so sentimental and the KHM gradually assumed more control over the craft and their assignments. When I took over they were being used for various jobs which had been done previously by local craft hired by the KHM. Naturally he was not very popular and it was generally assumed that he was involved in a bit of *affen-gescheft* (monkey business – a common phrase in Palestine) with the locals. The additional duties mainly consisted of towing the large wooden barges which were used when transferring the boarding platform scaffolding and other boarding equipment between the destroyers, fleet minesweepers and sloops which were on patrol to intercept illegal immigrant vessels, and carrying stores or work of a similar nature which had been done previously by a small harbour tug.

I enjoyed the extra work we were given to do, especially towing, as I had more opportunity to handle my craft and gain experience in manoeuvring under various circumstances and conditions. I learned to tow with the barge astern and with it alongside when manoeuvring in the harbour, especially in the confined space between the oil jetties. The more work I was given to do the better I liked it. On one occasion a large quantity of small arms and automatic weapons was delivered on board with instructions that it was to be ditched at sea in deep water beyond the 100 fathom line. They were defective weapons which the army did not consider to be worth repairing. However the Jewish terrorists would have made good use of them and if they had been ditched in shallow water they could easily have been recovered. A sergeant in the Palestine Police told me later that, if I had ditched the weapons in a pile in shallow water and had noted the spot, I could have made a lot of money by passing on the information.

In harbour the MFVs were berthed alongside LCT (E) 413 which was moored bow on to the quay and protected by a net boom. The landing craft, known as The Clank, was equipped with workshops and other facilities to enable it to act as a mother ship for the MFVs and other small craft such as the boats used by the naval divers and frogmen. The area on the quay immediately in front of the Clank was protected by a high wire fence and entry was gained through a gate which was locked at night. Nearby on the quay a canteen called the Flat Bottom Arms had been established in a Nissen hut.

Haifa had been kept free of terrorist activities due to the IZL and Stern Gang (Jewish terrorist organizations) being kept out of the city by Hagganah, the Jewish underground army, but this protection was later withdrawn and when I arrived the terrorist attacks by Jews and Arabs on each other, and on the British troops, were more or less a daily occurrence. It was not unusual to see tracer fire at night as the different factions engaged each other from the roof tops. On one occasion the Arabs filled an oil drum with explosives and rolled it down a steep hill intending that it should explode in the Kingsway, the main street in the port. Unfortunately, on the way down, it rolled into a corner building which contained a school and caused casualties amongst the children. Another time the Jews took up a position in a building opposite a dock gate and fired on Arab workmen as they were leaving the dockyard. A Royal Marine officer was injured in the incident and this resulted in the Marines putting a round through each window of the building from their Staghound armoured car. Our troops were liable to be shot or ambushed at any time whilst walking in the streets and everybody carried their personal weapons at all times.

We did not go ashore very often but when we did side arms were always carried and spare ammunition. Instead of wearing our holsters at the waist in the normal way we took the advice of the Palestine Police and fitted an extension between the belt and holster. This enabled the gun to be worn lower down cowboy fashion and, with the holster flap open and tied back, ready for a quick draw. There had not been any attacks made on naval personnel and, whilst I was there, there were two occasions when the Jews actually got officers on the shore staff out of serious trouble. One chap had taken his side arm off in a taxi and forgot to take it with him when he left the taxi to go into a bar, a court-martial offence and a mandatory year in jail. When he discovered his loss he told the barman what had happened. Fortunately it was a Jewish taxi and the barman made a quick telephone call which resulted in the weapon being speedily returned to its owner. The same barman performed a similar service for an officer who went out to find that his staff car had been stolen. A call to the right people and the car was returned.

The craft were quite secure and safe alongside the Clank inside the boom but at New Year we were on the alert in case the terrorists tried to catch us unawares when we were expected to be celebrating. All the officers gathered in the Clank's small wardroom having a yarn and a quiet drink, whilst awaiting the arrival of midnight and the traditional striking of sixteen bells by the youngest rating, heralding the arrival of the New Year.

It was round about midnight when the sound of gunfire was heard, to be followed by a sentry reporting that we were being fired on from the breakwater across the harbour. I dashed back to my craft and issued our armament, 1 Lanchester sub-machine gun and 6 rifles, and together with the other craft alongside, prepared to repel boarders. There had been rumours that an attempt might be made to blow up the motor transport fuel point located not far from our wire fence, and it was thought that the firing from the breakwater might be a diversionary tactic. I laid on deck in the bows of my craft, which were pointed towards the quay, and awaited developments.

Suddenly a figure was seen at the gate of the fence and, at the same time, there was the sound of a Lanchester being cocked ready to fire. Keith Saull, CO of the craft next to mine, was just about to open fire when there was a shout from the gate and the figure identified itself. It turned out to be the CO of the Clank who had gone ashore to find out the situation and had not informed anyone of his intentions. It was a very tense moment and Saull told me afterwards that Maclean, the CO had only escaped being shot by a couple of seconds. We had learned from the Palestine Police that the terrorists always had the advantage and that, sometimes, the only way to redress the balance in situations such as this was to shoot first and ask questions afterwards.

When the Jews first started their illegal immigrant operations the ships intercepted by the Navy were brought into Haifa and berthed alongside the oil jetties. After being de-loused, documented and given any other necessary assistance in the reception area on the jetty, the immigrants were put on board another ship which would take them to Cyprus to await their turn to be allowed authorized entry. By the time I arrived in Palestine the reception procedure had been altered. The Illegals were put alongside the cruiser HMS *Phoebe* which was moored in the harbour stern on to the breakwater. Documentation etc. was carried out on *Phoebe's* quarterdeck and the people put on board the transport which was berthed on her other side. The immigrants did not even have the satisfaction of reaching the promised land even if it was only an oil jetty.

When an illegal was being brought in to harbour my job was to follow astern and pick up anybody who jumped overboard in an attempt to swim to shore. The vessels which arrived whilst I was there were mainly large caiques and once alongside *Phoebe* it was fairly easy for my sailors to get on board. I was always keen to get the Jewish flag from the masthead but on each occasion it had inevitably been taken by the boarding party. However we did get hold of a ship's bell, a small yacht type, which our motor mechanic modified so that it could be unscrewed from the mounting when we were on patrol.

The people who organised the illegal immigrant movement had little concern for the well-being of the passengers who were packed into the grossly overcrowded, and in some cases unseaworthy, vessels. Many of the immigrants were old people from Eastern Europe who had probably never seen a ship before and, together with men, women and children, many of whom were sick, they were packed into confined spaces where there was little room for movement and a complete lack of adequate sanitary arrangements. The ships sailed from ports in various countries, Italy, France and Greece, and by the time they reached Palestine waters, and especially if they had encountered bad weather, the immigrants were usually in a very poor way, with the conditions below decks filthy and indescribable.

The Zionist sources, often American, who funded the immigrant movement at least made sure that the vessels were well supplied with a stock of a variety of tinned provisions. Whilst alongside my first illegal I happened to notice several boxes and cartons being whisked into my cabin and realised that they were being passed down by my sailors who had boarded the vessel. I turned a blind eye at the time and when we returned to our berth I found out what had been going on. The lads had used initiative in availing themselves of some items they had found loafing, tinned jam, M&V stew, corned beef, tinned milk and fruit juices. I told them it was all highly irregular but for a case of fruit juice the matter would be overlooked.

The craft were victualled by the shore base who supplied the basic rations of bread, meat, potatoes, etc. Any other items we fancied were obtained from the NAAFI canteen so, in effect, we governed our own standard of feeding. This was known as Canteen Messing as opposed to General Messing where the ship's Paymaster kept the crew's feeding allowance and supplied the catering. In Canteen Messing if a bill at the canteen was less than the total ration allowance a mess had a refund called mess savings. If it spent more than its allowance the members had a mess debt. In both cases the debt or savings was shared equally between the members of the mess.

Because we had quite a stock of food there was not a great deal being bought in the canteen and this was eventually noticed by the Base Paymaster. I was called to his office where he demanded to know what my crew was living on. I was a trifle puzzled at first until he pointed out that my craft had a very small canteen bill. It was not a very easy question to answer but, fortunately, he did not press the point, probably because he had a good idea of what we had been up to, and ended the interview by telling me firmly that he wanted to see some money being spent in the canteen.

My crew consisted of 2 petty officers, the Cox'n and the Motor Mechanic, 1 stoker and 4 seamen. The Cox'n was in charge of the victualling and other administrative matters affecting the crew. In small craft where no cook was carried the duty was often carried out by the ratings in rotation, however I was very fortunate to have a sailor whose mother had insisted on him learning to cook when he was a boy. Although personally not very keen on cooking AB Ferguson put his early training to good use and fed us extremely well. There was only one problem, an occasional shortage of china as a result of heavy rolling whilst on patrol in the Bay. This could sometimes put a strain on the meal service as I found out quite by accident when I noticed AB Holdway hanging around outside my cabin after he had brought my meal. When I asked him what he was waiting for he replied, "The plate, Sir, it's the only one left!"

A great amount of stores and equipment was being shipped out of Palestine prior to the final withdrawal of the British Forces. One day I was told to report to the KHM who informed me that the Arab workmen at the Naval Mine Depot at Mostir about 20 miles north of Haifa, had gone on strike because the British had refused to give them arms to protect themselves when their buses were attacked by the Jews. The *Fort Rosalie*, a Royal Fleet Auxiliary vessel, was at that moment in port waiting to load mine sinkers to be taken to Ceylon and the strike would delay her departure. I was instructed to take the two Sub-Lieutenants from the Clank, Scott and Neame, and my own crew plus twenty men from the Clank and another MFV, and proceed at once to the Mine Depot to load the train which was waiting to transport the sinkers to the docks.

I had no idea of how long we might have to stay at the depot so I took along plenty of food and a good supply of cigarettes. The men were all armed and we had a good reserve of ammunition in case we ran into trouble. I managed to get hold of a Bren gun from somewhere. In little over an hour the party was on its way in two 3 ton trucks arriving at the Mine Depot in the late afternoon.

The two civilian Naval Stores Officers showed me round the Depot and explained the method by which the sinkers were loaded on to the trucks, and the precautions that had to be taken to prevent damage to their wheels. The sinkers, each weighing 15cwt. and approximately 36 inches in height and 30 inches square with 4 small wheels on the base, were stowed in tiers inside a vast shed adjacent to the railway siding. The top tiers were lifted down to ground level by a Ransome mobile crane. A small 15cwt. crane, hand operated, with a fixed jib and fixed wheels which made it difficult to manoeuvre, was used to lift the sinkers on to trolleys which were then wheeled out to the trucks. Outside, alongside the railway track, was another hand operated crane which was used to lift the sinkers into the trucks. This crane was similar to, but much bigger and heavier than, the one in the shed. It was going to be a 'handraulic' operation with a lot of 'pullee haulee'. Worse was to come when I heard that the Arabs had put the mobile crane out of action when they went on strike.

There were cooking facilities of a sort which had been used by the Arab labour and the sailors had a meal before getting down to work. I put them into two watches, the Sub-Lieutenants each taking a watch, after we had devised a system of working which would make the best use of our man-power and ensure a continuous operation. The men had to be shown how to handle the sinkers to avoid damage to the wheels, and the method of placing the dunnage to avoid damage when the sinkers were placed on top of each other in the trucks. Each truck carried 20 sinkers and there were 20 trucks in the train. I remembered and tried to follow the maxim that Sam Williams was fond of quoting, plan the work and work the plan.

Petty Officer Rose, the motor mechanic, meanwhile had examined the mobile crane. Fortunately there was not a great deal of damage and he was able to get it back into working order, he also took on the job of crane driver. Rose had never operated a crane and his first attempts had everybody running for cover. The shed had an asbestos ceiling and it was soon full of holes made by the crane jib as it shot up and down whilst he tried to get the knack of operating the controls. However within the hour he had developed a gentle touch and was operating it like a veteran.

It took us some time to get the operation running smoothly. The small crane, which with a sinker weighed 1.5tons, was difficult to manoeuvre as was the larger one which also required a lot of man-power to place it in the right position for lowering the sinkers into the truck. As the night wore on we began to pick up a rhythm in the operation with more men working and shorter rest periods being taken, so that by morning we were loading a truck in just over 2 hours and looking to bringing this time down. During the forenoon Commodore Peachey paid a visit to see how we were progressing and we got a "Well done" for our efforts. The Commodore's visit had not been allowed to interfere with the job in hand but the same could not be said for the KHM when he arrived late in the afternoon. He told me to stop work to allow the men to have a rest and enjoy the few cases of beer which he had brought along. Morgan was an acting Lieutenant-Commander commissioned from Warrant Officer and he was inclined to be overbearing with his subordinates, especially in his position as KHM. I told him that if the work was stopped, if only for twenty minutes, the rhythm of the operation would be interrupted and as a result considerably more time would be lost. Although I was in charge of the operation he would have his way, and his total contribution to the clearance of the Depot was to cause an unnecessary delay.

Early in the morning of the last day, just as the last trucks were being loaded, I was feeling very tired having had little rest since arriving at the Depot. Some sailors were having difficulty in moving and manouevring the small crane which was carrying a sinker. I went to lend a hand but my added weight did not appear to be making much difference and I soon found out why. In my weariness I had been careless in placing my right foot in front of one of the crane's wheels, preventing the wheel from moving. I exhorted everybody to "bloody-well push", and they did just that – right over my foot. I let out a howl and caused considerable amusement as I went hopping around the shed on one leg and holding on to my foot which I felt had been crushed. Everyone was tired and my antics gave them all something to laugh about and, if nothing else, helped to raise morale.

I took a lorry and a couple of men and went back to the military hospital in Haifa where I arrived extremely dirty, dishevelled and in considerable pain. The Sister on duty could not have been more kind and sympathetic. Dirty as I was she put me straight to bed and, after finding out that I was extremely hungry, produced boiled eggs, bread and butter and lots of tea. The meal was delicious. Although it was badly bruised an X-ray showed that there was no significant injury to my foot; the big toe, which eventually became misshapen, had taken the weight and some nerves had been damaged.

The accident resulted in my being awarded a 'Certificate For Wounds and Hurts' (known as a Hurt Certificate), an old Naval document which, I believe, dates from the early 19th century. It was given to a man who was wounded or hurt 'To Certify the Right Honourable the Lords Commissioners of the Admiralty' that he 'was actually On His Majesty's Service' when the injury was received. This enabled him to make a claim on the Admiralty for a disability pension, or for further medical treatment should the injury give him problems after he had left the Service. An old hand told me that the Admiralty used to try and redeem the Certificate for £25 to absolve itself from further responsibility. It is a very imposing document and could be described as an early example of the 'Accident and Injury Report' in use today.

I was in hospital for only a very short time, but later on I had a longer stay, which enabled me to obtain some idea of the casualties being sustained by our troops from terrorist attacks, and of the problems confronting the medical staff at the hospital.

I had been bothered with a haemorrhoid and eventually I reported the matter to the KHM who sent me straight up to the hospital for treatment. Evidently he had once suffered with a similar complaint and said that he would not wish it on his worst enemy. I arrived in the late afternoon at the hospital where I was examined by a Major in the RAMC. He seemed to be rather impatient as he carried out an examination, and rather abrupt in his treatment when he took a knife, did something which made me jump, and sent me off with some cotton wool and instructions to keep myself clean. Whatever he did was not very effective and I continued to suffer. This time the KHM gave me a letter asking if I was fit to stand for 24 hours on patrol in a small craft.

Again it was late in the afternoon when I saw the Doctor who read the letter and then asked me, "Don't you want to go to sea?" This was a very insulting remark to make to an officer from another Service but I managed to contain my anger. He examined me again and said, rather grudgingly I thought, that he supposed I would have to be admitted, but it was a bit of a nuisance. I went back to collect my toilet gear and report to the KHM. Morgan was furious when he heard how I had been treated and said he would do something about it.

At the hospital I was put into a two bed ward which was occupied by an army 2nd Lieutenant, a national serviceman barely 20 years old. Accompanied by his sergeant he had been on patrol in Hadar (a Jewish quarter of Haifa) when a gunman stepped from a doorway and sprayed their Jeep with an automatic weapon. They were both badly wounded, the young officer had four bullet holes in his abdomen, but somehow they had managed to drive to the hospital, one working the pedals and the other steering. He had been in the hospital for some time and still had an orderly by his bedside to attend him when he became restless with pain. Later he told me that they had said on a couple of occasions that he would soon be going home but instead he had undergone further surgery.

I had my operation the next day and on the following day the Major came in to see how I was getting on. He was very pleasant and made his apologies for being so brusque. He went on to explain why he had been upset and, when I heard his explanation, I would have felt the same way if I had been in his shoes. The Major and a lady surgeon were the only surgeons in the hospital and as he always started his list at 5 p.m. I had been arriving just at his busiest time.

I saw an example of what our soldiers were going through, and what the Major had to contend with, one day whilst I was having a bath when I heard the roar of a car and a squealing of brakes as it stopped beneath the window. Looking out I saw a taxi standing below and as the door opened two soldiers, blood-stained and obviously wounded, more or less fell out and collapsed on the ground. This type of incident was quite common, as was the sight each morning of a row of men awaiting treatment, mainly for gunshot wounds. It all made me feel rather small with my very minor complaint.

Back on board my craft it was evident that my crew had kept themselves busy; she had been painted up, the decks were snow white and she looked a treat. In fact we all took great pride in keeping her 'tiddley' and if the paintwork was scratched when going alongside it would be immediately touched up. One thing which upset us when doing odd jobs was the state the deck got into when carrying stores and personnel, and the possible damage to paintwork and fittings. When carrying a party of Marines my lads were not slow in telling them to watch where they were putting their big feet.

The Royal Marine Commandos had formed a rear-guard around the vicinity of the docks in preparation for the final withdrawal in April 1948 and, along with the COs of the other craft, I received orders to return to Malta. I had been hoping to sail back in my little yacht but it was not to be and she was towed back by a destroyer. Because her Widdop diesel engine was American it was thought that there would be difficulty in obtaining spare parts, so 132 was taken out of operational service and suffered the humiliation of being used as the galley boat for the submarines in dry-dock.

If I had known beforehand I could probably have bought her for a very small sum and sailed her home. The General Officer Commanding in Malta had bought a sister craft which he converted into a very trim personal yacht

I was sorry to lose my Command and the 4/- per day allowance, however it had amounted to £24 over the period which was sufficient to enable me to go to Gieves and have a dinner suit made to measure. I have it to this day, 50 years on. I very much enjoyed my service in Palestine and I had been fortunate in obtaining an appointment which had provided interesting work and new experiences. Sometime later in Malta I heard the final outcome of my work at the Mine Depot. I ran into Sub-Lieutenant Scott who told me that the KHM, Lieutenant-Commander Morgan, had been awarded the OBE for his services in Palestine and it was said that the 'Mine Depot at Motsir' was written on the back of it. This was being a bit unfair, he had been in Haifa for a considerable time and must have done a lot of good work in charge of the port facilities when the arrival of illegal immigrant vessels was at its height.

I did not have long to wait before I was appointed to HMS *Chameleon,* an Algerine Fleet Minesweeper in the 2nd Minesweeping Flotilla which was about to start mine clearance operations in the Ionian and Aegean Seas. Again I was fortunate to be joining a ship engaged on active service.

Chapter 21

Minesweeping and Malta in Peacetime

Historically, for strategical reasons, the Mediterranean had always been the Navy's most important overseas station and a large fleet was always stationed at Malta. Although the strength of the Navy was gradually being reduced, when I joined HMS *Chameleon* at the end of April 1948 the Mediterranean Fleet was still a large force including aircraft carriers, cruisers, destroyers, frigates, minesweepers and submarines; much the same as it had been before the war.

To date most of my time had been spent on active service in a war environment but, with the Mediterranean Fleet more or less back to pre-war peace-time routine, I was now able to take part in many of the sporting, social and official occasions which were part of naval life on a foreign station, and which had been the subject of many of the stories which had captured my boyhood interest.

Again I was fortunate to join a happy and efficient ship and to be a member of a friendly and hospitable wardroom. The Commanding Officer, Lieutenant-Commander Watkins, was an experienced minesweeping type as was the First Lieutenant. They were both relieved within a few months, the new CO was Lieutenant-Commander Harris, a torpedo and anti-submarine specialist and destroyer man who was not very happy about being appointed to a minesweeper but it did not affect his enthusiasm and he was quick to learn. Keith Clark, the new First Lieutenant (Number One), had been serving as a Midshipman in HMS *Prince of Wales* when she was sunk by the Japanese off the coast of Malaya, and had been a prisoner of war in Singapore.

I was Second Lieutenant and Navigating Officer (Pilot), which was just what I wanted, and amongst other duties I was the ship's sports officer and managed the

Flotilla and the ship's football teams. Peter Peckham, the Third Lieutenant, joined *Chameleon* about the same time as myself, he was a cheerful rugger-playing chap who had played for the Navy, and we became good friends. There were two Sub-Lieutenants, Carne and Hedgecock. Carne came from a very naval family – his father was Captain of the cruiser HMS *Belfast*, an elder brother was a Lieutenant and a younger brother a Cadet at Dartmouth.

There were two engineer officers on board. The Chief was a Warrant Engineer Officer, a very nice person with a good sense of humour, Schofield, an RNVR Sub-Lieutenant, was a Cambridge University student doing his National Service. *Chameleon* also carried the Flotilla Medical Officer. Doc Irvine had been a pharmacist before putting himself through medical school and had worked throughout the war as an anaesthetist in a big London Hospital before joining the Navy. He was very popular in the Flotilla and had a good knowledge of the 1000 men in his practice.

The Flotilla consisted of eight Minesweepers, *Fierce* (SO), *Rifleman, Chameleon, Plucky, Rowena, Sylvia, Stormcloud,* and *Recruit*, and three Danlayers – *Sursay, Tocogay,* and *Vacesay.* Some of the ships had been engaged on the Palestine Patrol but with the ending of that operation the Flotilla was now at full strength and preparing to carry out extensive mine clearance operations in the Dodecanese Islands and around the coast of Greece.

During the following eighteen months a pattern of operations developed which resulted in eight or ten weeks sweeping, followed by a similar period at Malta carrying out maintenance and training.

When minesweeping the Flotilla usually worked from sunrise to sunset and anchored for the night at a suitable anchorage near the area being swept. At weekends one ship was detached to proceed to Skaramanga, the Greek Naval Base near Piraeus to collect the mail and any minesweeping stores which might be required. The remainder of the Flotilla would visit a suitable port nearby for shore leave and recreation. These were invariably small towns with limited facilities such as Kalimnos and Dragomisti, or the rather bigger Patras, but we were always made most welcome by the locals who had a considerable affection for the Royal Navy.

It was realised that there would be a shortage of beer in many of the places that were likely to be visited and that this might encourage our people to turn to the local drink 'Ouzo', a very cheap and potent spirit. In order to safeguard the younger and less experienced sailors each ship carried approximately 500 cases of beer in the magazine and took it in turns to set up a canteen on shore at the weekends. There was usually a proprietor of a cafe or hall who was prepared to allow his premises to be used by the Flotilla for which he was suitably reimbursed, the canteen manager of the duty ship being responsible for running the canteen.

It was *Chameleon's* turn to operate the canteen when we visited Port Laki in Leros and I was given the task of finding premises. I called on the Mayor and after some discussion he suggested that the Boy Scout Headquarters would probably be most suitable. I was surprised to find the Scout movement so active in a small island in the Aegean Sea and I was impressed by the examples of woodcraft and other types of handicrafts which were displayed on the walls. It was just like the average Scout hut at home.

Although minesweeping was, in effect, a hazardous occupation we all thought of it as just a job of work and rarely, if ever, discussed the fact that we might be putting ourselves in harms way. It was only when a mine, cut by the ship ahead, took longer than usual to come to the surface and suddenly appeared right under the bow, that one experienced a quickening of the pulse and realized that it was a hairy business.

HMS Chameleon

Swept mine exploded by gunfire

Clearance sweep in G formation – 2nd M.S.F.

Sailors on the minesweeping mess deck

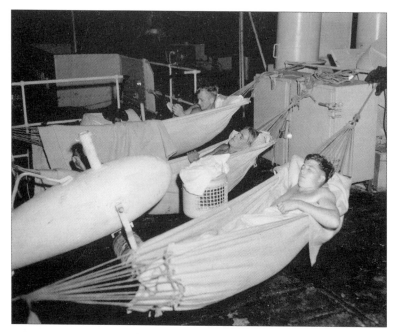

Sleeping on deck in hot weather

Cinema show on deck

Scrubbing decks

The positions of the enemy minefields had been obtained from records captured at the end of the war so that we were spared the more difficult task of locating the exact boundaries of each field. However the information had to be treated with caution as the mines had been laid some time ago and their positions could have altered in the interim.

The charts of the area were very much out of date, being based on surveys carried out around 1880 and in many cases there was no large scale chart available for the area being swept. When this occurred extracts from small scale charts blown up to a much larger scale were issued in order to facilitate accurate navigation and plotting of the ships' tracks. The final reports on the operations had to be extremely detailed and comprehensive in order to satisfy the International Mine Clearance Board that the area had been fully covered and was now safe for navigation.

Some of the mined areas were located close inshore and this quite frequently resulted in the minesweeping gear being fouled by underwater objects such as rocks and wrecks which were not shown on the charts. When this occurred the ship in question would ascertain the position of the obstruction as accurately as possible and forward the details to the Admiralty for subsequent promulgation in the Admiralty Notices to Mariners so that charts could be corrected and brought up to date. I enjoyed this elementary surveying which, due to the nature of our operations, was invariably carried out in an unorthodox manner using one's own technique according to circumstances and conditions. It often involved a combination of compass, radar, sextant and range-finder and working at speed in order to obtain an accurate position. I always had a feeling of satisfaction when I saw *Chameleon* as being the source when the chart correction was subsequently published in the *Notices to Mariners*.

During one cycle a Greek freelance photographer received permission to join the Flotilla and we were asked to accommodate him during his stay. He intended to take photographs of the minesweeping operations and life onboard the ships which he hoped to sell to *Picture Post* or *Life* magazines which were the principal photo-journal publications of the time. He was a very nice chap and stayed with the Flotilla for about a week, spending a day in each ship and returning to *Chameleon* in the evening. He took some excellent pictures of life on board and we were able to buy copies which no doubt helped to make his visit a financial success.

The photographer was very keen to take a close up picture of a mine exploding and one day, when we were engaged in mine disposal, he got his wish and also the fright of his life. He stood on the gratings on the port side of the bridge in order to get a clear and uninterrupted sight on the mine with the large box-type camera he was using and asked the Captain to take the ship as close as possible to the mine. The 'Old Man' manoeuvred to within about thirty yards of the mine in spite of my tentative suggestion, "We are a bit close, Sir", and as we prepared to open fire I moved round to the starboard side of the bridge and peered round the corner of the radar cabinet to watch the proceedings. I noticed everyone else was similarly engaged in seeking cover. The order, "Open fire", was almost immediately followed by an almighty explosion, the photographer went one way and his camera the other, both landing on the deck at the same time as a large piece of metal from the mine. Fortunately nobody was hit. It was thought that he had probably missed his picture but he was indeed a professional as the subsequent picture showed the water being blown out and up by the blast at the moment of detonation.

Vice-Admiral Denny, who was then Vice-Admiral Malta, visited the Flotilla for a week to witness our operations and spent a day on board each ship. When he boarded *Chameleon* at 6 a.m. just as we were about to weigh anchor, he was dressed in a most unusual rig of white shorts and white tunic instead of the usual shorts and shirt, or more formal Number 10s, white tunic and trousers. When he arrived on the bridge his first words after greeting the Captain were, "May I have permission to smoke?" Such is naval etiquette. The Admiral took a great interest in everything that was going on and frequently stuck his head under the canopy of my chart table whilst I was working, to ask questions or make observations on such matters as the age of the charts and when the area was last surveyed and by whom. He had the happy knack of putting people at ease and was very easy to talk to. However, when taking frequent fixes and plotting them I had to work fast, and it was sometimes difficult to get on with my work whilst he was chatting without appearing to be rude. After his visit he sent the Senior Officer, Captain Adams, a signal, repeated to the Admiralty, congratulating the Flotilla on the operations being carried out, and on being the most efficient unit in the Mediterranean Fleet.

The sweeping operations on the first cycle were carried out at the sea approaches to the Gulf of Corinth and between the island of Cephalonia and the Morea mainland,

and from May to August 331 mines and over 300 obstructors were swept from German mine-lays. During this period the 13,000th mine to be swept by British minesweepers in the Mediterranean was recorded.

In the summer the various units in the Fleet went on cruises performing the time honoured role of 'Showing the Flag' to foster good relations with the countries that were visited. At the end of the summer in 1948 the Flotilla called at Calvi (where Admiral Lord Nelson lost his eye) on the Island of Corsica. It was a picturesque town situated on a promontory at the end of a long, sweeping bay, and it reminded me of the castle which appeared in a well-known toothpaste advertisement, the narrow streets gradually wound round and upwards through the buildings and fortifications to produce the fairy-tale castle effect.

A French Navy liason officer came on board on arrival to give us some information on local traditions and customs which mainly concerned the female population. It seemed that the Corsicans were very jealous of their women and if they thought they were being insulted, chatted-up or otherwise interfered with they would think nothing of drawing a knife to avenge their honour. So before the liberty-men went ashore they were given a talk on how to conduct themselves with regard to the local popsies and told to keep out of trouble with their men-folk.

From Calvi the Flotilla proceeded to Villefranche, the small, exclusive holiday resort on the French Riviera. On arrival three ships were moored alongside each other in preparation for the cocktail party to be given on arrival for the local dignitaries and other guests who had received invitations from the British Consul. A party or reception of any kind on a British man-of-war was a social event in any part of the world and invitations were much sought after by local residents and British visitors to the town. Consuls could sometimes have a problem in knowing whom to invite or leave out without upsetting someone.

During sweeping operations it was the Senior Officer's practice to hold a cocktail party occasionally during our weekend visits to the neighbouring ports. To begin with I looked forward to these parties which were a pleasant break in routine but after the first two or three, in common with my colleagues, I found them heavy going. To be entertained on board a British warship was an exciting experience for the leading citizens of these small communities and their families and we did our very best to entertain them. However they were simple, unsophisticated people, shy and with little understanding of English so that it was difficult to keep up any sort of conversation. Sometimes the daughters would have a slight knowledge of English or French and we would have an amusing time trying to understand each other in a mixture of both languages with a spot of Hindustani thrown in for good measure. The Mammas, always in black, would sit quietly keeping a careful eye on their daughters; they may have spent their lives in the backwaters of the Mediterranean but they evidently knew all about young naval officers.

On the jetty at Villefranche, adjacent to the landing place, was a large cafe named Jimmy's Bar and this became the first stop for the libertymen when they went ashore and the last stop before they returned on board. Anyone who missed the last boat at night was allowed to doss down in the cafe, to wait for the first boat off in the morning. As approximately 600 men were entitled to shore leave every day Jimmy had a gold mine anchored just outside his front door. Because of currency regulations there was a limit on the amount of money that could be drawn, with officers restricted to £10 and the ratings to £5. Our sailors, however, were not to be put out by a shortage of cash. The rear premises of the cafe were gradually stocked up with sailors' raincoats and long bars of soap which Jimmy bought to sell on the Black Market, the sailors subsequently using kit upkeep allowances to replace the raincoats.

The following year when *Chameleon* visited San Raphael, just along the coast to the west of Villefranche, Doc went back to see Jimmy and he learned about the aftermath of the 2nd Minesweeping Flotilla's visit. It appeared that the Flotilla had consumed about three months supply of beer in one week and that Jimmy had been off work for three weeks due to a break-down after a week without sleep.

The following year, in addition to San Raphael, *Chameleon* visited Port Oneglia on the Italian Riviera where I had my first success as an interpreter. It was a small port approached through a narrow entrance between the breakwaters which enclosed the harbour and the Captain decided to moor stern on to the jetty. The pilot who came out to take us in to harbour was a small, bearded man dressed in a most flamboyant white uniform, all gold lace and medals, wearing a sword and looking more or less the image of General Badoglio, a well-known Italian General during the war who was much caricatured in the newspapers. He was an excitable little chap and it appeared that he was also the harbour-master. However he did not understand one word of English and the Captain had great difficulty in explaining that he wanted to moor stem on to the jetty. In the end I asked if I could have a go at explaining what was required. I pointed to my back-side and said, "Derriere premier", "Derriere premier." The harbour-master's face lit up as he began to comprehend the meaning of my gesturing and 'pidgin' French. Nodding his head in agreement he kept repeating with much enthusiasm, "Si, si, derriere premier, derriere premier", which was accompanied by much shaking of hands, The Captain got his wish and we moored stern on.

I witnessed a rather strange phenomenon in Port Oneglia. The wardroom had been invited to attend a performance at the local Opera House but being duty officer I was unable to go, however I arranged a film show on the foredeck to pass the evening. As I watched the film I noticed a large bright object, like a ball of fire, move rapidly from East to West across the night sky above the screen, and gradually descend until it appeared to come down in the sea. My immediate thought was that it was an aircraft on fire and I nipped up to the bridge and took a bearing of the direction in which it seemed to have crashed. The destroyer, HMS *Chequers* (Prince Philip was to join her a few months later) was in a neighbouring port and, being the Senior Officer in the vicinity, I reported the incident to her duty officer. The local authorities immediately instituted a search in the reported area whilst checking if any aircraft was missing.

The resulting search was negative and there seemed to be no satisfactory explanation for my *bal de feu* except the possibility that it might have come from the steel works in Northern Italy. I just wonder if I had seen my first and only Unidentified Flying Object.

Malta was the ideal place for a young batchelor to enjoy himself. There was always something to do and living was fairly cheap, although by the time one had paid mess and laundry bills and put something aside for a rainy day there was not a great deal left to throw around. There were several clubs of which most officers were members the main ones being the Marsa Sports Club, the Union Club and the Sliema Club. The Marsa had a race track, polo grounds and facilities for tennis and other sports. It also had very fine club premises, the entrance hall and staircase being covered with the crests of the scores of warships which had served on the station over many years. The Saturday night dinner dances were very popular especially in the summer when they were held outside in the gardens where it was pleasant to dine in a romantic setting under the stars, surrounded by trees and shrubs gaily decked with fairy lights.

The Royal Naval Hospital at Bighi overlooking Grand Harbour held an annual Ball which was one of the main social events of the season and I was very pleased to receive an invitation to partner a friend who was a Nursing Sister at the hospital. I met Marie at Number One's wedding where she had been a bridesmaid and I had been head usher and we subsequently became very good friends. Marie was a very attractive and popular girl with many friends, both service and civilian, and she took the opportunity to return their kindness and hospitality by inviting a large party to the Ball.

The day before the Ball *Chameleon* was at sea carrying out trials when a general signal was received from the C-in-C to the effect that the rig for the Ball would be Ball Dress. This was totally unexpected as Ball Dress uniform was in abeyance at the time and there had been no warning that it was to be re-introduced. This meant that I would need to wear a white waistcoat under my white bum freezer and miniature medals; which I did not possess, and as we were not returning to Valetta until the next day there was not going to be a great deal of time in which to get these very necessary items. However the Captain came to my rescue when he went through his kit and came up with a white waistcoat. As soon as we arrived in harbour my steward was sent post-haste to Gieves, the naval tailors, to have a set of my medals made up in miniature with strict orders not to return without them. True to form, and in keeping with their reputation, Gieves came up with the goods and Schembri arrived onboard as I was about to get ready for the do and beginning to get a trifle anxious.

The Ball was held on the tennis courts in the hospital grounds, the area being decorated with coloured lights and flood-lit. In keeping with the Corps tradition of being able to supply anything from a string trio to a full military band, and play anything from Bach to Berlin, the Royal Marine band of HMS *Vanguard* provided the dance orchestra. Its excellent performance was a major factor in the Ball being a great success with everyone having a happy and memorable evening.

It was the first time I had attended such a grand affair and I could have been daunted by the presence of so many Senior Officers and the great and the good. Earl Mountbatten, who was then a Rear-Admiral commanding the First Cruiser Squadron, and Countess Mountbatten were present together with Admiral Sir Arthur Power, the Commander-in-Chief, and Lady Power and other Senior Officers from the three services and their wives. Marie was a charming and hospitable hostess and with her guests being a friendly lot we very soon had a jolly party going on at her table.

It was whilst I was standing with a group of officers that I noticed a Commander taking a close interest in the medals I was wearing. As he looked up he caught my eye and, indicating my medals, remarked with a smile that I carried my years well and did not show my age. I did not understand what he was getting at until he quietly pointed out that the head on one of my medals was that of King George V instead of King George VI. It transpired that Gieves did not have a miniature of the Victory Medal so, in order to complete my set, they put a World War 1 medal in its place. I had been in such a rush to get ready that I never thought to examine the medals when I received them. The Commander was quite amused when I told him the story – it called for a drink, and I realized that there was such a person as the archetypal hawk-eyed naval Commander who never misses a trick.

I thoroughly enjoyed the Ball and later in the year I was offered the opportunity to repeat the experience when I met Commander Thring who had been my Commanding Officer in HMS *Tavy*. He had been promoted to Captain and was serving as Chief of Staff to the Flag Officer (Destroyers) in the Depot Ship HMS *Forth*. I invited him onboard for drink and sometime later I received an invitation from him to join his party and escort his daughter to the forthcoming St. Andrew's Day Ball, another big event in the social calendar. I had never met his daughter who, at that time, must have been about seventeen. I could not accept the invitation as I was due to take passage home before the end of November, which was maybe just as well as I could have been put in a bit of a quandry because I would naturally have wanted to take Marie.

Then again it was not every young officer who was asked by a future Admiral to escort his daughter to a Ball; there is no knowing where I might have ended up had I accepted the invitation. As it turned out the young lady became the talk of Kuala Lumpur when, 8 years later, she married an American businessman over twenty years her senior.

The Mediterranean Fleet Regatta was one of the main sporting events of the year and the spirit and pride in ship of a ship's company could often be judged by the response of officers and ratings in volunteering to crew for the various races. As Sports Officer my task was to get the departments – seamen, engineroom, miscellaneous and officers to enter for the whaler races, and then encourage the crews to turn out for the early morning training sessions that were conducted for several weeks beforehand in order to put up a good performance on the day. One of the ship's pets, a monkey named Tojo Malotte (Tojo after the Japanese of that name and Malotte after the local beer), was presented to the ship as the booby prize at a regatta held by the Flotilla during previous operations at Massawa in the Red Sea, and I was hoping that we might manage to do better this time. My father had often told me about the regatta held by the Grand Fleet at the end of World War 1 when no other ship would cover the £500 laid on the *Queen Elizabeth's* Royal Marines because they were such hot favourites in the cutter race.

In the summer of 1949 the Mediterranean Fleet Regatta was held at Navarino Bay in Greece where, in 1827, a British Fleet supported by French and Russian ships under the command of Admiral Codrington defeated a Turkish-Egyptian Fleet which eventually led to the liberation of Greece from Turkish rule. Prior to the arrival of the Fleet the Flotilla, which was engaged in the second cycle of sweeping operations, was given the task of sweeping a minefield off the approaches to the Bay. Mines were cut in 'G' formation and when the check sweep was carried out in 'A' formation one more mine was brought to the surface. There was no time left for further operations before the arrival of the C-in-C in *Vanguard* and we all held our breaths and counted our beads as she approached and entered the Bay. Fortunately all went well and there were no loud bangs.

The betting arrangements were operated by the Chief and Schofield, the Sub-Lieutenant (E), who set up as bookies at a table on the foredeck. Details of the bets were passed to the *Fierce* (Senior Officer) who acted as the Tote and worked out the odds on each competing boat. The races were held between the lines of ships at anchor, the boats being towed to the start line by ships' motor boats full of chucking up parties who followed the races cheering on their shipmates.

At the end of the regatta the ship which had collected the most points declared itself to be Cock of the Fleet and hoisted the symbol of a cockerel to the masthead. Later in the evening the Cockerel was taken in the ship's boat around the rest of the Fleet at anchor. As the boat passed each ship it was greeted with much good natured banter most often accompanied by a shower of spuds, small bags of flour or a jet from a fire hose. *Chameleon* did not win any races but we all did our best and enjoyed the occasion. And we did not win any more monkeys.

A couple of days after the regatta the Captain was told to report on board *Vanguard* and when he returned to the ship he told me that *Chameleon* had been detailed to take Sir Charles Norton, the British Ambassador to Greece, and Lady Norton to the Island of Zante and then on to a place called Lutraki. Lutraki was approached through the Preveza Channel where there was a 2 fathom patch and the Captain was concerned as to whether we would be able to get over it safely. I studied the chart of the place he had mentioned and the first thing that struck me was why should the Ambassador want to go to such an isolated spot on the west coast of Greece not even connected by main road to Athens. After studying the Admiralty Pilot for the area I found another Lutraki, this time situated at the Eastern end of the

Gulf of Corinth and only about 30 miles from Athens. It was a small resort and it was obvious that the Ambassador was going to land there and travel back to the Embassy in Athens by car. When I pointed this out to the Captain he got a bit of a shock when he realized that he might have taken Sir Charles to the wrong spot, and he immediately set out for the *Vanguard* to discuss the matter with the Fleet Navigating Officer. The Captain returned to the ship 'very nicely, thank you', having been the recipient of several large gins from a grateful officer whose future career might have been severely curtailed.

As we were leaving Navarino Bay with the Ambassador and his wife on board a message was received from *Vanguard* consisting of just one word, "Congratulations." The Captain was puzzled for a moment and then remembered that it was the time of the half-yearly promotions when every Lieutenant-Commander in the Navy would be anxiously waiting to know if he had been selected for promotion to Commander. They were only in the zone for 7 years and if not promoted during that time they were known as having been passed over and had to retire when aged 45. He was overjoyed to know that he had got his Brass Hat and that he was moving up the ladder, he subsequently left *Chameleon* to take up an appointment as Fleet Torpedo and Anti-Submarine Officer in the Home Fleet.

At Zante the Ambassador and Lady Norton went ashore to spend a few days with some friends whilst *Chameleon* went off to carry out exercises with HMS *Liverpool*, Rear-Admiral Mountbatten's Flagship of the First Cruiser Squadron. In the exercise *Chameleon* was given the role of a damaged Russian cruiser which *Liverpool* was searching for in order to prevent it from reaching the safety of the port of Taranto in Southern Italy. For the purpose of the exercise the Russian ship was given a main armament of eight 9-inch guns.

Chameleon was eventually found by the 'enemy' who closed in what appeared to be an attack with torpedoes. The Captain immediately sensed what *Liverpool* was about to do and, being a destroyer type he was able to anticipate her every move. With a "Watch this, Pilot", he began to manoeuvre his ship in such a way as to outwit *Liverpool*, and so thwart her attack that she was forced to turn away and disappear over the horizon. *Liverpool* reappeared on our port quarter, this time flashing her searchlight and signalling that she was firing at *Chameleon* with her 6-inch guns whereupon we replied that fire was being returned with 9-inch guns. This seemed to take *Liverpool* by surprise as she immediately broke off the action and again turned away. Shortly afterwards the exercise was terminated. It was subsequently heard over the grapevine that Mountbatten was not at all pleased with the outcome of the exercise and it was probably just as well that the Captain had already received his promotion.

We returned to Zante to pick up the Ambassador and, before proceeding to Lutraki, a couple of days at anchor afforded the opportunity for all hands to enjoy swimming parties on the quiet, clean and attractive beaches that bordered the anchorage. We sailed early in the morning with an estimated time of arrival at Lutraki of 6 p.m. Before reaching the entrance to the Gulf of Corinth Lady Norton remarked that the sea looked so inviting that she would like to go for a swim. The Captain decided to stop and "Hands to Bathe" was piped, the dinghy was lowered as a safety boat, and very soon the hands and Lady Norton were cavorting in the water. I was not too happy at having my voyage plan interrupted and I remained on the bridge, keeping one eye on the clock and the other on the swimmers in the water. Suddenly I saw a black fin not far from the swimmers in the water and I immediately thought it was a shark, but then thought it was probably a porpoise (as I had never heard of sharks being in the Mediterranean) in which case I did not want to raise a false alarm and start a panic amongst the bathers. By this time it was too late to do anything if it was a shark but fortunately the Captain decided it was time to clear the water and proceed on our way. I had kept my suspicions to myself and I spent a few anxious minutes willing the swimmers to hurry up and get inboard. Many years later I read an article by a French underwater explorer who said that he first came across sharks at the beginning of his career whilst working in the Aegean Sea.

As we entered the Gulf of Corinth Lady Norton, who was a most charming and affable person, pointed out places of interest to the Captain and gave him details of their historical significance. The 'Old Man' had quite a job in giving her his full attention and maintaining his usual courteous manner whilst at the same time keeping an eye on where the ship was going. All he could do was to say now and again, "All right, Pilot?", as I conned the ship through the narrow bottle-neck which was the entrance to the Gulf, and swung the ship in large alterations of course first to starboard, then to port, and then again to starboard as we threaded our way between the spits and bar which lay at the entrance. Our route lay in a straight line down the centre of the Gulf, but Lady Norton asked frequently if we might go a little closer inshore when she would be able to point out something of interest. She was a mine of information about the history of the area and contributed greatly to a most enjoyable passage. In spite of the delay with the swimming party and several deviations from the planned route it was exactly 6 p.m. when the ship anchored at Lutraki which was noted by the Captain with a, "Well done, Pilot."

Football was the main sporting activity in the Fleet although all other sports and forms of recreation had their various competitions and trophies. Being responsible for football I was kept busy organizing and attending the matches involving both *Chameleon* and the Flotilla teams when in Malta and during minesweeping operations. Although I had played football as a small boy I had no real knowledge of the game having been devoted to rugby, and I relied to some extent on my committees with regard to team selections; my main role being to run up and down the touch-line shouting words of encouragement and exhorting, "Don't just stand there – do something!"

HMS Chameleon refulling at sea

Mediterranean Fleet football team – 1949

Chameleon's football team – 1948

The Bookies

The Greeks were very keen on football and during the sweeping cycles we played matches against the local teams at the ports where we happened to be spending the weekend. Some of the pitches were rather rough and over the period our sailors had the experience of playing on every type of surface from the grass in the stadium of Izmir's 2nd division team to the stoney ground of the village square at Kalimnos which was normally used as a vehicle park. At Syra, one of the oldest ports in Greece which we visited several times during our operations, there was a large military barracks whose Commanding Officer very kindly offered the Flotilla the use of their sporting facilities whenever we were in port. There was always a match with the Greek Army team and the ships were able to play off inter-ship matches in the Flotilla League.

Football matches were more or less mandatory during good-will visits so that during the course of a year there was hardly a time when players were not involved in one way or another. In addition to playing for his ship an outstanding player could be called upon to play for the Flotilla, Destroyer Command, the Navy team and the team from Combined Services and it was not difficult or unusual for such a person to suffer from football fatigue.

In the Mediterranean Fleet there was intense rivalry between the ships and between the various Squadrons and Flotillas. There were three trophies to be played for. The Fleet Cup was the main competition involving the winners of the various leagues, i.e. the Cruisers, Destroyer Command, Shore Stations, etc. The Fleet Knock-out Cup was a knock-out competition involving all the ships and establishments and the Destroyer Command Cup was contested between the Flotilla teams of the Destroyers, Frigates and Minesweepers. In addition each Squadron and Flotilla had its own trophy.

During the 1948–49 season the 2nd MSF won the Destroyer Command Cup and was runner-up to the 2nd Frigate Flotilla in the Fleet Knockout Cup and to

H.M.S. *Liverpool*, Rear Admiral Mountbatten's flagship of the 1st Cruiser Squadron, in the Fleet Cup. This game was played at the Corradino sports ground overlooking Grand Harbour in front of a large crowd including the top brass of the three services. The score was 1–1 at full time but unfortunately we lost to a late goal towards the end of extra time. We were very disappointed at losing as it was the first time for many years that a small ship flotilla had won the cup. Both teams received congratulations from the C-in-C on a hard fought match played in a sporting manner.

It should not be thought that all the time in port was spent in social or sporting activities. In Malta officers and ratings received instruction and training at the signal school, the anti-submarine attack teacher, depth charge driller and other facilities much the same as in war-time. Frequently a day would be spent at sea exercising with a submarine and carrying out a practice shoot at a surface target under tow and at a drogue towed by aircraft. Operations such as transferring stores and personnel at sea and taking in tow would be exercised, and whenever the Flotilla was on passage the ships would carry out exercises such as 'Officer of the Watch Manoeuvres' and 'General Drill.'

The maintenance and appearance of the ship was of prime importance but by the time men had been detailed off for various parties the First Lieutenant was sometimes left with very few hands to work their part of ship. Painting Ship was an operation which involved all hands with the exception of the cooks and one telegraphist whose duty was to play records over the SRE (ship's recreation equipment). On one occasion I was standing on the upper deck when the Buffer (Chief Bosun's Mate) came striding along with a look of thunder on his face. I asked him what the trouble was. Pointing to the sailors who were swaying to and fro plying their brushes in time to the music he said, "That 'Sparks,' I'll have his guts for a necktie, it is not a waltz I want, it's the post-horn bloody gallop!"

One of the most important events during the year was the annual two-day audit of the ship by the Senior Officer of the Flotilla and his Staff. On the first day the ship's company was inspected at Divisions after which a complete and thorough inspection of all internal spaces and upper deck fittings and equipment was carried out. The staff officers – Navigating, Gunnery, Engineer, A/S and Signals inspected the equipment and records of their various departments and the ratings were given the opportunity to examine their Service Certificates and Conduct Sheets.

On the second day the inspection party boarded at 6 a.m. when the ship proceeded to sea to carry out exercises with a submarine and aircraft. The Staff would also carry out a programme of exercises in which various situations and conditions were simulated to test the reaction of the ship's company. It was a busy day for all hands. At the end of the day the officers were interviewed individually by the Senior Officer and the Captain and their progress, performance, etc. would be reviewed. They would also be given the opportunity to discuss any matters of a personal nature with the Senior Officer.

On completion of the second cycle of operations at the end of March 1949 the Flotilla visited Izmir in Turkey for five days of rest and recreation. Shortly after our arrival in the late afternoon all ships received a signal from the SO giving details of invitations which had been received from various people and organizations who wished to entertain the officers and men in the Flotilla. The local British residents had even organized a canteen where the sailors could have free beer during the visit. Some of the invitations were for two or three officers from each ship, and Peter and I chose to attend a dance at a tennis club at Buca which was some distance out of town.

The visit to Izmir was only one of many memorable events that took place during my peacetime service on the Mediterranean station. It was to be the happiest two years of my sea-going career during which time I experienced all that made the life of a naval officer so interesting and rewarding.

Chapter 22

LEAVING THE SERVICE

———

After a spell of leave which enabled me to spend Christmas and New Year of 1949 at home I was appointed to HMS *Montclare*, a Submarine Depot Ship, which was based at Rothesay in the Firth of Clyde.

HMS Montclare

Montclare was in Rosyth Dockyard nearing the end of her annual docking and repair period so I did not have very far to go when the time came to join her. However I did not have the same feeling of anticipation and excitement that I had experienced previously when joining a new ship. The measures to reduce the size of the Navy were beginning to take effect and many ships were being scrapped or laid up and put into the Reserve Fleet, with the consequent result that there was a growing shortage of sea-going appointments. This was no doubt popular with some officers and especially those who were married, but to someone like myself, who wanted to go to sea and advance one's professional knowledge and see the world with the hope of encountering some unusual experience or adventure, it could be a very depressing prospect.

In the existing situation I had been extremely lucky to receive another sea-going appointment after a two year commission abroad and I appreciated my good fortune, although I realised that, being a Depot Ship, *Montclare* would spend most of the time secured to a buoy and would rarely go to sea. It was this thought which was the cause of my seemingly low spirits.

Montclare was a large passenger ship belonging to the Canadian Pacific Steamship Company which was taken over by the Navy at the outbreak of the war to be used as a mother ship for submarines. Her large cargo holds were converted into workshops and stores and fitted with machinery and equipment necessary for their repair and maintenance. She was a sister ship of the *Montrose* which was noted as having been the ship in which Crippen, the famous murderer, attempted to escape from the country before the first World War. Wireless had just come in to use at sea and it was the first time it was used in the apprehension of a criminal; Crippen was arrested when the ship arrived in Canada.

When I arrived on board I found that I was to be the officer in charge of the Quarterdeck Division responsible for the discipline and welfare of approximately 90 men, the maintenance of the Quarterdeck part of ship, and also a watchkeeping officer. In destroyers and smaller ships in harbour the watchkeeping officers took their turn as Officer of the Day for 24 hours, but, in cruisers and above they kept their normal four hour watches on the quarterdeck where they were responsible for running the ship's routine and had to be fully acquainted with more or less every activity that was taking place. Before taking over my first watch I was given a couple of days to find my way around the ship, the situation of the various compartments and spaces and to get some idea of the ship's routine.

The Commanding Officer was on leave when I joined the ship and I did not meet him until I was performing my first period of duty as Officer of the Watch. I will never forget the introduction. I had been told that the Captain would be using the forward accommodation ladder when he was leaving the ship in the evening to visit a submarine and I had gone forward in readiness to see him over the side. He came along the deck and stood in front of me. "Who are you?", he said. "Lieutenant Stewart, Sir." "Are you Brown's relief?" "Yes sir." "Are you Officer of the Watch of *Montclare*?" "Yes Sir." "Then go aft and attend to your duties."

The Captain's manner and attitude on our initial meeting was totally different to that of my previous Commanding Officers who, even when I was a Cadet and

Midshipman, showed a friendly interest in making me feel welcome. It was not long before I realised that it was nothing unusual in his case. He was a much decorated officer with the DSO and two bars and the DSC and bar from his exploits whilst in command of submarines during the war. He had the reputation of being a hard man; an excellent submarine commander but not a popular officer.

Although the atmosphere in the wardroom was friendly enough there was not the same close relationship and sense of chumminess amongst the officers that I had become used to through my experience in small ships. It was only to be expected as there were many more officers and the submariners who lived on board when their boats were alongside, kept very much to themselves. Submariners were a different breed; once they had volunteered for submarines they rarely, if ever, returned to General Service except in the event of their failing the Commanding Officer Qualifying Course, traditionally known as the Perisher.

When on watch on the quarterdeck the most anxious period occurred at 9 a.m. when the Captain, who lived ashore in Rothesay with his family, was due to come on board. In the Navy it is a crime, and in effect bad manners, both to keep a boat waiting to depart and for a boat to be late on arrival so that it was important that the Captain's barge should arrive alongside the jetty just as he was stepping from his car. This operation had to be carefully timed and organized by the Officer of the Watch who was also responsible for ensuring that the various senior officers (heads of departments) who had to be on the quarterdeck to meet the Captain when he came on board, were in attendance. They had to be informed at just the right moment so that they did not have to waste time standing around waiting for his arrival.

There was a good view of the road along which the 'old man's' car would be travelling and when it passed a certain point the barge crew would be called away. They always seemed to take ages to man the boat after which they would burn cotton waste around the engine to warm it up, prompting visions of the whole thing going up in flames. All the time the car would be drawing nearer to the jetty and when the barge eventually departed it was watched anxiously as it made its way inshore, the impression always being that it would never arrive in time or, worse still, it might even break down.

Somehow the barge always arrived at the jetty at the same time as the car and the Officer of the Watch would give a sigh of relief as it was seen to be returning to the ship with the Captain on board. The next part of the operation was to have the senior officers in attendance and this was done by informing them over the loudspeakers that they were required on the quarterdeck. In spite of a repeated request for their presence invariably there would be no sign of them as the barge came alongside. The Officer of the Watch would be standing at the top of the accommodation ladder saluting as the Captain was being piped on board, when out of the corner of his eye he would see the various officers appearing miraculously as if from nowhere. Although there were never any slip-ups there was always a sense of relief, and one could be left feeling a bit of a wet rag, by the time the whole business was over.

Periodically *Montclare* put to sea to take part in exercises either with the other ships in the Home Fleet or to act as a target ship for the submariners who were undergoing the Perisher course for command. The ship so seldom went to sea that we used to joke that we would first have to find the wheel and then someone who knew how to steer before we could leave our berth at the buoys.

Whenever a submarine was on passage unescorted, or carrying out exercises by itself, it was required to report to the Operational H.Q. at specified times. If a submarine failed to surface and report at an arranged time and it became evident that it might be in difficulty, a search and rescue operation was immediately put into motion. A signal, SUBSMASH 1, was broadcast by the Admiralty to all ships and establishments who responded in accordance to the roles allotted to them in the emergency.

A rather amusing incident occurred in *Montclare* on one occasion during a Subsmash exercise. When the signal was received *Montclare* sounded her siren ordering all personnel on shore to return to the ship and certain nominated people then boarded the destroyer HMS *Tenacious* and the frigate HMS *Woodbridge Haven*, which were based at Rothesay, to proceed with all despatch to the scene of the emergency. Doc Kelly, a Surgeon Lieutenant RNVR, was one of the people detailed to go in the *Woodbridge Haven* but, unfortunately, he was in Greenock at the time being fitted for a new uniform. When the Surgeon Commander reported to the Captain that Doc was absent he was told to go himself and sail with the *Woodbridge Haven* which was already under way and leaving the anchorage. Dashing down to the quarterdeck where the Captain's barge, fortunately, was waiting alongside, he leapt on board and, throwing out an arm and pointing at the fast receding *Woodbridge Haven*, shouted the unforgettable order to the cox'n, "Follow that frigate !"

One day I received a surprise visit from a sailor who had served with me in *Chameleon*, he was passing through on his way to join another ship and when he heard I was on board he asked to see me. He found me in the bath. 'Wee' Benny Houston had been a stalwart of the ship and flotilla football teams and he subsequently played for the Navy in Malta after I had left the ship. He was a small chap but a very fine football player. Benny came from Glasgow but although the family had lived in Coventry for many years he had never lost his accent or Glasgow humour.

We went to my cabin for a yarn and of course I was keen to hear how the Flotilla team had fared after my departure. it appeared that they had only to win the last match to retain the Destroyer Command Cup but, although they were leading by 2 – 0 at half-time, they lost the match. When I asked him what at gone wrong he said, "We thought we had it won and fell away in the second half and you weren't there to shout at us" I thought it was one of the nicest compliments that I had ever received.

With the continuing run down of the Navy and ships being taken out of commission, a surplus of officers began to build up and the Admiralty made it known that officers could apply for voluntary retirement subject to their approval. I had become rather unsettled in *Montclare*; I had joined the Navy to go to sea and all I seemed to be doing was acting as a sort of station-master on the quarterdeck and, what was more important, I was not being given much opportunity to further my professional knowledge. My previous appointments had all been in ships which had provided interesting duties and a variety of experiences and, in retrospect, I had not yet appreciated that in any profession or occupation one has to take the rough with the smooth, and be prepared to endure periods of boredom in work not altogether to one's liking.

I had been taking stock of my position and I had been considering the future. Like myself, many officers had obtained Extended Service Commissions in the hope of being granted a permanent commission at the end of their period of service. With the reduction in the Navy it was easy to see that few permanent commissions would be on offer and that it would be a lottery as to who would be selected, much would depend on age and seniority. I was 27, a senior Lieutenant and I came to the conclusion that not many of my seniority would be required otherwise in two or three years there would be a glut of Lieutenant-Commanders. Even if I was fortunate to be selected (I had already received accelerated promotion and I had received very good reports from all my COs) the probability was that there would be retirement at the age of 45. I decided to leave before I became any older when it would be more difficult to get started in a new career.

When I told the Commander that I wanted to retire in order to sit for a Master's Certificate of Competency (Merchant Navy) he tried to talk me out of it, noting that the schoolmaster on board would give me all the assistance required to pass the examination. However I had made up my mind and in May 1950 my request to retire was accepted. I was interviewed by the Captain before I left the ship and, as he said goodbye and wished me well, he remarked to the Commander that he thought the Admiralty were wrong in encouraging people like myself to retire as the Navy would be losing many young officers with invaluable wartime experience.

And so ended my career in the Royal Navy. My ambition had been realized and for ten years I had enjoyed the life of variety, adventure, danger and romance which had been portrayed in the many stories about the Navy that had caught my youthful imagination.

Taking passage on the ferry to the mainland I began to feel a tinge of regret about leaving the service and doubts started to arise as to whether I had made the correct decision. I was to regret my action even more so some six weeks later when the Korean war started and there would have been the opportunity for active service in the ships that were taken out of reserve to go to the Far East.

It was not until I saw a crowd of sailors in Waverley station in Edinburgh who had arrived on a train from Rosyth to go on weekend leave, that I fully realized that I was now outside and on my own and no longer one of the family. I had grown up in the Navy, it had been my home and I had been more or less sheltered from the realities of civilian life. As far as I had been concerned I had never been earning my living, I looked on my pay as pocket money for doing something which I wanted to do and enjoyed doing. Now I would have to set about earning my living like everybody else.

Chapter 23

LIFE OUTSIDE THE SERVICE

———

I was not really keen to return to the Merchant Navy; though I had only given my wish to obtain a Master's Certificate as a reason for retiring from the Navy, but when a chap in the village, who was a Second Engineer with a company which operated ships on behalf of the New Zealand Shipping Company, suggested that I should join his company which offered good conditions of service and only four month trips I decided to give it a try.

I was accepted and travelled down to Bristol to join the *Kaimata*. After the spick and span of a warship the sight of my new ship was depressing. She was a Fort type cargo ship, a class mass produced during the war, extremely dirty and untidy and the scruffy steward I encountered on boarding did not provide a very good first impression. I found that I would be expected to sail in the ship to Canada where I would be required to transfer to the *Kaiwana* (a sister ship) and serve for two years on the run between Canada and New Zealand. When I told the Superintendent that I had been given to understand that the trips would be of only four months duration he was highly amused. He said, "Good God laddie, you won't get four month trips anywhere nowadays." I told him, politely of course, that having recently spent two years in the Mediterranean there was no way I was going to spend two years in a ship like the *Kaimata*. There were other aspects that I was not happy about and I returned home with the firm conviction that I would find it difficult to start again in the MN after my experience of the Navy.

I wrote to several companies but without much success. At that time most of the big international companies and trading houses took their management trainees

straight from school so that in most cases I was too old, also the first people to go to
university after the war were graduating at the time and that did not help matters.

For a time I was rather depressed but I eventually decided to have a go at breeding
pigs and I bought a small cottage and steading on the hills just outside Denny in
Stirlingshire. My aim was to keep sows and sell the piglets when they were weaned at
about 6 to 8 weeks. It was an old cottage but well built with a stone flagged floor in
the kitchen, a small room off the kitchen which I used as a dining room, and a sitting
room and bedroom downstairs. Upstairs had been floored and lined to provide a
bedroom and a small cupboard for the Elsan toilet. There was no electricity, toilet
facilities or running water in the house when I bought it and I had to put in a water
supply. It was too expensive to put in electricity so I used paraffin lamps.

The steading was a bit of a ruin and required a considerable amount of repair. I
did everything by the book and thereby learned a lesson about budgeting; add 50%
or more to your final figure. Inside the steading the walls of the five sties were cement
washed and each sty was fitted with a 2-inch steel pipe farrowing rail to prevent the
sow from laying on her piglets. Along the length of the steading, at the front and rear
of the sties, were two passages. The front for feeding the sows and the rear one for use
as a mucking area. Doors in the sties could be opened and secured across the passage
to isolate each sow's mucking space and, when closed, the sows were kept in their sties
whilst the passage was being mucked out. At the rear of the steading there was a small
paddock where the sows could root about.

I started with two pedigree large white sows, in the hope that the gilt weaners
would be in demand for breeding, and one ordinary large white. My intention was
to feed them on potatoes with a little meal until about 3 weeks before farrowing
when they would be fed mainly on meal to increase the milk for their young. The
potatoes I intended to use were brock potatoes, unfit for the commercial market but,
unfortunately, shortly after I started they became very scarce and I had to buy ordinary
ware potatoes which were more expensive. This plus unforeseen increases in meal
prices was to have a considerable effect on my budget.

I made another one of my mistakes during this period in not taking a part-time
job of some description in order to have some money coming in. As it was I was living
on my small amount of capital which was fast being depleted. It was all very well having
a clean and tidy house but that did not pay the bills.

The first three litters were very successful and produced 29 piglets all of which
survived. The aim was to get the piglets on to meal as soon as possible and to this end
I put a 'creep' (wooden partition) into each sty which prevented the sow from eating
their meal. This enabled the weaners to put on weight quickly and at 6 weeks they
were weighing 50lbs. I budgeted on selling the weaners for £8 which was the market
price when I started up. However when I took them to Stirling market I began to
learn that there was more to breeding pigs than feeding them; one had to be able to
sell them for the right price.

In the sale ring the weaners looked in good condition and well above the weight for their age but bidding was low compared to other lots and I could only get £5 for them. I found out afterwards that this was because I was unknown, a new boy to the trade and not in the circle. I could not helping thinking of the saying that was common amongst seamen which was indicative of their opinion of the treatment they received in their dealings with people on shore, "Here's a sailor, let's rob him."

When the time came for the second litters to be born the weather had become much colder and this was to have a considerable effect on the success of my project. There was no heating in the steading and although the farrowing was successful and I delivered 28 piglets, many died subsequently due to the intense cold although I took various measures to keep them warm.

It was obvious that the operation was far too small to ever become economically viable. All my capital had been used up and I still owed the builder for the work carried out on the steading so I decided to give up before I became deeper in debt.

When I wanted to sell the property Hendry, the lawyer, was too busy to see me and handed me over to his assistant. The price received was not sufficient to pay off the builder and the assistant could only advise me to go bankrupt.

I had Hendry's bill checked by another lawyer who said that he thought I had been overcharged. However he advised me not to query it as Hendry was also a director of the building firm and could make things awkward for me by pressing for immediate payment. I was told to say nothing to the builders about my situation but to send them something each week, whatever I could afford, towards their account and that would probably satisfy them. This I did for a couple of years until my father came to my assistance and paid off the balance. I think my father was rather disappointed when I decided to retire from the Navy although he understood my reasoning. He was more at a loss to understand why I did not want to return to the Merchant Navy as he realised, more than I did at the time, that the sea was the career I was best suited for.

Work was to start on the construction of a hydroelectric scheme which involved building a damn and a considerable amount of tunnelling and other operations in the surrounding area down to Loch Earn at St. Fillans. As this would lead to an influx of construction workers to the village and an increase in business, father asked me to join him in the hotel and take over the supervision of the bar, assist him in the kitchen, and generally try to learn all aspects of the business.

Before I joined him in the business at the beginning of 1952 father arranged for me to spend 6 months at the Fortingal Hotel, about 35 miles away at the head of Loch Tay, where there was a French kitchen. That is one in which the food was prepared, cooked and served with the various sauces and garnishes which were distinctive of the French style of cooking which was then considered to be the acme of *haute cuisine*. Although father was a skilled and very experiences French chef (he had been second chef to Escoffier who was considered to be the standard reference for all French cooking) the hotel was serving the traditional and more economic British fare which was common to the vast majority of small family hotels, and which did not require the full range of culinary skills which he wanted me to experience.

Mr. Heptinstall, the proprietor of Fortingall Hotel, was a well-known and highly respected chef and the hotel had an excellent reputation amongst gourmets for the high standard of cuisine.

Because of the nature of the dishes being served the meals were expensive – lunch was 12 shillings compared to five shillings in an ordinary hotel – and this could sometimes be quite a shock to people who stopped on the off-chance to have a meal and who did not appreciate the cuisine.

Mr. Heptinstall always took one or two trainees each season and seemed to work on the assumption that, if he took people with common sense and intelligence they would be able to follow his instructions and, with him keeping an eye on them, they would be just as useful as an experienced person who would have to be paid higher wages.

I was not entirely green when I started at Fortingall as I had picked up a certain amount of basic kitchen practice through watching my father over the years. Ever since I had been a small boy I had been in and out of his bakehouse and kitchen talking to him whilst he was at work, and often he had given me little tasks to do whilst I was standing around.

I worked from 6 a.m. to 9 p.m. seven days a week with a couple of hours off in the afternoon between clearing up after lunch and starting to prepare the dinner, and by the end of the season I knew what it was like to work day in and day out in the heat of a busy kitchen. I had quite enjoyed cooking but I had no real interest in food for itself and I think that at the back of my mind I was wondering if I could spend my life at it in the same way as my father had done.

When I went home and took over the bar I found it a bit of an ordeal. It seemed to me that when a regular customer wanted a change of scenery he would pick on the slightest excuse in order to be able to say he was going down the road and would not be back – this sometimes happened when he was refused a drink after hours. To me it all seemed so childish but I found there was more to being a barman than pouring beer out of a bottle into a glass. One had to be tolerant, patient, understanding and diplomatic, whilst at the same time ensuring that the bar was at all times run in a firm and orderly manner and that the customers knew who was in charge.

I took over the bar in the Royal Hotel at the end of the season in 1952 when business was rather quiet and there was only local trade to contend with. I managed quite well by myself (a part-time barman came in for the evenings) and I gradually began to learn the job and to appreciate the difficulties attached to it. One problem was always clearing the bar at closing time especially at night. To begin with when I shouted, "Time gentlemen please!", I expected everybody to stand up straight, right turn and march smartly out of the bar. I soon found that some of the customers would see how far they could go in trying to get just one more and that one had to be patient and tolerant yet firm in refusing to serve after hours.

Father had the bar re-designed and enlarged in preparation for the anticipated increase in business which would come with the hydro scheme. When the work was finished it was one of the most attractive hotel public bars in Perthshire. The walls were lined with light-oak panelling and fitted with a small shelf on which people could rest their glasses. Small tables and chairs were placed adjacent to the cushion-covered oak bench which formed the seating around the room. The bar counter, 18 feet in length, was of oak with a formica top and it had 3 beer taps at each end. A new type of plastic flooring was installed which was considered to be hard wearing and easy to clean. For optimum results it had to be cleaned with wire wool and I did this every Sunday morning when the bar was closed, it was quite a job as it involved over 3000 square feet. On other days, when the floor was not too dirty an ordinary mop sufficed.

When the hydro workers began to arrive I engaged a full-time barman Bob had been born in India, where his father had been a hairdresser, and educated at Boroughmuir School in Edinburgh. He had a second class qualification in Forestry but he was a bit of a wanderer and flitted from job to job. His last position had been at the Station Hotel in Perth so I contacted the manager to find out something about him. I was told that he was an excellent barman but to watch my stock! When I engaged him I paid him one pound over the going rate and gave him a half bottle of whisky on a Saturday night when he went off to the local dance when the bar was closed. These initial moves on my part seemed to have the desired effect as I had no problems with bar stock or shortage in the till. Bob turned out to be a good hand; he did not watch the clock and was very willing to lend a hand at whatever was required, whether or not it was within the job description of barman.

It became known that the hotel was primarily residential and that I would not permit any undue noise or rowdiness and this was the reason some chaps would move on during the course of the evening. I don't suppose I was a very popular mine host – I lacked the common touch – but I had the satisfaction of running a clean, well ordered bar serving a good drink and we had the major share of the trade in the village.

Father once told me that he thought my naval service, with very little contact with civilian life apart from social occasions, had tended to make me rather insular. I remember him saying that every minister should spend 6 months behind a bar to get down-to-earth knowledge of human nature, and I certainly found the experience to be an education in itself.

I found that dealing with a person who was maudlin or under the influence, especially if he was turning 'nasty,' required a lot of tact and diplomacy and I did not have the patience which was required, especially if the proceedings were drawn-out and the chap was uncooperative.

In 1954 I got married and the idea was that we should learn the business and eventually take over from father and mother when they decided to retire. However after about a year it became apparent that my continuing to be closely involved with my family in the business was having an effect on my marriage and this, combined with the realisation that I was not cut out to be a 'mine host' – especially in a bar – made me decide to move away and find another job.

In one way I was very sorry to leave. I had become much closer to my father whilst working alongside him and we had made up much of the time lost during the ten years I was in the Navy. We had managed to do many things together, we played golf, went curling and I accompanied him on different occasions to funerals or when visiting distant relatives and on business matters. Father was Master of the Lodge of Freemasons in the village and he put me through my four degrees which was an emotional experience for both of us. He was a keen and practising Mason throughout his life, as were both my grandfathers, and he truly lived by the Masonic creed.

I had been keeping an eye open in the newspapers for a suitable job and I was successful in obtaining a position as assistant contract manager in the Sheffield office of a large firm of industrial caterers.

The company I had joined, Peter Merchant Ltd., was at that time the largest firm of Industrial Caterers in the country operating approximately 800 canteens and restaurants in many varied industrial and business concerns. Peter Merchant had started off with a barrow which he took round building sites selling tea, sandwiches etc. and over the years, by hard work and initiative, he developed his small operation into a business which specialized in industrial catering during the time that the provision of canteen facilities in the work-place was becoming an accepted practice.

In each division a contract manager (the appointment of an assistant was a recent innovation) was responsible for new business, negotiating contracts, checking on client satisfaction by making regular visits to senior management and ensuring that any complaints were speedily rectified. The company advertised in all the top quality business and industrial publications; there was no door-knocking or cold calls and initial approach was always by letter at director level. Leads were often sent to us by head office but we had to carry out an extensive mail campaign from our own office and continually send follow-up letters to possible clients. The company postage bill ran into thousands of pounds.

The Sheffield office was responsible for an area stretching from Harrogate to Northampton and from Dewsbury on the Lancashire border across to Hull on the East coast. In 1955 Sheffield was a main centre for steel production and other heavy industries and, in consequence, it was a very dirty and unattractive city. It was a complete change from a Perthshire village but one has always to go where the work is to be found and as the saying goes "Where there's muck there's brass."

When making the initial visit to a client to view the premises and obtain the necessary information on which to base an estimate, a contract manager had to be very careful in carrying out his survey. The client would either be running the canteen himself and employing his own staff or he would have another firm of caterers. In both cases he would be anxious not to upset the existing staff by the knowledge that the catering was under review and we usually made our visit in the guise of being a personal friend or business associate of the director showing us around. A good deal of information was required: numbers using the canteen, variety of dishes, snacks etc., their prices and popularity, number of staff, hours of duty and wage rates, trolley and staff services, whether the work force lived close by and were able to go home at lunch-time were some of the things we had to find out and memorize. At the same time the lay-out of the kitchen and service facilities had to be noted along with the type and capacity of the equipment which was available.

After a routine visit to a client, which was more or less an exercise in early public relations, I had to make out a report and send it to head office with a copy to the group manager. A black report would indicate that the client was satisfied with our service whilst a red report would list itemised complaints or areas of dissatisfaction. In the event of a red report I was not allowed to visit the client until the complaint had been rectified and I had been notified by the group manager. So I had to do a certain amount of chasing up (which required a good deal of tact and diplomacy) in order to be able to return to the client as soon as possible and then report to head office that the problem had been dealt with to the client's satisfaction.

I had about seventy or eighty clients who had to be visited every three months which involved a good deal of travelling. This was probably the best part of the job as it got me out of the office and satisfied my wanderlust and I was able to see something of the country. It was also very interesting to visit firms engaged in different areas of industry and business and to sometimes be given the opportunity to see the work in progress.

At first sight it appeared to be a good job. £650 a year, car and meal expenses and first class accommodation when staying away from home. However at the end of the day there was really little job satisfaction and it seemed to me a waste of time and money to travel all the way from Sheffield to Norwich to spend 15 minutes chatting about this and that. Occasionally there would be a feeling of elation if I had managed to secure a lucrative contract, or if I had been successful in negotiating price or subsidy increases with a particularly difficult client but this did not occur very often.

After a year with the company I felt I was not achieving very much and, more important, there did not appear to be much of a future in the company. Many of the contracts were not financially viable but the company retained the clients for prestige purposes and this was beginning to cause a drain on the company's financial position. There was too much centralised control which meant increased administrative costs which had, in the end, to be borne by the clients and they were beginning to query the need for them. These together with several other factors gave me an uneasy feeling that there would eventually be drastic changes in the company structure and operational methods, and my fears subsequently proved to be well founded when the company was eventually taken over by one of our smaller competitors – Gardners Ltd.

It was during a visit to Dow-Mac at Stafford that the seeds were sown which eventually resulted in my returning to sea. My contact, Mr Lewis, who was a retired Wing Commander R.A.F. was a big rugby-playing type and an extremely nice person to talk to. Whilst we were chatting away he asked me what I was doing in such a job and why didn't I go back into the Navy. When I told him my reason for retiring (fleet reduction, etc.) he suggested I should try the R.A.F. Air Sea Rescue. The entry qualifications demanded a Master's Certificate of Competency and although I did not have one my naval service would entitle me to a Master's Certificate of Service. This was the same qualification with the exception that one could not command a Home Trade Passenger Ship. One would be able to command the *Queen Mary* but not a small ship of 2,000 tons plying between Leith and London. I believe this limitation was put on the certificate to prevent retired naval officers stealing these jobs from Merchant Navy officers. Mr Lewis was very friendly with the Group Captain in the R.A.F. who was then in charge of recruitment and suggested that I should write to him and make some enquiries.

The Board of Trade was extremely careful regarding the issue of Certificates of Service to ex-naval officers. To be eligible for a certificate an officer had to produce evidence of the exact amount of time he had spent at sea, and provide details of his duties on board each ship especially with regard to bridge watchkeeping, navigation and pilotage, and ship handling experience. Because of the amount of specialization in the navy and the many different jobs to which a naval officer could be appointed it did not follow that, because an officer had many years of service, he had the necessary sea-going experience to command, or carry out the duties of a deck officer in, a merchant ship. Needless to say the certificate was not looked upon with much favour by the shipping companies and the general opinion amongst Merchant Navy officers, who had to pass the difficult Board of Trade examination for a Certificate of Competency with its 75% pass mark, was that it was very handy for papering a wall.

The Admiralty attested to my sea-going appointments and this, together with my 'flimsies' (given to an officer by his commanding officer on leaving a ship or appointment and certifying to his conduct, ability, duties and performance) and record of service with the British India Company seemed to satisfy the authorities who gave me a Certificate of Service without more ado.

I did not go any further with regard to the Air-Sea Rescue but I had started to think about returning to sea. We were not very enamoured with Sheffield and the procedure regarding car expenses had been altered in such a way that it was no longer economical to run my big car. I had to sell it and buy a smaller one which upset out. finances with the result that we were not having much of a life. I noticed in the newspapers that the Caltex Oil Company required officers for its fleet of oil tankers and this gave me the idea of going back to sea for a year to get experience to sit for a Certificate of Competency as Master (Foreign Going). I hoped that this might assist me in obtaining a position ashore in the administrative side of the shipping industry. I did not visualise myself remaining at sea.

I sent off an application and subsequently attended for an interview in London. I was rather apprehensive as to how I would get on as I had been away from the sea for 6 years, I had no cargo experience and I was 33 years of age which might count against me in view of my lack of previous experience. It was fortunate that I held a Second Mate's Certificate of Competency as some shipping companies had a jaundiced view regarding ex-naval officers and I would at least be able to produce a B.O.T. qualification.

The interview with the manager of operations, Captain Pointon, went very well and I told him that whilst I was prepared to start at the bottom again I did not expect to stay there. I would be looking for early promotion subject to satisfactory reports from my commanders. Captain Pointon said that I would go to the top of the list of Third Officers as I would be the only one with a Master's Certificate, albeit only a Certificate of Service, but the company would want me to pass the examination for one of Competency after which I could expect quick promotion. I would be paid as holding a Master's Certificate which meant a few extra pounds a month. Leave was earned at the rate of 90 days after 12 months service at sea but this was commuted to 75 days with 15 days pay in lieu of the remaining 15 days. I was to find that this was the cause of some dissatisfaction as the 15 days pay had already been earned and there was no compensation for actually giving up the leave. I would also be entitled to 3 months leave whilst studying for the examination so all in all I could expect to be at home for about 6 months which would give me time to investigate the possibilities with regard to shore employment in the shipping industry.

I was sad and downcast at having to leave my family for such a long time and I tried to cheer myself up by reminding myself that it would only be for a year. As it happened things worked out very differently and it was only after a couple of years, when I accepted the fact that I would be remaining at sea, that I settled down and began to enjoy my new career.

Chapter 24

INTO THE TANKER TRADE

———

The Caltex Oil Company had been formed before the war by the Texas Oil Company (Texaco) and the Standard Oil Company of California (Socal), each company having a 50% holding. Texaco had large oil reserves and Socal had the marketing outlets, especially in Europe and the Far East, so that Caltex became a marketing subsidiary for both companies. Caltex also had an interest in the Bahrain Petroleum Company (Bapco) and Bahrain was the home port for the Caltex Fleets of Tankers when I joined the company in December 1956. At that time Caltex were operating four fleets under the British, Dutch, French and Panamanian Flags, the British company, Caltex Trading and Transport Company Ltd., having been formed in 1951/52.

During the war America had built a large fleet of oil tankers to supply the invasion forces during the anticipated final assault on the Japanese mainland. It was thought that this would be a very bloody affair and that, amongst other things, there would be severe losses of shipping during the operations. However with the dropping of the atomic bomb and the Japanese surrender the military assault was not required, and at the end of the war America had a fleet of approximately 500 oil tankers, many of which had never been used, and far in excess of her own requirements.

In the immediate post-war years there was a severe shortage of merchant shipping and the oil companies leased, bought or chartered these oil tankers from America whilst new ships were being constructed to their own designs and requirements. Newly formed companies also used the American ships which, in some cases, continued to form the back-bone of the company for many years. The Caltex fleet was started with these tankers and it was augmented in the years to follow by new building. In

1968/69 the Caltex fleets were divided up between the parent companies, Texaco and Socal (Chevron), the British fleet becoming part of the Texaco-International Fleets under the name Texaco Overseas Tankships Ltd.

These American war-time tankers were a considerable advance on the average pre-war tanker especially with regard to carrying capacity, propulsion machinery and cargo pumping arrangements. The American ships, which were known as T2s being turbo electric and fitted with electric centrifugal pumps, could carry 15,000 tons of cargo and discharge it at a faster rate compared to the pre-war ship of 8,000 tons with its steam up and down pumps. Having a small merchant fleet in relation to the size of the country the United States was short of an adequate supply of trained and experienced seamen for the rapid expansion of shipping which took place when the country entered the war. The tankers were designed to be operated by quickly trained and relatively inexperienced personnel. This was especially true of the engine-room where auxiliary machinery, pumps etc. were duplicated so that if one item malfunctioned another would automatically cut in without any breakdown in the engine's performance.

In the wheel-house on the bridge there were large posters and diagrams showing the various lights and shapes to be displayed, and the Signals to be sounded and illustrating the action to be taken, in various situations. At first sight this appeared to be an insult to a professional seaman, but when one considers how little training many of the officers must have had when the ships were first put into service it was only common sense to have the basic rules on display which could be referred to by anyone who was at all in doubt. There was one other important departure from the design of pre-war merchant ships and that was in the officers' accommodation. The cabins were fitted with adjoining toilets and showers instead of the traditional communal bathrooms, and there was a smoking room/lounge for the officers to use instead of having to meet in each other's cabins where people would be crammed together sitting on a bunk and any available space.

The ships, which were named after towns and cities, were manned by Indian seamen recruited in Bombay. The various companies employing Indian seamen had their own pools of men from which the crews were made up by their local personnel manager. This was a complete departure from the traditional system whereby deck and engine-room serangs (boatswains) selected their own men, often from their own villages, with the result that the senior ratings did not have the same power and influence over their men as had been the case when I first served with Indian crews some 17 years earlier.

I noticed that changes had taken place in their life-style during the intervening period and this was to continue during the next 25 years that I was with them. They had become more westernized in their dress and eating habits; they took their meals separately in a mess-room instead of all sitting around, and helping themselves from, a communal tray on deck. More of the sailors spoke English so that there was not the same need, or requirement, for officers to learn to speak Hindustani as there had been in BI and they would go ashore by themselves instead of in a crocodile led by the serang who paid for all their purchases. At one time pedal sewing machines were much sought after by Indian families and the sailors tried to obtain them to take home to their wives and mothers. Over the years this gave way to the purchase of more sophisticated goods such as radios, tape recorders, cameras, etc. which they would sell on their return to India.

I was very pleased to be serving with Indian seamen again. I had always admired the loyal and valuable service they had given to British shipping for nearly 150 years and during two world wars. Some people preferred white crews being of the opinion that Indian seamen were less efficient and had a lower work rate and output. It was my experience as Chief Officer, and subsequently Master, that they never failed to respond in a willing manner when called upon to turn out unexpectedly and/or work long hours when the occasion arose, and that one could always rely on them to do their best. They certainly never ever let me down.

There was one occasion which may serve to illustrate the mistaken impression some people had of Indian seamen. I was Chief Officer of the Texaco *Plymouth* during 1966/67 and for about 10 months I had been carrying out a comprehensive maintenance programme aimed at bringing the ship up to a high standard of appearance and condition. The programme had just been completed when we received orders to take a cargo to Boston, Mass. in the United States. It was the first time the *Plymouth*, which was only six years old and one of the biggest ships in the company, had visited America and as many of the senior management had never seen the ship several of them came up to Boston from Head Office in New York to have a look over her.

I was very proud of the ship as we entered Boston harbour on the Saturday morning. She looked a picture; I had been blessed with good weather for a few months and all the paintwork was bright and free of rust stains, cargo tank valve wheels were brightly painted in their various colours and steam pipes were bright with silver paint. As the electrician remarked, "She looks like Codona's circus." The crew accommodation and other interior spaces had been painted recently and, as usual, were clean and tidy. As we steamed up the channel we passed an outward bound Gulf Oil tanker which was a veritable rust bucket and the comparison must have been a good advertisement for Texaco to the many yachts and pleasure craft which were in the vicinity, and which came even closer to have a look at our ship.

I did not have the pleasure of showing the visitors around when they boarded the ship on arrival as I was busily occupied with starting the cargo and other matters and it was left to the Chief Engineer to do the honours. However I met them just before they left and, after congratulating me on the condition of the ship, one of them remarked that they never knew that an Indian crew could keep a ship to such a high standard. It was this sort of remark that used to upset me. I told him that with the right leadership and encouragement the Indian seamen were as good as, and often better than, those of other nationalities.

Finally, at Whangarei, the oil terminal in New Zealand, where the crew accommodation, galleys and toilets of visiting vessels were always thoroughly inspected by the Port Health Authority, the *Texaco Southampton*, of which I was assigned Master for 7 years, received many commendations, and on one occasion the official remarked that she was the cleanest vessel he had seen for three years. When remarks like this were conveyed to the crew their pride and pleasure were evident, and it was always nice to be able to let them know that their efforts had been noted and appreciated by others.

The officers had been drawn from every corner of the Merchant Navy. Being a new and rapidly expanding company many had left old, established companies in order to find quicker promotion, others like myself, had been ashore for a spell and had returned to sea for one reason or another, whilst some had been dismissed by their previous employers. During the first five or six years promotion had been quite rapid as more ships joined the fleet and when I joined the company Chief Officers were expecting to be promoted to Master after only four years in the rank. This was a considerable difference to pre-war practice in the larger companies when the average time spent in each rank from 2nd Mate to Master was 10 years and very few men reached the position of Master before the age of 45. There had been a considerable sorting out of personnel during the initial years and I heard many entertaining stories of some of the characters who had joined the company, and who had gone up, up, and out for various reasons. For some time after I joined there continued to be a steady turnover of mainly junior personnel who were always looking for greener pastures, and who left to join companies where it was rumoured that there were better conditions of service and prospects of promotion.

Because the officers had served in a variety of companies, each of which had its own way of doing things, standards varied from ship to ship depending on the background of the senior deck and engineer officers. This variation of standards was poor training for the initial entry of deck and engine cadets in the first few years of the company being established and, to my mind, some of the senior officers set a very bad example to their juniors in their manners, conduct and general approach to their responsibilities. After my experience of BI, the Orient Line and the Navy I found it all very strange and disconcerting and for the first two or three years I was not very happy in my new surroundings.

However, I began to enjoy my new occupation. I had plenty of experience of bridge watchkeeping duties, navigation and pilotage, general seamanship and ship maintenance, but tanker operations were completely new to me and there was a great deal to learn, especially if I wanted early promotion. I had to become familiar with pipe-line systems, the location and purpose of valves in the tanks and pumproom, methods of loading and discharging cargo and ballast, and how to operate pumps in order to obtain the maximum discharge rate. There was also much to learn about the different types of petroleum products that were carried. The order of loading and discharging different products or grades in order to avoid contamination, precautions which had to be taken when loading kerosine in order to prevent static build-up in the tanks and possible explosion and the precautions necessary when loading high sulphur crude oil which was extremely toxic, were only a few of the things I had to learn about my new trade.

Then there was the preparation of the tanks to receive cargo; the general operation of tank cleaning. The amount of cleaning required for each product to be carried, the cycle of the tank-washing (Butterworth) machines and the amount of scaling and sludge lifting that was required was another area of operations which had to be, mastered. Above all I had to learn and remember the myriad of safety procedures and practices which had to be observed in every phase of tanker operations. No matter how efficient or conscientious personnel might be there was always the possibility of forgetfulness, carelessness, complacency or cutting corners and I soon found out that, for peace of mind, one had to be a bit of an old woman and check, check and double check, and encourage others to do the same, in order to ensure a safe operation. It was on the job training and it was on my third trip when I was promoted to Chief Officer and I was responsible for all cargo, ballasting and deck maintenance operations that I really started to learn the trade.

I had never been mechanically minded and it was a bit of a shock to discover that the deck officers were responsible for the pumproom and for controlling the pumps during pumping operations. In old established companies such as BP and Shell this had been the responsibility of the Engine Department; the Chief Officer deciding which tanks were to be discharged and the Chief Engineer lining up the pumproom accordingly. Deck officers were only responsible for the control and operation of the cargo tank valves. The steam reciprocal pumps were able to pump a mixture of air and product and a tank could be stripped dry without damaging the pump before switching over to a full tank. I was given to believe that the deck officers being responsible for the pumproom and cargo discharge was an American innovation brought about by the advent of the new steam, and electrical, centrifugal pumps with their greater pumping capacity. These pumps quickly lost suction if air got into them and they were easily damaged if starved of product. It was therefore important that they be closely monitored and controlled, especially when two or more pumps were working in tandem. As the quantity of product in the tanks decreased this required bleeding from full tanks in order to maintain a full flow to the pumps, whilst at the same time maintaining suction on the nearly empty tanks without allowing air to get into the suction line and thence into the pumps.

The ships in the fleet were engaged in what might be called three trades. The black oil ships carried crude oil to refineries in various parts of the world, and also fuel oil. Refined products such as gasoline, diesel oil, aviation fuel and kerosine were carried in the white oil ships, whilst lubricating oils were carried in four smaller tankers which had been specially built for these products.

When I joined the company the majority of the fleet was engaged in the carriage of refined products from the BAPCO refinery in Bahrain (cargoes were also loaded at the BP refineries at Abadan in Iran and Fao in Iraq) to Caltex terminals in countries around the world which did not have refining facilities. In the years to come Caltex, and then Texaco, established refineries in the UK, South Africa, Australia, New Zealand, India, Kenya and other emerging nations so that the white oil trade gradually diminished and the carriage of crude oil increased. Concurrent with this change in trading pattern was the advent of the super-tanker of 60,000 tons which could replace four normal size vessels, and subsequently the VLCC (Very Large Crude Carrier) which ranged from 100,000 to over 250,000 tons and led to a reduction in the number of ships required in the fleet.

Chapter 25

SS *CALTEX WELLINGTON*

———

I joined the Caltex Wellington in Bahrain on 14th January 1957. There were several other people joining at the same time and we travelled out by BOAC in an Argonaut aircraft, one of the early post-war four engined airliners which had a maximum speed of about 280 mph but which were extremely reliable and reputed to be able to fly on one engine. There were more modern aircraft in service at the time and the Argonaut was referred to as the steam eagle. Air travel was still very much a novelty to most people (I had only been up three times before) including the cabin staff who were very enthusiastic in going about their duties in what was still a relatively new occupation. One noticed as the years went on and air travel became more commonplace that, although the standard of service was maintained and in some ways raised, the camaraderie between passengers and crew –resulting from the feeling that they were all taking part in something new – was never the same. This was no doubt due to both the occupation and mode of travel becoming more mundane and larger aircraft making personal attention more difficult.

As the ship arrived alongside the oil jetty where we were standing awaiting her arrival, the first thing I noticed about oil tankers was that there was no respite for the crew on arrival in port. There was a good deal of activity on deck as sailors prepared to connect up cargo hoses, operated valves for the discharge of ballast, prepared to land laundry and take on board stores. As soon as we had boarded, the relieving personnel started immediately to take over from those being relieved. It was a short hand-over as the agent was already standing by to take those leaving the ship to a hotel to await the flight home. It did not take long for the chap I was relieving to show me around the bridge and hand-over the couple of books that held the inventories of the signalling equipment and lifeboat equipment for which, as 3rd Officer, I would be responsible.

The Master, Captain High, had been a Master in the Esso Lake Fleet of small tankers operating in Lake Maracaibo, and he was running a battery charging business before returning to sea with Caltex. The Chief Officer had also served in the Lake Fleet as Master before joining Caltex. He suffered from the opposite complaint to insomnia, he could not stay awake, and my first impression was that he was a very poor type of officer. This was confirmed when I reported to him that men working overside were not using safety lines, only to receive the reply that I was not in the Navy now! He was eventually relieved after a couple of months and left the company. This was the first of many reminders in my early days that things were done differently to the Navy and, I may add, not always with the best results.

The Junior Chief Officer had been Chief Officer of a large modern tanker, the *Golden Arrow*, and had left her to sit for the Extra Master's Certificate, a very difficult examination and a qualification which was held by few people. He had passed half the examination and had come away in a less responsible position in order to devote more time to study. He was a nice chap, if a trifle facetious, and he gave me a lot of assistance with my own studies. The Second Officer was an older chap with a somewhat chequered career if one could believe his story. After leaving Dartmouth he joined the RAF to train as a pilot but in the middle of his training he had to leave on medical grounds. He then joined the Royal Fleet Auxiliary (tankers owned by the Admiralty but chartered on commercial voyages when not required for Fleet duties) and sailed in them during the shipping slump in the Thirties, when some ships were fully manned by men with Master's or Chief Engineer's Certificates. He too was a nice chap but inclined to drink too much at times. He had trouble reading his sextant when we were taking sights at noon and would always agree with our readings without declaring his own. He too left the company shortly afterwards.

The *Wellington* was a black oil ship engaged in carrying crude oil from Bandar Mashur in Iran, at the north end of the Arabian Gulf to Bahrain. It was not a popular run as the round trip took only three or four days and there was little time between ports to carry out essential deck and engine maintenance and other departmental work. There was no time to relax, either at sea or in port, and everybody was rather depressed at the thought of being on the run for some time to come. Fortunately an incident occurred during the second trip after I had joined which took us off the run and resulted in a variety of interesting voyages during the following 12 months.

Whilst leaving the berth at Bandar Mashur the rudder was damaged, with the result that the ship had to be towed back to Bahrain where the tow was transferred to a company vessel, the *Caltex Dublin*, which continued the tow to Bombay for repairs. It was decided to carry out the annual docking and repair period concurrent with the rudder repairs so that our stay in Bombay lasted for four or five weeks.

SS Caltex Wellington

I had never visited Bombay but unfortunately I was not in a position to do any sight-seeing or have many runs ashore. My main aim was to save money, so that recreation was limited to visits to the Marine Club for a game of snooker and the odd walk into town when, on one occasion, I had tea in the Taj Mahal Hotel. Bombay was dry at this time and the only way one could obtain alcohol was to have a medical certificate. In the Marine Club it was rather amusing to see tough seamen of various nationalities sitting morosely over their soft drinks and no doubt longing for a long, cold beer.

The Chief Officer was relieved in Bombay and his relief was a different type of chap altogether and turned out to be a most hard working and efficient officer. Mr. Dewar came from Helensburgh where his father was a tailor. The family home had at one time belonged to Bell who built the *Comet*, the first steamship on the Clyde, and the house still contained the brass handrail of the engine-room ladder. He had served his apprenticeship with the Anchor Line, a well-known Glasgow company engaged in the transatlantic cargo/passenger trade.

Mr. Dewar set a good example of the style of leadership which would encourage the sailors to give their best performance. With four deck officers the Chief Officer did not keep a bridge watch so he was able to be on deck all day supervising, and often taking part in, the work in hand and it was quite common to see him squatting down and chipping the deck with a hand hammer along with the rest of the crew. Needless to say this was not expected or required of an officer, especially a senior one, but he enjoyed the physical work and an extra hand was always appreciated and helped to expedite the work. He was a few years older than myself and we became good friends and I learned a great deal about tanker practice from him. I tried to follow his example when I became Chief Officer although in my case it meant putting in over twelve hours on a normal day as I eventually had to keep the 4 to 8 bridge watch in the morning and evening. However I did not mind as I enjoyed the work and my responsibilities and I obtained considerable satisfaction from ensuring that various tasks and operations were carried out safely and efficiently.

From Bombay we returned to Bahrain to load for our next voyage which turned out to be to Port Swettenham in Malaya. This was rather fortunate as there was the possibility that I might be able to see my sister Chris and her family who were living on a rubber estate at Sungei Buloh to the north of Port Swettenham.

The ship arrived in Port Swettenham on Merdeka Day (Freedom Day) when British rule came to and end and Malaya became independent. To celebrate the occasion we had to dress ship which meant running a string of flags from the bow up to the foremast head, then along to the mainmast head and down to the stem. Very few people had seen it done before so I showed them how to do it 'Navy Fashion.' The flags were clipped together in three sections, there were plenty on board as we carried the flags of many countries in addition to the usual signalling flags, and down-hauls were rigged to each masthead and attached to each section of flags which were laid out on deck. Sailors were stationed at each down-haul and at other places along the deck to ensure the flags did not catch on any obstruction and that each section went up smoothly at the same time. Although it was new to the sailors they soon got the hang of what was required of them and when I gave the order, "Hoist", I was very pleased with the result. Each section reached the mastheads at the same time and, although it might possibly have been done more quickly, the operation went smoothly and there were no snags.

Mr. Dewar said he would cover my watch for me and, with Captain's permission to go ashore and stay until the following morning, I was able to go with Chris to her home at the Rubber Research Institute plantation where her husband, Teddy, was the assistant manager. Teddy took me around the estate and I saw the rubber being tapped from the trees and the work being done in clearing the surrounding forest for further planting. I also got a first hand view of the type of conditions I had read about in accounts of the war in Malaya and Burma, and I could better appreciate the difficulties that had faced our soldiers when they were fighting the terrorists in Malaya prior to independence.

There was a large leper colony near the estate and Chris took me to visit the doctor in charge who was a friend from our childhood days in Troon. I was introduced to a gentleman who had been a barrister in Singapore and who was a former pupil of the Royal High School. The patients, in spite of their terrible disfigurements, all appeared in good spirits and positive, and I came away thinking that if I was ever ill and felt pain in the future I should remember this colony and realize I had little to complain about.

After a further trip to Port Swettenham we went to Japan calling first at Kudumatsu, a port in the inland sea, before going to Osaka for engine repairs. My first contact with the Japanese people left me a trifle perplexed. Although the war had been over for 12 years I was still acutely aware of the atrocities which had occurred during the fighting and of the tortures and hard treatment which had been inflicted on our prisoners of war. It was difficult to associate these actions with the seemingly mild, polite and industrious workmen who came on board to carry out the repairs. Ashore many of the women wore the traditional Japanese dress in which they appeared shy, demure and totally feminine and it was hard to believe that they were the same people whose men-folk had such an evil reputation.

I soon realise that there were many things that we could learn from the Japanese and that they were ahead of us in many ways. The wash-rooms and toilets provided for ships' crews were tiled throughout and spotlessly clean with showers and sunken baths, and well heated with a constant supply of hot water. In the UK dockyard toilets and wash-rooms were invariably cold, dingy, dirty and uninviting with an uncertain supply of hot water and one was loath to use them. In Japan workmen bathed and changed out of their working clothes at the end of the day before going home, whereas in Govan and Clydebank, for example, the men went home in their working clothes which continually dirtied the seats of the tramcars, with the result that other passengers' clothes became soiled. In common with most other countries the Japanese ship-yard officials were quite happy for the ship's staff to carry out other items of maintenance and repair concurrent with the work being done by the yard. It was a different matter in the UK where the trade unions insisted that all work of whatever description had to be carried out by shore workmen. This stipulation meant that ship's staff were idle and unproductive whilst in the yard and thus uneconomic, and many companies preferred to send their ships to other countries rather than put up with the restrictions imposed by British yards. Over a period of time this was a factor in the decline of the shipyard industry.

I had always wanted to visit Australia having met so many Aussies during the war, so I was delighted when the next voyage was to Botany Bay with a cargo of crude oil for the new Caltex refinery. I liked the long trips – the round voyage would take about six weeks – as they enabled me to get down to a regular routine of study for the Master's examination. I was off watch from noon to 8 p.m. and I put in several hours every day.

At that time the route from the Gulf to Botany Bay was normally via Ceylon, the Malacca Straits, The Java Sea, Thursday Island and the Great Barrier Reef. It was about 300 miles longer than the route across the Indian Ocean to Cape Leeuwin and round the southern part of Australia but the extra fuel consumption and the time involved was compensated for by the amount of shipboard maintenance that could be carried out in the fine weather, and the avoidance of possible storm damage in the heavy weather that was generally experienced in the Australian Bight. It was more economic to purchase provisions in Singapore than in Australia where prices were much higher, and it became the practice when passing Singapore for a barge to rendezvous with the ship and for the stores to be loaded whilst the ship continued at slow speed.

With the advent of bigger, deep-draughted vessels which could not navigate the shallow waters at the northern end of the Barrier Reef, south about became the normal route in loaded condition. Masters were given the choice of route for the return ballast passage but they were expected to proceed south about unless there was a requirement to call at Singapore.

The passage through the Malacca and Singapore Straits, past the islands off the south-east coast of Sumatra and along the north coast of Java was very picturesque. After leaving the Singapore Strait the route lay south through the Gaspar Strait and into the Java Sea. In the early 19th century these waters had been swarming with Chinese and Malay pirates whose junks and proas, under long sweeps, would surprise a vessel in a calm at night or a vessel which may have run aground. Although the vessels might be armed the crew would eventually be overcome by sheer weight of numbers and, after being looted of all valuables, the ship would be burned scuttled and sunk. 'Dead men tell no tales!' The tea clippers passed through these waters when using the Sunda Strait on their passage to and from China. Although the attacks by fleets of pirate vessels had diminished by the eighteen sixties, the heyday of the clipper ships, piracy was still very common and the crews had to take precautions and continually be on guard against surprise attack. Most of the clipper ships were armed with two or three small iron guns which were loaded with canister and grape and most effective against crowded proas. They had a supply of muskets, pistols, cutlasses and pikes; it was also standard practice to keep a supply of boiling water on the galley stove ready to repel boarders. The greatest risk of piracy occurred in restricted waters when the wind came ahead and a ship had to anchor, sometimes in deep water and sometimes close to the shore and the pirates' nests, in order to save herself from being swept back, or shorewards, by the strong currents.

The coast of Java and the islands of Indonesia were heavily wooded from the mountain peaks to the water's edge and at night I could see the ribbons of fire on the mountain sides which were the result of lava erupting from the active volcanoes in the region. I saw my first south sea island schooner in the Java Sea. The small, white vessel with its white sail looked quite romantic when seen from a distance and in a tropical setting, and it appeared to be similar to the ones I had seen in films or I had read about in adventure stories. However as we drew nearer and I was able to get a better view my romantic notions were soon dispelled. Instead of being clean and tidy with clear decks and everything ship-shape, the craft was loaded with what appeared to be copra and it was extremely dirty and in a poor state of repair.

From the Java Sea the passage continued through the Flores Sea and the islands between Indonesia and New Guinea to Thursday Island off the North-East point of Australia. At one time Thursday Island had been the centre of a thriving pearl fishing industry and the natives were a mixture of the various races who had arrived over the years to become pearl divers.

Thursday Island was the Pilot Station for the pilots who guided the ships through the reefs which barred the entrance to the Coral Sea and the Pacific Ocean, and also through the channels of the Great Barrier Reef which runs some 1,500 miles along the north-east coast of Australia to Fraser Island north of Brisbane. My first trip down the Barrier Reef was a most interesting experience both from the scenic and navigation points of view. The initial stage of the route south lay close to Cape York peninsula and, with never a ship in sight, the bleak sandhills and surrounding scrub land only served to illustrate the sense of loneliness and isolation which pervaded the area. Further south the land rose gradually to form the mountains around the more populated area of Cairns and Townsville. As we passed through Whitsunday Passage between a group of islands a 'Bon Voyage' signal was hoisted at a lighthouse. It was the practice for the keeper's family to make a signal to passing ships which were a welcome sight in their isolated environment. The children received their early education over the schools radio service but they eventually reached an age when they had to stay on the mainland and attend school in the normal manner.

The Torres Straits pilot service was a private company owned by the pilots and licensed by the Queensland government. The pilots served the ships running between the ports on the Barrier Reef – Brisbane, Gladstohe, Townsville and Cairns – joining at Sydney or Brisbane for the north-bound passage. The pilots had all been shipmasters and had made many passages up and down the reef in command of their own ships before joining the company. It was a very good, if responsible, job for anyone interested in the skills and practices involved in navigating in restricted and confined waters and there was also the attraction of frequent, if sometimes short, periods at home depending on the rota.

From the outset I was very interested in the possibility of one day being a pilot and I subsequently kept a record of all my trips up and down the reef and tried to learn as much as I could from the various pilots. There were very few lights or navigation marks, some of the reefs were marked by beacons but many had only a clump of mangrove to indicate their positions, and there were others which lay just under the surface and whose presence was only made known when there was a sea running and the water was disturbed. However, by the time I had completed ten trips up and down the reef I had become Chief Officer and established in the company and I realised that becoming a pilot was not a practical proposition.

Steaming into Botany Bay for the first time was another memorable experience. The terminal jetty was just around the corner on the port side of the narrow entrance and only a few hundred yards from the spot where Captain Cook had first stepped ashore. There was a monument situated in the small park which had been laid out to commemorate the event. Once again I was able to let my imagination take free reign and visualize the scenes which must have taken place when the first convict ships arrived in 1788.

As soon as the ship had berthed everyone was caught up in the busy arrival routine that I was to come to know so well in the future especially as Chief Officer and Master. The first person to board was the Port Medical Officer who had to examine everyone on board before anyone could come on board or go ashore. As it was important that there should be the minimum delay between arrival and the start of the cargo discharge the Chief officer was kept busy chasing up people who were dilatory in arriving for examination whilst, at the same time, organizing the shipboard preparations for discharge. During this time the jetty personnel and other officials, ship chandlers and repair people were all waiting impatiently to come on board to carry out their various duties and business. I could not help comparing the whole arrival procedure with that of a naval ship when it arrived in port. There the most important matter to be dealt with was the amount of leave that should be granted to the ship's company.

Several of the jetty operators and supervisors had emigrated from the UK after the war and had served in the Forces. One chap had been a Sergeant in the Royal Marines and another had been a Stoker in *Cassandra* when she was torpedoed off the North Cape and *Tavy* had escorted her back to Murmansk. Over the years I was to make good friends amongst the operators and agents and I always looked forward to meeting them at the end of a long trip, and to hearing news of ships and colleagues who had called at the port since my last visit. It was much the same in Singapore and other places which were regular ports of call for company ships and I came to know various agents, ship chandlers and other people involved in the ship's operations and requirements very well. I always had the feeling I was meeting old friends again when they came on board, especially if I had not seen them for some time.

The remainder of my time on the *Wellington* (in the MN one serves on a ship, in the RN one serves in a ship) was taken up with voyages to Aden, Djibouti, Mombassa and finally a voyage to Swansea where I was relieved after 13 months to go on leave.

The passage through the Suez Canal was my first visit to the area for nearly 14 years and many changes had been made since Nasser had nationalized the canal in 1956. At that time it was thought that the Egyptians would not be able to operate the canal and that they would have difficulty in finding pilots from amongst their own people to replace the mainly British and French pilots who were leaving because they would not be able to send their money out of the country. It had been the usual practice for ships to proceed singly through the canal after arrival at Port Said or Suez, stopping and making fast to the canal bank as required to allow traffic to pass in the opposite direction. The Egyptian authorities replaced this method of operating with a convoy system whereby one north-bound convoy left Suez each morning and two south-bound convoys left Port Said, one in the morning and the other in the evening. The operation was so timed that the convoys would pass each other in the Great Bitter Lakes.

Pilots of all nationalities were recruited to take the place of the pilots who had left and to keep the service running whilst Egyptian pilots were being trained. Eventually all the pilots were Egyptian nationals and, as the job was looked upon as being of national importance, they were not allowed to leave the service of their own accord. It was generally accepted that the Egyptians operated the canal much more efficiently than the old Suez Canal Company which had been controlled by the British and the French.

As I passed through Port Said harbour after the canal transit there was still evidence of the fighting that had taken place a year earlier and it was particularly sad to see the remains of the statue of De Lesseps (who built the canal) which had been tom down by the mob when the canal was nationalized. As we passed Navy House, the ferry across to Port Fouad, the site of the Officers Club and other familiar places my thoughts went back to the war years and the many happy times I had enjoyed in the port.

As usual the reliefs were waiting on the jetty when the ship arrived in Swansea and, as I had been away for 13 months, I did not waste any time in handing over to the new Third Officer. I did not know it at the time but, in a few months, I was to meet him again as a shipmate.

Chapter 26

UPS AND DOWNS

———

In February 1958 I enrolled at the Nautical School in Aberdeen to prepare for the Master's examination. I was entitled to three months paid study leave in addition to the normal service leave of 75 days so I would have time in hand if I failed at the first attempt and had to re-sit at a future date.

Once again it was a case of attending the school during the day and putting in two or three hours work at night. So much depended on my getting the Certificate and at 35 years of age studying did not come easy, it was very much a case of cramming in order to pass first time. I sat the examination at the beginning of June and passed the signals and written examination although I had a slight moment of panic over the latter. Returning to the school from the examination centre we were comparing answers to the paper on magnetism and compass deviation and correction. I found that whilst I had the same answer as the other chaps I may have failed to read the question correctly, as I could not remember seeing a figure in the question that was necessary to carry out the calculation. The instructor tried to put my mind at ease by telling me that I had made a mistake in my answer to the way I had read the question but that my answer was correct for the way the question had been written. All very involved.

However I was convinced I had made a mess of it and went back to school at the beginning of the following week to continue working for the next examination. On the Monday, at the end of the day's work, we were discussing the examination and our possible results with Captain Mackay, our instructor. Without saying anything he left the room and returned shortly afterwards holding a piece of paper. He said he had just telephoned to try and get the results to put us out of our misery. He read out the first two names and then, looking at me directly, he said, "Stewart, passed." I got the surprise of my life and the books went up in the air. I felt a great sense of relief as I had been sure I would have to re-sit the whole examination. When I passed the oral part of the examination my joy was complete and I subsequently received my Master's Certificate.

Certificate of a Master Mariner

At the end of my leave in August I was re-appointed to the *Wellington*, this time as Second Officer, joining the ship at Killingholme, near Hull. The Master, who was only a few years older than myself, was newly promoted having assumed command when I left to go on leave. He was a popular chap but he was irresponsible and lacked imagination, at least as far as navigation was concerned. I soon found out that he was rather fond of breaking the boredom by going close inshore to view the scenery. We took a short cut through a narrow passage subjected to strong tides and currents when leaving the Channel, and when passing through the Straits of Hormuz into the Arabian Gulf we went through the Gap, a very narrow passage between a large off-shore rock and the mainland instead of using the normal route. There was nothing inherently difficult about taking a ship through these narrow channels provided everything went according to plan. However, if there was an engine breakdown, a failure of the steering gear, compass or other equipment the ship could be in serious danger with no room to manoeuvre and little time to effect repairs. The *Wellington* was an old ship, as were all the T2s, and it was only commonsense, apart from good seamanship, to keep off the land and avoid all possible hazards when it was possible to do so. In my mind I reckoned that before the year was out he would find himself in trouble and, sadly, my fears were eventually confirmed.

I was glad to leave the ship when we arrived at Singapore a few weeks later and I found that I was to transfer to the *Bombay* with promotion to Junior Chief Officer. I was more than pleased when I found that I would be sailing once again with Mr. Dewar who had joined the ship after his leave. About a month later we were listening to the news and heard that a tanker had broken down whilst passing through the Suez Canal and that traffic had been disrupted for some time. Sure enough it was the *Wellington* and she eventually came to grief when she ran aground on a shoal in the Arabian Gulf a few months later. It was a navigational mistake on the part of the Officer of the Watch but Captain Maclean had to accept the final responsibility. He performed so well in getting the ship back to Bahrain that the company decided that demotion to Chief Officer would suffice instead of the normal instant dismissal. However Maclean took exception to this relatively light punishment and left the company. I often wondered if he went back to making lead soldiers in his gas cooker which was his occupation before he decided to return to sea and joined Caltex.

I had only been on board the *Bombay* for about three months when I was paid off sick in Sydney with stomach trouble which turned out to be a duodenal ulcer. I left the ship a couple of days before Christmas and spent the next six weeks in a private nursing home in Sydney. I had a room to myself and seldom saw, let alone spoke to, other patients unless a door was open and I happened to glance in as I went to and from the bathroom. There was no reading material available and my sole means of passing the time was reading the daily paper from cover to cover and listening to a small radio which was loaned to me by one of the nurses. The England cricket team were in Australia for the Ashes and I heard every ball of three Test Matches as I listened to the commentary on the radio. The marine manager of the terminal came up to see how I was getting on and I had a couple of visits from the agent, but apart from that I had no other visitors and I finished up speaking back to the radio. It was all very boring but the rest in bed and the diet did the trick and the ulcer disappeared. We were allowed three months paid sick leave a year so I was sent back to the UK to convalesce and be examined by the company doctor.

The flight from Sydney to London took sixty hours stopping at nine places enroute. At each stop passengers left the aircraft to stretch their legs and were given free refreshments by the airline – first class passengers were given a choice of spirits or soft drinks whilst economy class were restricted to soft drinks only. I was travelling first class and I found that the chap sitting next to me was a Sergeant in the Royal Marines from HMS Albion (a commando carrier) in civvies and going home on compassionate leave. He was able to give me news of my school friend, Doc Wilder, whom I had last seen in Malta some 10 years previously when he was attached to a Marine Commando. He was now PM0 (Principal Medical Officer) in the *Albion*.

On arrival in London I was met by a chauffeur-driven limousine and taken to the Rembrandt Hotel in Knightsbridge where a reservation had been made in case I did not feel up to travelling that night. In the event that I was able to continue to Aberdeen the head waiter had been instructed to prepare hot milk to sustain, me on my journey. Caltex, and later Texaco, spared no expense in looking after the health and welfare of their employees.

At the end of my sick leave I had to undergo a company medical examination to be passed fit for sea-going. The specialist told me that the ulcer had responded to treatment but advised me to give up the sea, even if it meant a drop in income, as the ulcer could possibly recur if I was subjected to stress which seemed unavoidable in my present profession. I was really alarmed at this suggestion and at the thought that he might not pass me fit to return to sea. At my age and with my commitments and responsibilities, it would have been extremely difficult to take a drop in income whilst starting in a new career. I explained my situation to the doctor who calmed my fears by saying that, at present, I was perfectly fit for sea-going duties; he was only giving me his advice and it was up to me to make my own decision.

Chapter 27

LIFE AS A CHIEF OFFICER

––––

In 1960 I was promoted to Chief Officer and joined the *Caltex Adelaide*. As there were four deck officers the Chief Officer did not keep a bridge watch but was employed on day-work and had all night in which was one of the items which had attracted me to the Company. However I had only been a year in the rank when the complement was reduced to the normal level of three officers and I was back to watchkeeping.

A Chief Officer put in a long day; never less than 12 hours and often anything up to 18 or 20 hours when loading, discharging or tank cleaning. There was a good deal of paper work involved – inventories, work records, defect lists, cargo plans, medical log, etc. which I preferred to do in the evenings after I had come off watch. This left me free to get around the ship during the day and give closer supervision to the work in hand. I enjoyed my work and my aim was to get my ship looking as smart and tiddley as possible but this could be a very frustrating process. One would arrive in port after a loaded passage with the decks and fittings looking smart and well painted, only to have the whole effect nullified on the return ballast passage by the dirt, oil and grease, and mechanical damage resulting from the tank cleaning and sludge lifting operations.

Up to this time I had served exclusively in ships engaged in the black oil trade where the handling of homogeneous cargo was fairly straight forward, but henceforth, for the next few years, I was in white oil ships carrying several different grades of petroleum products which I found to be a much more interesting trade. Great care had to be taken to ensure that there was no contamination between the different products whilst loading, discharging, and in transit, and the condition of the war-time T2s, by this time 17 years old, presented many problems. Due to corrosion over the years the bulkheads between the tanks were very thin and their integrity was affected by many corrosion holes and fractures which made it very difficult to keep products separated. During the periods between the biennial shipyardings for maintenance and repair these defects had to be repaired by the ship's staff and, as the engineers were usually busy with matters in the engineroom, the work had gradually become the responsibility of the Chief Officer in order to avoid delays. The repairs were carried out using plastic patches, or plastic steel named 'Devcon'; a new product recently on the market and in which we believed the Company held most of the shares as we used so much of it.

On the ballast passage the bulkheads and pipe-lines (they were similarly affected) would be tested for leaks and marked accordingly, and once the new cargo orders had been received and the cargo plan decided upon the bulkheads separating the various grades would be repaired as required. Scaffolding was not carried in the ships at that time and I would sometimes have to work from ladders at heights of over 35 feet above the tank bottoms. Invariably it was very difficult to rig safety lines because of the lack of suitable attachment points, and at extreme heights with the ladder nearly vertical it was hazardous work. I often had to work with the chest close to the ladder to retain balance whilst leaving the hands free to receive the repair materials and tools from the sailor who was standing behind on the ladder. The leaks had to be patched on both sides of the bulkhead and, if the tank on the other side of the bulkhead contained ballast, I would sometimes go swimming. The materials were placed in a bucket and floated across in a lifebuoy to the position of the leak which would be just above the water level and I would carry out the repair whilst treading water or trying to support myself by any piece of structure that was handy.

After the bulkheads separating the products had been repaired I always prayed for good weather as too much movement in rough seas could open up the fractures. The same thing could happen when berthing if the pilot caused the ship to land heavily on the jetty when going alongside. On one occasion heavy contact with the jetty opened up fractures which only became apparent after the loading operation had started. Before further repairs could be carried out the product in the relevant tanks had to be transferred and the tanks gas-freed which, apart from the extra work involved, caused considerable delay. When the product was transferred back again and the bulkhead inspected it was found that the repair was tight, but that yet another leak had started elsewhere. This sequence of events went on for over three days in temperatures of up to 120°F, it was August, the hottest time of the year in Bahrain. I had hardly any sleep and I eventually passed out just as the work was successfully completed. One of the Dutch T2s took 10 days to load a cargo.

I thoroughly enjoyed the physical work involved and I gained a great deal of experience in carrying out various types of repairs and in the removal and replacement of valves and sections of pipe-line. The latter was usually done by the engineers but if they were very busy to cut down delay, we would have a go ourselves and shout for help if we ran into difficulties. There was a great deal of work required in cleaning and preparing the tanks for cargo, whether clean or black oil and I very soon discovered that, in tankers, the popular image of a Chief Officer in peaked cap and brass buttons was very far removed from reality. One would have thought that the dirty work would have been performed by the junior officers whilst the senior stood back and kept his hands clean but nothing could be further from the truth. Cadets worked on deck and in the tanks when tank cleaning, but as soon as they obtained their certificates they became bridge watchkeeping officers and thereafter had little involvement in tank work until they became Chief Officers. However, there were so many safety regulations and practices to be observed that it was important for the Chief Officer to be closely involved in every stage of tank cleaning and repair activities in order to give the tight supervision that was required to ensure safe operation.

In the early sixties many of the Company's ships were sent for drydocking and repair to Palermo in Sicily which was the home of the Mafia, the criminal organization which, through protection rackets, threats and extortion virtually controlled many areas of business and commerce in Italy and the United States. It was in Palermo that I first met two genuine American gangsters. Pete and Charlie were employed by the shipyard to act as interpreters and as a line of communication between the work force and the ship's personnel. They were both Sicilians who had emigrated to America and had been members of Al Capone's gang when they were arrested and sentenced to long terms of imprisonment – Charlie had been convicted of murder. When they were eventually released they were deported back to Sicily.

Pete and Charlie were both rather ordinary types, not at all one's idea of a tough mobster as seen in the Hollywood films, although in some I had seen Charlie's prototype, short, fat and not very bright, usually employed as a messenger or 'gofer.' It was generally assumed that the Company had come to some arrangement with the Mafia (who were rumoured to have large holdings of Texaco shares) which enabled the Company representative to have considerable authority over the work force in the shipyard to prevent any labour problems arising. Hayward, an American and one quarter Cherokee Indian, was an extremely forceful character reputed to hold both an American Master's and Chief Engineer's certificates, and he seemed to have the power to fire any workman who incurred his displeasure. As it was most unusual for a Company representative to be able to do this in a commercial shipyard it was presumed that the Mafia had brought pressure to bear on the management, which had no other option but to comply with Hayward's requirements.

In a shipyard, the Company's policy was to repair only those bulkhead and pipe-line leaks which were seen to be active on arrival, temporary repairs carried out by the ship's staff were never touched and the area of bulkhead or section of pipe-line was not renewed. Whilst this policy reduced the cost of shipyarding, held certain tax advantages, and thus helped the ship' economic performance, it did nothing to reduce the amount of work and worry imposed on the ship's staff, and one could never leave the Yard in the knowledge that the ship was tight. After a few days enroute to the loading port, with the working of the ship, old temporary repairs would again become active and new defects would appear where new metal had been welded to old.

When I left the *Adelaide* the *leak* chart showed 145 bulkhead leaks and 45 pipe-line leaks repaired by ship's staff, by which time she was on her way to the scrap yard after 18 years service. I met a Chief Officer from BP tankers who had never seen a leak in all his years of service; BP was reputed to take their ships out of the clean oil trade after 12 years.

During the years 1961 to 1968 several T2's were scrapped and in 1968 the remainder were *jumboised*. The bridge and part of the midship accommodation was removed and re-sited aft on the poop, and the hull cut off at the poop and replaced with a completely new bow and tank section which increased the carrying capacity by some 7,000 tons to over 23,000 tons. At this time the ships were 24 years old and were still operating with their original boilers and engines. They continued to do this for a further 10 years or so until they were gradually taken out of service and scrapped as the fleet was run down because of operating costs. By 1983 the Texaco fleet had been drastically reduced from 19 ships at the beginning of 1982 to 5 ships and one of these was a T2; the *Melbourne* still steaming with her original boilers and engines after 40 years in service.

The Company had started a building programme in the mid fifties beginning with 4 small motor ships for the carriage of lubricating oils from Trinidad, followed by four Liverpool class and two Newcastle class steam turbine ships for the clean oil trade. These clean oil ships carried about 20,000 tons of cargo, the normal capacity at that time, but in 1959 two ships of the Bristol class with a cargo capacity of about 33,000 tons were constructed making them the largest product carriers in the world. With the building of more oil refineries in various parts of the world there was a demand for large crude oil carriers and at the beginning of the sixties the super-tanker came into being. The Company built four – the Plymouth and Brisbane of 45,000 tons followed in 1963 by the Greenwich and Southampton of 57,000 tons. In 1962 I was appointed to the Liverpool and thereafter I was lucky to be given a newer or bigger class of ship until 1968 when I was appointed to the Westminster, the Company's first VLCC (Very Large Crude Carrier) which was 101,000 tons.

Compared to the T2s the ships were relatively new when I joined them and I obtained a great deal of pleasure in trying to bring them up to a high level of appearance and condition. On joining I would draw up a list of work to be completed by the time I was due to be relieved. Progressing the work from day to day, over the succeeding months, helped to make the time pass more quickly and gave me a great deal of satisfaction as each stage of the programme was completed and I saw the ship's appearance improving until it reached the standard I was aiming for. In some respects it was not so much a job as a hobby.

During these years I visited many ports that I had never been to before and this was one of the advantages of serving in the tankers of a major oil company as opposed to general cargo and passenger ships in liner companies which were on regular runs. In East Africa there was Mombasa, Dar es Salaam, Beira, Lourenço Marques and Tamatave in Madagascar. In New Zealand, Auckland, Whangarei, Dunedin and Napier, where people still observed the old custom of coming down to the jetty to see a ship from 'home.' In addition to Sydney, Melbourne and Hobart, I saw all the small ports on the East coast of Australia – Port Kembla, Cairns, Townsville, Gladstone, Newcastle and Brisbane.

I paid my first visits to Singapore, Hong Kong, Bangkok and Saigon which I was to see quite a lot of during the Vietnam War. I had always wanted to visit the United States and I managed to get to Portland, Maine, Boston and Philadelphia where I was able to see the Declaration of Independence, the famous Liberty Bell and the room in which the first Congress took place. There were also several ports in Europe that were new to me. Hamburg, Amsterdam, Rotterdam, Frederikshavn and the Kiel Canal and I had the experience of navigating the thick ice which is a feature of Stockholm in the winter months. The varied runs ensured that life never became boring and I always looked forward to the arrival of the voyage orders in the hope that we might be visiting pastures new.

My last ship as Chief Officer was the *Westminster* which I joined in 1968. She was the first ship in the Company to have an automated cargo control system with hydraulically operated valves which, together with the pumps, were controlled from a panel in a Cargo Control Room. The tanks were fitted with equipment which transmitted the ullage and temperature of the oil to gauges in the Control Room and the whole system was designed to enable the ship to be loaded/discharged by one person from a centralised position. A feature of the *Westminster* was the tunnel, surrounded by a cofferdam, under the main deck which ran for the full length of the ship so that one could go from the accommodation aft to the fore part of the ship without having to go along the upper deck. The tunnel contained the hydraulic equipment and controls to the pipe-line valves and sluice gates between the tanks.

I joined the ship in Zeebrugge on completion of her maiden voyage and quickly found that she had suffered many teething problems during the trip. The hydraulic system was most unreliable with valves and sluices opening and closing regardless of their control settings, so much so that Tom Shields, who had been dragged back from his leave to take the ship on the maiden voyage (the chap standing by had resigned at the last minute) had resorted to pieces of string to hold the control levers at open or shut as required in an attempt to counteract the problem. I subsequently spent a great deal of time in the tunnel opening and closing valves by means of a hand pump. Some of the equipment in the control system had been supplied from abroad and we always seemed to have technicians on board fault finding and repairing some piece of equipment or a system.

SS Texaco Westminster

All in all the automated cargo system was a big disappointment and because of its unreliability, it was of no great help in reducing the number of personnel required during cargo operations. It was a question of check, check and double check at all times to guard against overflows and pollution when loading, loss of suction and possible damage to the pumps when discharging, and many other situations which could arise through faulty valves and gauges. When in ballast it was quite common to wake up in the morning to find the ship listed one way or another, or the trim altered, through valves and sluices creeping open during the night. Eventually she became known throughout the fleet as the *Westmonster*.

The VLCCs had fewer cargo tanks than the preceding super-tankers and due to the size of these ships the tanks were extremely large, some had a depth of over 100 feet, and were often compared to the interior of a cathedral. Tank cleaning had continued in much the same war as in the smaller ships although the operation took much longer because of the areas to be washed. However it was subsequently found that we had been skating on very thin ice when two 200,000 tonners of the Shell fleet had massive explosions whilst carrying out tank cleaning operations. During tank cleaning jets of water from the washing machines generated a mist of minute water particles charged with static which was discharged to earth when the mist came into contact with the ship's structure. Through the enquiry into the Shell explosions it was discovered that in very large tanks the mist could form clouds which could produce a thunderstorm effect if they came into contact with each other. If this happened the resulting spark (lightning in a natural thunderstorm) and mixture of gas and air in the tank, if it was within the explosive limit, could cause an explosion. This finding brought about the introduction of new safety requirements and procedures in the operation of VLCCs which involved filling the tanks with an inert gas (usually fumes that were vented through the funnel but which were now washed and treated by special equipment before being introduced into the tanks) to produce an atmosphere which would not support combustion. During loading, discharge and tank cleaning operations the inert gas was introduced or expelled as required and in such a way as to ensure that the space between the oil level in the tank, or the tank bottom if empty, and the upper deck was completely filled and that all air/oxygen had been expelled. It seemed that the size of the *Westminster's* tanks had been just on the limit for enabling the static to be discharged to earth and for preventing mist clouds forming, but great care had to be taken when introducing any metal object, which was not bonded to the structure, in case it caused a spark. This of course was a basic safety precaution in any size of tank vessel.

I was promoted to Master after 6 months in the *Westminster* and although I was offered an appointment to a VLCC 5 years later (the Company had built several 200/250,000 tonners) I preferred to stay in smaller ships. To my mind the VLCC had no character and did not even look like a ship, more like shoe box with a block of flats perched on the end. They were unwieldy and difficult to manoeuvre and because of their deep draught they were always looking for water. In bad weather their sheer bulk and weight made it difficult for them to ride the seas which they would slam into as if hitting a brick wall, and reducing speed to prevent slamming could result in a loss of steerage way putting the ship at the mercy of the seas. They could be a lot of worry. And finally their pattern of trading was very limited and the runs could become very boring – invariably Arabian Gulf round the Cape of Good Hope to Rotterdam or Milford Haven.

The *Westminster* did distinguish herself on one occasion just before I left her. We arrived off Milford Haven to find that we could not berth because the tugs were on strike for some reason or another. The refinery was running low on crude and, as our cargo was urgently required if the refinery was to continue operating, the pilot said that if the Captain agreed he would have a go at berthing without tugs.

There were very strong tides around the entrance to Milford Haven and we went in at the beginning of the ebb when we would be able to use the tide in the berthing operation. Arriving off the berth we dropped the port anchor – I had to take care not to anchor the ship – and sent the mooring ropes away, the boats just making it to shore before the action of the current on the rope bight dragged them astern. Then it was a case of veering the anchor cable, heaving in the mooring ropes and using the ebb current to gradually push the ship alongside the jetty. She landed up with the cargo manifold right under the shore discharge pipes – in perfect position. At that time we were the biggest ship in the world to berth without tugs in a harbour (we were bigger in tonnage than the *Queens* who had berthed without tugs in New York) and the T.V. people came down to record the event.

Chapter 28

IN COMMAND AGAIN

———

Due to officers leaving the Company, for one reason or another, I gradually climbed the seniority ladder until I was one of the Golden Six, the senior Chief Officers in line for promotion. In 1967 the Caltex Fleets had been divided up between the parent companies, Texaco and Standard Oil of California, and shortly after this re-organization several of our senior Masters retired, or their services were terminated, and by 1969 the Golden Six had all been appointed to command after a minimum of 9 years as Chief officer.

In 1965, when I had been Chief Officer for 5 years I was tempted, and given the opportunity, to join another company which offered prospects of immediate command. The P&O (Peninsular and Oriental Steamship Co.,) the large passenger liner company, had formed a subsidiary company named Trident to operate oil tankers. Whilst I was loading in Bahrain there was a Trident tanker berthed on the other side of the jetty and I happened to see the name of the Master on the loading sheet in the jetty office. His name was Bunn, the same name as the Chief Officer I had sailed with when I was a Cadet in BI and I wondered if it could be the same person. I went on board and I was pleased to discover that he was indeed the same person and, what is more, that he remembered and recognized me. Captain Bunn told me that he had retired from BI as Vice Commodore of the fleet when he was about 56 years of age but as he could not live on his pension of £900 he had decided to go back to sea. Trident had been starting up at the time and he was appointed senior relieving Master.

When Captain Bunn found that I had five years experience as Chief Officer and much of it in product carriers he encouraged me to leave Caltex and join Trident where he said I would get command within a year. The company was very short of experienced officers to take over the new ships that were coming into service and people were being promoted with very little experience. The next person due for promotion was his Chief Officer who had only been a year in tankers. It was an attractive thought. I knew that having been a BI Cadet (P&O and BI were one company) followed by naval service would be an added advantage if I applied for a position; P&O had close ties with the Navy and many of their officers were in the RNR

However, I had heard the stories that were being related by the terminal operators in various ports regarding Trident tankers, and the way they were being operated by the P&O personnel who viewed tankers as a bit of a come down in comparison to their traditional passenger trade with its more sedate way of life. I had also taken notice of the state around the decks of the Trident ship when I went on board and of the storage space in the centrecastle underneath the midship accommodation. In my own ship this space was extremely clean and tidy with everything neatly stowed, and leaving a clear and well painted deck area where one could have held a dance. On the Trident ship this space was a mess, dirty, with gear all over the place and everything on top and nothing handy.

It did not take me long to decide to stay where I was and as things turned out I made the right decision. Within a few years P&O got rid of their tankers, and at the same time made many officers redundant when the passenger/cargo trades were overtaken by air travel and bigger and faster container ships, which led to a reduction in the size of their fleet.

My first command was the *Texaco Wellington* which had recently been jumboized and had the accommodation and bridge re-sited on the poop thus making her an all aft job, a term in use at the time. After the bigger and more recently constructed ships in which I had been serving the *Wellington* was a complete change. During the jumboization little had been done to improve or enlarge the accommodation for officers and ratings which was then over 25 years old, and very depressing after the relatively spacious quarters in the more modern vessels. The crew washrooms and toilets were a sad sight. The steel had lost its 'skin' so that in spite of continuous maintenance and painting, the bulkheads, ship's side and pipe-work were continually rust-stained and it was impossible to maintain a smart and hygienic appearance.

The ship was still steaming with her original boilers and machinery and subject to break-downs which often occurred in the most inconvenient places. On one occasion, when we were leaving Singapore, I had just dropped the pilot and was proceeding across the flow of traffic to get into the correct traffic lane when the Chief Engineer rang the bridge to tell me that he had a problem and would have to stop the engine. When I told him where we were he gave me thirty minutes before the ship would black out and lose all power. Fortunately there was a pilot boat handy and I was able to dodge the traffic, pick up the pilot, and get back to the anchorage before we conked out. There was a similar occurrence at Port Kembla, south of Botany Bay, in Australia.

I was approaching the entrance to the anchorage, which was located between the mainland and a group of rocks and small island which lay close offshore, when I was told that there was a problem with the engine's manoeuvring controls. There was just sufficient time and space to put the wheel hard-over and head back out to sea. After twenty minutes or so the Chief Engineer reported that we could proceed as usual but I decided to steam out to sea and lay stopped for the night. We had been steaming for about thirty minutes when it was reported that they were still having trouble and would have to stop and shut down the engine. It was a further 16 hours before the problem was located and rectified.

SS Texaco Wellington – Jumboized

These incidents early on in command of unreliable ships made me extremely safety conscious and I may have gained the reputation of being a bit of an old woman when it came to navigation and ship-handling. Unless circumstances warranted close approach to the land I always kept well off, at least 20 miles, so that in the event of a break-down there would be less fear of drifting ashore before the engineers had time to effect repairs. I also gave orders that, whenever there was sufficient sea-room, all traffic was to be passed at a distance of not less than two miles in case the steering gear should fail at a critical time. Comprehensive instructions were posted on the bridge, in the engine-room and at the steering gear for the change-over to emergency steering and the procedure was exercised every week, unexpectedly, so that all bridge and engine-room personnel were thoroughly trained in what to do should there be a failure of the primary steering.

My first voyage in command was one which was to become fairly regular for the next two years or so. Bahrain to Penang, Singapore, Saigon and Bangkok, returning to Singapore to load for Saigon before returning to the Gulf. I enjoyed the run as I liked the people in the area, it gave the crew an opportunity for shore leave and we got an extra 5 days pay each time we went into the war zone at Saigon. The American ships running to Saigon got extra pay for the round trip from San Francisco.

The first call at Penang gave me a hair-raising experience. I had arrived an hour after the latest time for crossing the bar at the entrance to the port but the pilot thought that there would still be enough water for us to get across, even though the tide was on the ebb, and thus save a delay of at least twenty-four hours. I could see the mud being churned up astern as we proceeded at full speed across the bar and I began to worry in case we ran aground. I thought my fears had been realised when the ship started to heel over to starboard, as though she was going to turn over, as we drove through the mud. The engines were quickly put to half speed and I held my breath until she came upright and we found ourselves in deeper water at the other side of the bar. I had the unfortunate experience of having to send for a diver to inspect the ship's bottom for damage during my first voyage in command. However there was no harm done and the passage through the mud at least had the effect of cleaning the bottom of barnacles and marine growth which could effectively reduce the speed of the ship through the water.

I first visited Vietnam in 1961 when we took a cargo to the Caltex terminal a few miles down river from Saigon. The war had not yet started at that time and it was a peaceful and interesting passage up the winding river with its heavily wooded banks and many small tributaries and creeks. The Caltex and Shell terminals were adjacent to one another and each had a small berth for the barges and local craft which carried tins of kerosine and gasoline to villages situated on the river banks. It seemed idyllic with the American terminal manager practicing his golf strokes on the sward in front of the terminal building and his only apparent worry being the performance of his Texaco shares on the stock exchange in New York.

The situation was totally different when I paid my next visit in 1969 at the height of the Vietnam War. Being in a war zone there was always the possibility of the ship coming under attack during passage up the river and at the berth, and the precautions that had to be taken added a certain amount of excitement to the proceedings. At the start of their campaign the Americans had sprayed the country-side with a chemical defoliant in order to wipe out the jungle which offered concealment to the enemy and to make his movements more visible. The jungle on either side of the river had now largely disappeared and all that remained were isolated clumps of bushes and mangroves which could be seen for several miles around. However, they were sufficient to conceal the Viet Cong who used them when making rocket attacks on river traffic.

At Vung Tau, at the entrance to the river, we anchored to complete the port formalities and await the sailing of the small convoy up the river. I got quite a surprise when the customs officials demanded ten cartons (2000) of cigarettes in addition to the usual bottle of whisky; normally one expected to give out only a couple of cartons but it seemed there were various people ashore who had to get their cut. I received a bigger shock when we reached the berth and found that a further ten cartons had to be given to the customs officials from Saigon. The agent told me that the custom officials were so poorly paid that they had to sell the cigarettes on the black market as an additional source of income; he reckoned that there were over fifty varieties of cigarettes on sale in the streets of Saigon. Sweetening the customs also encouraged them to turn a blind eye to any trading which went on between the Indian crew and the locals. One ship which did not give enough sugar was fined two thousand pounds.

Before proceeding up river the ship was issued with several sets of military protective equipment to be worn by the bridge personnel in case the ship came under attack during the passage. The equipment consisted of steel helmets and liners, flak jackets, and thick cumbersome body armour worn around the stomach to protect the vital organs. I found the helmet extremely heavy, much heavier than the British battle bowler of World War 2, and made do with the liner which was much fighter and not so sore on the neck muscles. Wearing all this gear in the hot weather made for a most uncomfortable trip up the river and on subsequence visits we gradually reduced to just wearing flak jackets.

There were several US naval units in the anchorage at Vung Tau, mainly repair ships and auxiliaries. I was not very impressed by them. Even allowing for the fact that there was a war on it seemed that little attempt was being made to maintain a reasonably smart appearance, and the sight of the crews, dressed in a variety of rigs and lolling around the decks only added to the general impression of scruffiness and inefficiency. In accordance with normal practice I dipped the ensign as we passed but our salute was not returned even although there were men hanging about under the ensign staff. During the many visits I made to Saigon our salutes were rarely returned by the US Navy.

Ships proceeding up and down the river were occasionally being subjected to rocket attacks from small groups of Viet Cong who infiltrated the area during the night, so I took several precautions to ensure, as far as possible, the safety of the ship and personnel. With the exception of those on duty on the bridge all personnel were told to stay below decks in the accommodation and, if practicable, to stay away from the vicinity of the ship's side and keep to the alleyways in case the hull or superstructure was hit. The fire pump was kept in continuous operation with water going overboard in readiness for immediate switching to fire hoses which were connected and laid out around the ship. The lifeboats were swung out ready for immediate lowering, and men were stationed at the emergency steering position in case the primary steering on the bridge was put out of action. During the passage up the river we were escorted by helicopter gun-ships which patrolled the area adjacent to the river on the look-out for any signs of the enemy. The choppers passed quite close overhead and I got a very good view of their heavy armament of rockets, and of the soldiers sitting at the heavy machine guns at the open doors on each side of the fuselage. At various times we met up with some of the small gun-boats which patrolled the river, nosing up the side creeks and into the mangroves in search of possible infiltrators. Because of the thick weeds and river debris which could foul propellers they were powered by water-jet propulsion from pumps which forced water through narrow pipes located at the stem of the craft. The boats, which were fast and quick to manoeuvre, were equipped with heavy machine-guns which were invariably covered, probably to protect them from the climate, which did not make for a fast response should they suddenly meet the enemy. The crews did not appear to be very alert and had probably become complacent through lack of enemy activity, but they all wore side arms and I saw one chap wearing a gun-belt with twin holsters cowboy style.

The situation at the terminal, which was ten miles south of Saigon, had changed radically with the onset of war. A tall fence surmounted by barbed wire enclosed the terminal area to which entry was strictly controlled although it was difficult to ensure that there were no members of the Viet Cong amongst the terminal personnel and the labourers loading the river barges. It was rumoured that the terminal barber was head of the local Viet Cong for that area. The road to Saigon was open and reputed to be safe during the day, but the Viet Cong appeared at night and were said to be in control during the dark hours. Needless to say I did not grant any leave even during daylight hours.

Just outside the terminal fence and not far from the jetty a heavy howitzer had been positioned which used to blast off a few rounds periodically, usually at night when there were signs of activity to the north. At night I was given a taste of my own medicine from Palestine days, when patrol craft dropped grenades near the ship as a defence against frogmen who might attempt to place limpet mines on the hull. It was not too bad when the tanks contained oil, just a dull thud, but with empty tanks the noise would reverberate throughout the ship and one would think that a pipe-line had fractured or there had been an explosion. A favourite practice of the Viet Cong was to fashion a mine out of an oil drum and float it down on the current towards a ship alongside, or make it fast to the ship's anchor cable by a length of rope which allowed it to drift down with the tide and land alongside the hull. This actually happened to the *Wellington* after I had left her to go on leave and she had to be taken to Singapore for repairs to the rudder. To guard against sabotage the shadow area at the water-line was illuminated as far as possible and sailors patrolled the ship's side continuously inspecting the water below with the aid of torches.

From Saigon we would go to Bangkok and then to Singapore to back-load another cargo for Saigon before returning to the Gulf. The passage up the river to Bangkok was very interesting. On the port hand the bank was heavily wooded with little clusters of the native wooden houses, sometimes on stilts, at intervals along the water's edge. To starboard the country was open and flat and the golden roofs of several temples could be seen in the distance. The berth was some distance from Bangkok and too far away for me to leave the ship for any length of time to go sight-seeing. My visits ashore were therefore limited to the occasional trip to the agent's office for an 'on the house' telephone call home.

I suppose it is every Shipmaster's hope that at some point in his career he will have the opportunity to make some money by claiming salvage after finding a ship broken down at sea and towing it to port. A lifetime could be spent at sea without coming across such a situation and to have the chance to test one's seamanship, but I was fortunate to be given the opportunity during my first period in command.

A sister ship was outward bound from the Gulf when she broke down with boiler trouble in the Arabian Sea just at the onset of the south-west monsoon. The current was setting her in a north-east direction towards the land in the region of Karachi at a rate of 36/48 miles a day. Although there were tugs available at Karachi and Bombay they would inevitably claim salvage if called upon to render assistance and this would cost the Company a great deal of money. If at all possible shipping companies preferred their own ships to render assistance to each other, especially if there was no risk of immediate danger, and as I was enroute to the Gulf and only a couple of days steaming from the ship in trouble I was directed to go to her assistance.

There was a lot of preparation to be made as we steamed towards the rendezvous. The anchor cable was broken and ninety feet taken out and dragged down to the poop to be attached to our end of the towing wire which also had to be taken from its reel in the f'c'sle and laid out in bights around the poop. Ideally, the towing wire should have been secured to the anchor cable of the ship being towed, so that the cable when paid out into the water supplied a spring to the tow-wire and allowed it to form a catenary rather than a direct pull, thus taking a lot of stress off of the wire.

On arrival at the rendezvous I found that the tow (I forget her name but I will say it was the *Sydney*) had been unable to raise and maintain steam so she was unable to use her windlass to handle her anchor cable. This meant that I had to use her towing wire. *Sydney's* lifeboat was used to pick up my messenger ropes and take them back to be connected to her wire which was then brought on board and secured to my cable which was then veered into the water.

The tow was connected just before sunset and I had the task of turning 180 degrees to get course for Bombay. We had got to the *Sydney* just in time as she was over the 100 fathom line and drifting closer to land all the time. Once on course the tow followed nicely although she took up a pattern of weaving from the starboard quarter to right astern which may have been due to the rudder having been stopped in a hard-over position. I had remained constantly on the bridge, taking only the occasional cat-nap on the settee, but I had to go down to my office to prepare messages to be sent to Bombay concerning arrangements for our arrival when disaster struck.

The sound of running footsteps told me something was amiss and I arrived on the bridge to find that the tow-wire had parted and the tow was now broad on our port quarter. I told *Sydney* that I would pass him my wire but he said it would not be necessary as he had managed to raise steam and would be able to proceed under his own power. The sailor watching the towing gear on the poop said that the *Sydney* appeared to be moving under her own power as she crossed astern and this confirmed that she had been responsible for parting the wire. The Captain did not offer any explanations but I found out later, from someone who had been on board, that *Sydney* had been testing her engines. It appeared that the engineers had started steaming without telling the Officer of the Watch who, suddenly finding himself going faster than the towing vessel, had to take action to avoid overtaking and had consequently parted the towing wire.

We were all very disappointed at losing the tow (I jokingly blamed the Second Officer for spending his salvage money before we had completed the job), but as it turned out it was all for the best. We arrived in Bombay at 10 a. m. the following morning and after re-fuelling and completing formalities, I was preparing to sail about 4 p.m. when I received warning that a cyclone was about to strike a few miles south of Bombay. Although some distance from the centre, the port was lashed by torrential rain and high winds for a few hours which delayed our sailing and, when finally clear of the port I ran into a heavy swell and rough seas. If the *Sydney* had not been able to proceed under her own steam we would just have been arriving at this time with her in tow and, in the prevailing weather, the towing wire might well have parted and she would have been in a hazardous situation.

I received a "Well done" for our efforts and a bonus of half a month's pay plus a great deal of valuable experience.

Chapter 29

SHIPBOARD ADVISORY TEAMS

――――

At the end of 1971 I was offered a shore assignment at Fleet Headquarters in London to draw up the guidelines for a new safety project which was being introduced in conjunction with the other Texaco Fleets. The aim of the project was to increase safety awareness and emphasise the need to adhere to Company safety practices and procedures, and to provide a channel of communication on safety and any other operational matters between fleet personnel and FHQ.

The project was originally named Texaco Shipboard Safety Advisory Teams but it was subsequently changed to Texaco Shipboard Advisory Teams (TSAT). A team would consist of a Master and Chief Engineer who would visit the ships and inspect safety equipment, show safety films, monitor adherence to Company regulations in such matters as cargo loading/discharge, bridge and engine-room procedures when entering/leaving port, emergency organization and drills. The team would hold safety meetings at which time any departure from Company procedures or requirements that had been noted would be raised and the matter would be discussed with the ship's staff. The object of the exercise was not merely to find fault – there might be a valid reason for omitting or amending a Company procedure which experience had shown to be out of date, and it was the team's job to convey and explain this to FHQ. It was hoped that by standing back and watching others at work and noting any mistakes or omissions that were made, the team members would recognize the deficiencies in their own performance which they had not been aware of, and they would be that much more safety conscious when they returned to sea.

When considering the project, management had realised that many in the fleet would look upon the teams as spies from head office, and that some would resent the idea of someone looking over their shoulders with the apparent intention of criticising their performance. In order to gain their co-operation and to get them to appreciate that the team was there to assist them, and to explain and expedite their requirements in head office, a great deal of tact would be required especially when dealing with the Masters and Chief Engineers. It was therefore quite a surprise, and a compliment, to be told by the manager of operations that I was thought to be the person most suited to initiate the programme of ship visits and to take out the first team.

I was a bit apprehensive about taking on the job as I knew, or I had heard about, some of the difficult characters amongst the Masters and Chiefs and who, at best, might be uncooperative and resentful. However it was a new adventure and it fulfilled my desire to always be trying something new and to gain experience of whatever kind. It also provided the opportunity to get home at the weekends, and also the opportunity to gain an entry and insight, however slight, into the world of ship management which had been my ultimate aim when I returned to sea.

Whilst drawing up the guidelines I attended meetings with representatives from the other FHQs who were preparing their own guidelines to ensure that there was a common approach to the subject. I acted as secretary at the meeting, keeping the minutes and preparing the final report and I continued to do this at subsequent International Fleets Headquarters meetings which were held in Oslo, Monaco, and London during the following eighteen months. I had the opportunity to attend trade exhibitions and bring myself up to date with the latest advances in safety and life-saving equipment and protective clothing and I spent a week at the Siebe Gorman factory for instruction in the maintenance, calibration and proper use of breathing apparatus which was coming into general use in the fleet. I would then be in a position to give instruction or advice to people who were not fully familiar with the equipment.

John Newberry was the Chief Engineer assigned to the team and we decided to cut our teeth and try out the project on the Texaco Durham and the Texaco Gloucester, the two vessels which were employed in home waters around the UK coast, before visiting the foreign-going ships. It would be a dummy run and it would enable us to get our act together. We set off laden with safety films, tape-recorder, polaroid camera, spare tapes and films and wondered how we would be received on board. Our only armament was a letter to the Master which explained our mission, gave us authority in certain matters and asked for the complete co-operation of all those on board. As it turned out we were well received and made to feel at home. Little word of the project had got about and we were able to fully explain the concept and allay any fears before they were aroused.

We received quite a shock from our inspection of the two ships. The safety, life-saving and fire-fighting equipment was in a very poor state and it was obvious that there had been no routine inspections or maintenance carried out for some time.

The life-boats were especially bad with the gear in a poor condition and badly stowed, so that they would have been of little use in an emergency, either to those on board or in giving assistance to a vessel in trouble. There also seemed to be a general lack of safety awareness and safety consciousness on board and many basic tanker practices were not being observed. These ships were mainly employed in carrying fuel and diesel oil cargoes which were fairly innocuous and it could be said that the omission of certain safety practices did not constitute any real hazard. What gave cause for concern was the possibility of personnel being similarly relaxed in their attitude to safety when they returned to vessels carrying crude oil and other dangerous cargoes.

The coastal ships were hard running with short passages between ports and quick port turn-around which gave the hard-working officers little opportunity for the inspection and maintenance of equipment which, on foreign-going ships, was carried out during the longer passages between ports. This fact was emphasized in the reports submitted to management on completion of our inspections.

The reports contained several pages of defects with recommendations as to which ones were to be attended to by ship's staff or the relevant department in FHQ. The opportunity was also taken to report on the general condition and appearance of the ships (which was not strictly within our terms of reference) and the amount of upgrading required. Our poor findings and the recommendations we had made caused quite a stir in the office and we were not at all popular with some of the departmental heads, especially the engineering department, who had to work to very tight budgets which allowed little leeway for unplanned expenditure. However we did not have time to see if any action was being taken on our recommendations as we were soon off to visit the foreign-going ships.

The first port of call was Portland, Maine, in America where the *Southampton* was discharging before going on to Boston. It was the month of January, the depth of winter when the temperature dropped to 20 degrees and more below zero and so cold that the paint covering on the after accommodation forward bulkhead came off in large sheets exposing the bare metal below. Carrying out our inspection was a cold, miserable job and taking photographs was especially difficult, as heavy clothing had to be opened up in order to be able to hold the polaroid under the armpit to obtain sufficient warmth to develop it.

From Boston we flew to New York and spent two days there inspecting the *Greenwich* and the *Plymouth* which were in shipyard for minor repairs. John and I had served in these ships and we were unpleasantly surprised at their appearance as we approached them in the dockyard, and we became more depressed as we went around on our inspection. They were indeed in a sorry state of repair and appearance and by the time we had finished we had compiled lists of defects, repairs and maintenance required for both ships which would have served as specifications for shipyarding. This deterioration in appearance and condition was not altogether due to lack of interest or inefficiency on the part of ships' personnel or indeed the management in

FHQ Ships reported their requirements regarding repairs, renewals, equipments and stores to the various departments in London who had to operate within budget levels allocated by the Texaco head office in New York. Sea-going personnel tended to blame the office staff when repairs were not carried out or stores and equipment were not forthcoming but this was not really fair or equitable. Although London argued their corner and stressed the needs of the fleet, in the end they had to accept the limitations imposed by accountants in New York who, not being seamen, had little appreciation of the effect that a growing list of defects could have on a ship's operational efficiency and appearance, and on crew morale.

My arrival on board the *Ghent* at Port a Pierre in Trinidad was somewhat undignified and provided a good example of more haste less speed. As the ship was at anchor we boarded from a tug and whilst stepping on to the accommodation ladder I fell into the sea. In spite of having been given cautionary advice from John to take my time I jumped too soon and, although I landed safely and grasped the ladder chain with my left hand to steady myself, the weight of the heavy brief case in my other hand caused me to over-balance and in I went. Fortunately I held on to the brief case which contained amongst other things, the tape recordings of the previous inspections. John was a big, strong chap and he quickly had me on board by the scruff of the neck and he breathed a sigh of relief when he found the tapes were safe. Some of the crew had been watching the tug's approach but by the time I arrived on deck, soaken and bedraggled, they had all disappeared. Word soon got around, however, and the incident caused a great deal of amusement amongst the British crew and, if nothing else, helped to raise their morale. At a subsequent safety meeting I passed it off by saying that we had put on a demonstration of an unsafe practice but, unfortunately, nobody had bothered to attend.

At midnight, after the safety meeting, the emergency alarm was sounded when smoke was discovered coming from one of the crew cabins. It was a classic case of a fire having been started through someone smoking in bed. When John and I arrived on the scene we found some people crowding round the cabin door to see what was going on and others walking around the alleyways, disorganized and apparently wondering what to do. There was nobody running out hoses or taking other precautions in the event of the fire spreading, and it became obvious that the emergency organization was very poor and that the crew had received little training in dealing with specific emergencies by simulating situations at fire drills. What was most disturbing was the action of the junior engineer who discovered the fire. In the belief that the Second Engineer would think that the safety team was just carrying out an exercise and that he would not turn out when the alarm bells were sounded, the junior first called the Second Engineer to convince him that it was a real fire before activating the emergency alarm, thus causing an unnecessary delay in tackling the fire and which could have had serious consequences.

We sailed with the *Ghent* to the Texaco refinery on the Delaware river near Philadelphia where we transferred to another ship for the return trip to Trinidad.

After returning home from Trinidad John and I joined the *Hamburg* (one of the new VLCCS) at Rotterdam and took passage to Las Palmas where we transferred to the *Cardiff* which was on her way to Cape Town. From there we returned by air to London where we received rather a cool reception as we were evidently supposed to stay with the *Cardiff* until she arrived in the Gulf. It was just as well that we did return as, on making enquiries, we found that little action was being taken on our reports. In order to establish and maintain the credibility of the TSAT, it was important that fleet personnel should see that management was making a positive response to valid suggestions and requests, as well as giving instruction and advice on matters which required action on the part of the ship's staff. When this was pointed out I was made TSAT co-ordinator with the job of planning and organizing team visits and expediting action within the office on the teams' reports.

Subsequent teams were required to report on appearance and condition as part of their terms of reference and the first team to do this officially gained something of a reputation for themselves. The comprehensive and in-depth inspections carried out by Captain Campbell and Chief Engineer Harland and the resulting long lists of defects and repairs, accompanied by the sometimes scathing comments contained in their reports, made them most unpopular with the maintenance and repair department who called them 'The Wreckers'

From the outset, copies of the TSAT reports were sent to Texaco Headquarters in New York and, whilst it may have been purely coincidental, they may have been instrumental in the decision by the New York management to initiate a programme to upgrade the fleet. In the upgrading programme New York required a monthly statement showing the expenditure of the various departments – maintenance and repair, safety, accommodation refurbishment and training, together with the progress being made in the individual ships. I was given the job of collating all the information and producing a report for submission to our deputy managing director who had the overall responsibility for the programme.

I was therefore well and truly 'working in the office' and I thoroughly enjoyed the experience as I was gaining more and more knowledge of what was entailed in ship management. I was given other jobs to do such as interviewing prospective candidates for Cadetships and giving a presentation at a seminar on the TSAT. Whilst working in the office I stayed at a hotel in Knightsbridge and travelled home at the week-ends.

In 1973 Texaco was installing a submarine pipe-line and mooring buoy at Trinidad for the discharge of VLCCS, and whilst this work was in progress it was proposed to anchor them so that they could discharge their cargoes to smaller tankers alongside for transhipment to the terminal, or to ports on the east coast of America. Once again I was assigned the task of producing guidelines for the transhipment operations, this time in co-operation with one of the staff from New York and a local representative. A similar type of operation was being carried out by Shell Tankers in the English Channel when the lightering ship berthed on the VLCC whilst both ships were under way, providing the weather conditions were suitable. Before going to Trinidad I was given the opportunity to sail with the lightering ship to observe the operation.

Shell had adapted two ships to be used for lightering. Davits were fitted on the port side of the main deck to carry the large pneumatic fenders which were essential in preventing damage to the ships, and shore-type loading booms which were quick and easy to connect/disconnect and self adjusting, were installed to be used in place of hoses which took time to connect and required frequent manual handling. The ships were also fitted with a separate system for pumping ballast which allowed the cargo loading and ballast discharge operations to be carried out concurrently. This ensured that if the transfer operation had to be aborted, for whatever reason, the ship would have sufficient deadweight at any stage of the operation to enable her to proceed at a satisfactory and safe draught and trim.

The procedure for berthing was for the VLCC to proceed on a steady course and at the minimum speed required to maintain steerage way whilst the lightering ship approached from astern, lowering and positioning the fenders before going alongside. Once the berthing was completed the VLCC anchored in a suitable spot whilst the cargo transfer took place. On completion the lightering ship unberthed from the VLCC, which remained at anchor until the next visit by a lightering ship. The VLCC then weighed anchor and got under way to repeat the berthing procedure.

Because of various factors we had to adopt a somewhat different procedure at Trinidad. After the VLCC had anchored the fenders were placed alongside by a tug, and tugs were used to berth the lightering vessel. It was in the unberthing operation that the first difficulty came to light. It was found that the VLCC kept swinging into the water being displaced by the lightering vessel as it was being pulled away from alongside prior to moving off. The tugs did not have sufficient power to separate the vessels quickly enough to a sufficient distance where the smaller ship could move off safely ahead without fear of collision.

It was obvious that more powerful tugs would be required, not only for this operation but also to be available in the event of an emergency situation arising in the area involving a VLCC. More powerful tugs were sent down from America but there were one or two anxious moments during the early transhipment operations.

The first three transhipments involved British, Greek, and Japanese VLCCs and I acted as co-ordinator between them and the ships of Texaco's Panamanian Flag fleet (which had Italian officers) which were employed as the lightering vessels. I spent about a week on each VLCC and it was very interesting to compare their performance, efficiency and equipment. I was very impressed by the Japanese ship which had only been in service for 6 months. She had a much smaller crew than our VLCC and consequently she was fitted with labour saving equipment which made for quick and easy operation. For example the heavy metal accommodation ladder, which was permanently positioned at the ship's side, could be swung out and adjusted for height by two sailors with the aid of compressed air driven machines, whereas in our ship the ladder was stowed inboard and had to be hoisted and swung outboard, and positioned, by means of the derrick which required the full deck crew. All the Japanese crew members on deck were equipped with walkie-talkies and if I required the hoses to be adjusted or the moorings tended, a word to the Chief Officer and a sailor would speed along the deck on a bicycle and attend to the matter.

Even allowing that the Japanese ship was only 6 months old I was still impressed with her accommodation. The galley bulkheads and fittings were of stainless steel and spotlessly clean, as were the galley staff in their smart white working uniforms. The entrance to the officers' lounge was through a glass screen which was engraved with Japanese artistry and a similar screen separated the lounge from the dining saloon. The lounge was fitted with a well-appointed bar complete with moquette covered bar stools and deep, comfortable sofas and armchairs. There was a rack containing copies of Japanese newspapers which had been received on a facsimile machine. The crew were also well provided for with regard to recreational facilities. In the library, which also served as a hobbies room, there were several paintings and other items of handicraft which caught the eye, and showed that some of the sailors pursued worth while hobbies in their off-duty hours.

During my temporary assignment to the London Office I was offered a permanent position as an assistant marine superintendent in the operations department which would eventually have led to a career in management. It was what I had always wanted but unfortunately I was not in a position to accept the offer. It would have meant moving to London and, although I would have been with my family all the time, the move would have caused a serious disruption in the children's education at a time when two were preparing for university and one had just settled down in a new school. Another factor was the drop in salary which I could not afford. Masters received a much higher salary than all but the most senior management personnel. Although I was disappointed it all worked out for the best, by remaining at sea I was able to do more for the family and I was to enjoy many more years in command.

A few years later I did have one more assignment in the London office as Fleet Safety Superintendent when, for eight months, I sat in for Captain Wheeler who was suffering a period of ill health. This time instead of living in a hotel I had to find my own accommodation and ended up in a bed-sit in Notting Hill.

Chapter 30

A Master Again

―――

My office assignment ended rather unexpectedly when I was told that I would have to return to sea because of a temporary shortage of Masters. I was offered a VLCC but although there was a certain prestige in commanding these big vessels I preferred the smaller Japanese built ships of the *Plymouth* and *Southampton* classes with their conventional appearance and finer lines which made them more manoeuvrable. They also had more spacious accommodation and their size allowed a more varied voyage pattern.

At the end of 1973 I returned to sea in command of the *Plymouth* and in 1974 I was appointed as permanent Master of the *Southampton* and I remained in command of her until 1982 when she was scrapped during the drastic reduction of the Texaco Fleets which hastened my retirement. I became very attached to the *Southampton* as I returned to her after each leave period and, in effect, it was as if I had my own yacht. Being the assigned Master I was responsible for her condition and operational performance even whilst I was on leave. Senior deck and engineer officers were also assigned to the ship and, as there were always two of them on board whilst I was on leave, we were able to ensure continuity in the way the ship was operated. Work, maintenance and training programmes agreed by the ship's management team were progressed and various operational and emergency procedures which had been instituted continued to be observed.

Before joining the *Southampton* I was sent at short notice to relieve the Master of the *Wellington* which had suffered boiler trouble during bad weather whilst outward bound from the Channel and had only just managed to reach El Ferrol on the north-west coast of Spain.

SS Texaco Southampton

On the bridge of Southampton

After loading in the Mediterranean we proceeded on a voyage round the west coast of Africa calling at several ports I had not yet visited. The first port of call was Dakar and it was interesting to see the place that had been a Vichy stronghold during the war, and which had been the objective of the expedition in 1940 which had been so unsuccessful. The next call was at Freetown and as I took the ship into the anchorage I was reminded of my first experience of command, the ship's motor life-boat, and how much I enjoyed running to and from King Tom pier. I also remembered, with a great deal of sadness, the very many large and stately liners, then in use as troopships, that used to fill the anchorage when they called at the port on their way to the Middle and Far East. Their like would not be seen again in such numbers.

Abidjan on the Ivory Coast was the next discharge port. The town was a little way from the harbour but it looked a nice place with many fine buildings. After a call at Lome in Togo we proceeded to Lagos where I had my first experience of being boarded by pirates. At that time Nigeria was in the early days of independence and had embarked on a massive development programme which required the import of large quantities of goods and building materials. The port facilities were not large enough to cope with the amount of shipping involved and this resulted in ships having to anchor outside the port and wait, sometimes for several weeks, until a berth became available. These ships became the target for gangs of thieves who would creep alongside the ships at night and board from their small boats by climbing up the anchor cable or by ropes attached to grappling hooks. The ships tried to deter the thieves by having powerful water jets continually directed down the hawse pipe and anchor cables, illuminating the water area around the hull and having a security watch visible on deck. Crews were advised not to try to apprehend the thieves if they did manage to get on board (they usually made off if discovered) as it had been found that they would not hesitate to use knives and other weapons to avoid being detained.

In our case the thieves appeared to have boarded by rope to the main deck at the break of the forecastle where the paint locker was situated and, having broken the padlock on the door, stole some drums of paint. The Chief Officer discovered the theft when making his rounds after taking over the watch at 4 a.m. The area was in full view of the bridge and any movement should have been spotted by the bridge personnel if a proper watch was being maintained. The subsequent investigation showed that in spite of being warned verbally and in my night orders for the need for vigilance, the Second Officer, who was on watch at the time, had spent most of his time yarning with the quartermaster and had neglected his duty of ensuring that a strict security watch was kept and that my orders were being obeyed.

A final call was made at Douala in Cameroon where I had the pleasure of meeting, and giving lunch to, friends of my sister who had met them whilst she was living in the town where her husband worked for the Development Corporation. Then it was on to Capetown for stores and refuelling for the last leg of the voyage to the Arabian Gulf.

I returned to the *Southampton* in 1975 and for the next seven years I enjoyed a varied voyage pattern and visited several new ports. Crossing the Pacific Ocean and visiting the west coast of America was a new experience. In Long Beach, California, I saw the *Queen Mary*, at one time the pride of the British merchant fleet and the finest ocean liner afloat, now reduced to a floating museum, amusement arcade and wedding parlour. The Chief Engineer went across to see over her but I preferred to remember her as she was in her heyday. As a boy I saw her in the fitting out basin in Brown's shipyard on the Clyde.

Another trip across the Pacific took me to Anacortes, at the head of the Juan de Fuca Strait, in the State of Washington on the north west coast. A couple of months previously there had been a big oil pollution incident on the east coast and the American Coastguard had since instituted rigorous safety inspections on all tankers before they were allowed to discharge cargo. Fortunately *Southampton* passed the inspection, but during the course of it the inspectors found several items which would have to be rectified by the time she called again at a port in the United States. On the passage back across the Pacific the tanks had to be cleaned, scale and sludge lifted, and gas-freed so that hot-work could be carried out in effecting the repairs. At Singapore the material for carrying out the repairs and renewals was brought on board and a riding crew of four joined the ship to assist in carrying out the work. In all about 700 feet of piping on deck was renewed on the passage between Singapore and Bahrain. In a tanker very thorough checks for gas have to be carried out before any hot-work (burning, welding, etc.) can take place. In shipyard this was done by a qualified chemist who issued a gas free certificate for the space, or area of the ship, where the work was to take place, on other occasions it was the Master's responsibility. It was a worrying time.

Botany Bay in Australia was a frequent port of call. We were always routed south about but I still had the option of returning via the Barrier Reef and Thursday Island. On one occasion, for some unknown reason, I put off ordering the Reef pilot until it was too late and I had to return south about via the Australian Bight and Cape Leeuwin. Just as we reached the Cape news came through of the cyclone which had devastated Darwin in the north. Going to the chart I did some calculations and found that if I had proceeded via the Reef I could have been caught in the cyclone area.

Another time I arrived at Cape Leeuwin just as a cyclone was moving down the west coast of Australia and about to speed up and turn south east across the Cape. The sea was a greasy calm with a long low swell as we put more ballast in the ship and filled the ballast tanks full so that there was no free surface to affect the ship's stability. Then it was full speed to the south west to get across the front of the cyclone into the navigable semi-circle where the wind direction would blow the ship away from the centre. About midnight the ship was rolling heavily and shipping heavy spray whipped up by winds which, according to our position and the reported centre of the

cyclone, must have been in the region of 100 m.p.h. In the following hours, as the
wind backed, I was able to alter course gradually round to a northerly course and by
six a.m. the weather had moderated considerably as the cyclone moved away in an
easterly direction losing strength. It was an anxious few hours but my ship behaved
very well and responded each time I murmured a few words of encouragement as she
was belaboured by the elements.

Another incident occurred due to bad weather this time off Botany Bay. For
some time the Australian maritime unions had been insisting that only Australian
ships should be used to transport crude oil to the refinery and to carry cargoes
between Australian ports, and to this end they frequently delayed foreign ships
and refused to berth them or handle their cargoes. I arrived off Botany Bay at the
beginning of one of these strikes and for four weeks I stayed outside the port awaiting
orders to berth. I would steam out to a position about 60 miles offshore (within
TV range), stop the ship and allow her to drift to within 20 miles before returning
to seaward.

Meanwhile the refinery was running low on crude oil and there was a real
fear that it might have to shut down and that Sydney and the surrounding area would
suffer a shortage of gasoline and diesel fuel oil. One day, when the ship had just
reached the limit of her drift inshore, there was a sudden deterioration in the weather
and within a few hours a severe gale was blowing and I had to steam out to sea to
ride it out. The following morning the weather had moderated a little and the Chief
Officer took some men on to the main deck to manhandle the heavy accommodation
ladder (which had been on deck ready for berthing) into the centrecastle to repair
some slight damage. I went down off the bridge and told him to get the men off the
deck and they were just moving off when a rogue wave came on board and scattered
them like ninepins. There were no broken bones but several sustained severe bruising
and, as it turned out, there was the odd hairline fracture. I headed in towards Botany
Bay and asked the agent by telephone to arrange for a doctor to meet the ship just
outside the entrance as I knew that the authorities did not like to have large crude oil
ships in Sydney harbour for fear of a pollution or other incident. However on this
occasion the agent received permission for me to enter the harbour and land my men
for medical attention.

About an hour after I spoke to the agent the Radio Officer reported that there
was a shore telephone call for me. It turned out to be a reporter from the Sydney
Morning Herald newspaper wanting to know details of the injuries sustained by the
crew and any damage that the ship had suffered in the storm. I had to be very careful
in what I said as apart from bad publicity for the company there were legal matters to
consider. When the ship arrived in port I found it was the centre of a great deal of
attention. The doctor came onboard to examine the men and found that only two or
three required further examination ashore. When they landed they found a TV station
had sent a crew to record their arrival. That evening, in spite of my orders to the officers

that no visitors were to be allowed on board, there was a knock at my door and there was the Third Officer with, of all people, a reporter.

He was quite a nice chap, obviously after a story and he was anxious to know what damage had been caused to the ship by the storm in addition to how the men had been injured. I was a bit put out to have my professional ability questioned, we had ridden out the weather very well with no damage to fixtures or fittings. I explained that I could not say very much because of the legal side of things, insurance, etc., but if he looked around the deck he would see that nothing had been bent. The following day there were items in the newspapers on how the strike had forced the ship to remain at sea, resulting in her being caught in the storm and the subsequent injuries to her crew members. It may just have been a coincidence but the strike was lifted that day and the following morning I took the ship round to Botany Bay where we were welcomed once again by a TV crew. I had been asked by the agent to give them my full co-operation (good publicity!) which I was pleased to do. I had to be interviewed and beforehand we discussed the type of question I would be asked. The interview took place on the wing of the bridge and the only question I hedged on was, "What do you think about the action of the people that forced you to wait outside for so long?" The final question was on the lines of what did I miss most during the time we were waiting to berth. I said, "A chiropodist and a barber." The interviewer laughed and asked me why. I replied that my feet were killing me and look at my hair. I half hoped that I would be inundated with calls from chiropodists offering to attend to my feet but there was a deadly silence, then again Channel 10 was not a very popular station.

I had another opportunity to lend assistance in a towing operation involving two of the Company's ships. My sister ship, the *Greenwich* had gone to the assistance of the *Plymouth* which had broken down with serious engine problems in the Indian Ocean west of Sumatra and, as I was in the vicinity, I was told to rendezvous with them to see if I could assist in any way. I contacted the *Greenwich* by radio and her Master, Ernie Adams, whom I knew very well, told me he had *Plymouth* in tow and was proceeding nicely but, as he had a voyage of some 1200 miles ahead of him, would I pass him my insurance hawser as a spare in case anything went wrong.

The insurance (towing) hawser in *Southampton* was a very heavy wire six inches in circumference and six hundred feet long. The wire was taken from its stowage in the forecastle space and flaked down along the main deck and up to the poop, together with several mooring ropes, in readiness for the transfer operation.

The *Greenwich* and her tow were proceeding at six knots in fine weather when I met her at the rendezvous. I took up station close ahead of her and streamed two lengths of polyproplene mooring ropes (approximately 1100 feet) as a messenger, with a float secured to the end, for her to pick up from her forecastle with a grapnel. This was the interesting and tricky part of the operation as I had to adjust my speed to maintain exact station on the *Greenwich* and manoeuvre the ship as required to keep the tail of the mooring ropes close to her bow so that it could be grappled on board. The inboard end of the messenger was secured to one end of the towing wire and a further two lengths of mooring rope attached to the other end. As the *Greenwich* heaved in the messenger the towing wire was paid out followed by the attached mooring ropes. Once the wire was on board the *Greenwich* she secured the messenger to the other ropes and we pulled them back on board. The whole operation took about two hours.

Whilst I was in the process of passing the wire another ship, the 140,000 tons Bibby Line *English Bridge* passed by and the Master was so amazed at the sight of three Texaco tankers in line that he altered course to take a look at what was going on. The *Southampton* and the *Greenwich* were identical and the *Plymouth*, although some 10,000 tons smaller, was very similar in design and it must have appeared to him that we were carrying out fleet manoeuvres. He took some photographs and sent them to our head office. In his accompanying letter he said, "In all my years at sea I have never seen anything like it. As a professional seafarer the sight of those three Texaco Masters handling the situation filled me with awe. It really stirred the blood".

It was around this time when I was returning to Singapore, via the Sunda Straits in Java (passing the famous volcano Krakatoa), that the ship was again boarded by uninvited guests. It was a dirty morning with rain squalls and poor visibility as we passed the Horsburgh lighthouse and headed west along the Strait to Singapore. The ship was at light draught with a freeboard of about 28 feet and, in addition to the bridge team for arrival in port, there were extra lookouts on the bridge wings because of the poor visibility. About 6 a.m. the Second Engineer called the bridge and reported that he had found a Chinaman wandering around the accommodation. He carried no papers or identification of any kind and it appeared that he was by himself and was the only person to board.

The police in Singapore did not get much information out of him. It seemed that he had boarded by climbing up a rope, secured by a grapnel, from a small craft which had come alongside undetected by either the lookout or the officer manning the radar set. Picking up small craft on the radar in the prevailing conditions of rain squalls which cause a great deal of interference is always difficult and it was not surprising that it was not spotted on this occasion. The incident served to show how easy it must be for a gang of pirates to board a ship at sea and rob and threaten the crew and worse. The police told me that if I wanted to charge the man I would have to appear in court now or at a later date. As this would have meant delaying the ship it was decided not to press charges, however, knowing the Singapore police they would no doubt have dealt with him in their own way.

An important area of a shipmaster's responsibilities was the health and welfare of the officers and crew. In addition to ensuring that their accommodation, cabins, toilets, galleys, etc. were kept in a clean, tidy and sanitary condition, he was also responsible for ensuring that the proper treatment was administered in cases of illness or injury. A qualified medical practitioner was only required to be carried in ships with 12 or more passengers or more than a hundred crew members, and in the vast majority of ships the Master was, in effect, the ship's doctor. Apart from a course on First Aid (which no one ever failed) when sitting Second Mate's Certificate, officers were not trained in this aspect of their duties and any knowledge gained was through experience and with the help of the *Shipmaster's Medical Guide*. This was a very helpful publication which listed various diseases and common types of illness, their symptoms and the appropriate treatment, and the methods of dealing with various types of injuries. The only drawback being, that one first had to make a guess at the illness and then see if the symptoms applied to it, rather than the various symptoms being listed in tabular form with the relevant illness and treatment being indicated alongside. This method was adopted at a later date.

Traditionally, it was the Chief Officer who was in charge of the medicine chest and to whom people reported when sick, however in the event of serious illness or injury the Master was more closely involved. Over the years, both as Chief officer and Master I had to deal with a variety of cases. Whenever one was in doubt the international Medical Organization in Rome could be contacted and it had various specialists on call to give advice by radio. This service was of great assistance on several occasions. The ship could also head for the nearest port but such a deviation in the voyage had to be carefully considered as it would result in lost time and incur extra costs. This would not be welcomed if it was found that the patient could have remained on board safely until the ship arrived at her destination. The well-being of the patient was, of course, paramount and one would err on the safe side but, at the same time, there was a certain amount of worry as too many deviations could put one's judgement in doubt.

As is often the case one learns from experience. One evening I was called to the Serang's (boatswain) cabin where I found him complaining of a burning pain in the region of his chest and upper abdomen. He had few teeth and as he had recently been eating I put it down to indigestion (I sometimes had the same symptoms and suffered from that complaint) and a check in the Medical Guide appeared to confirm the diagnosis. The following morning at 6 a.m. I went along to see how he was getting on and found him in distress – gasping for breath and obviously on the way out. I asked other crew members why I had not been called earlier and they told me a few minutes before I arrived he had been quite normal, drinking tea and eating a little bread. He died a few minutes later. I had sent for the Captain who diagnosed a heart attack and said there was nothing I could have done to save him, and this was confirmed by the doctor when we called in at Aden to land the body. However I was upset with myself for not thinking of the heart in the first instance; when I subsequently consulted the Medical Guide and looked under heart attack the symptoms were exactly those of the Serang.

There was a similar occurrence in my next ship when we had just left the jetty in Botany Bay. Again it was the Serang, sitting on the windlass platform gasping, and pulling his shirt open as if to get air and complaining, "Too much pain, Sahib." I knew what it was this time and shouted to the bridge to get the doctor from shore and at the same time dropped the anchor. The doctor arrived within twenty minutes and gave the Serang an injection but did not hold out much hope for him. He died in hospital the next day. Fortunately we were back in Botany Bay in time for his funeral.

On one occasion, a couple of days after leaving the Arabian Gulf bound for Australia, my Chief Officer, who had just joined after a spell of sick leave, became ill with a recurrence of kidney trouble and was unfit for duty. The following day the Second Officer also became unfit for duty when an old injury to his knee began to trouble him and his leg became badly swollen and extremely painful. They were both bed rest cases and this left me with just an uncertificated Third Officer to share the bridge watch for the remaining sixteen days of the voyage.

Other serious cases ranged from two broken legs with compound fractures sustained a by a Second Officer when a mooring rope parted, mental breakdown suffered by a Third Officer who was a Scientology convert, to the collapsed lung in a young engineer officer. Perhaps the most worrying was the occasion when my Chief Officer had to be rescued from the pumproom where, because of his own negligence and failure to observe safety procedures and precautions, he had been overcome by gas.

The Chief Officer had been found unconscious under the gratings at the bottom of the pumproom lying in the foetal position with his face in the oily water. As soon as he was taken on deck I started artificial respiration and I soon found that procedures do not always go according to the text book or in training class. Attempting mouth-to-mouth rescucitation I found that I could not open the patient's mouth as his jaws were locked and his teeth clamped tight together. His nose was cleaned out and an attempt to give him air by that route was to no avail. Whilst this was going on he was gradually turning blue and an officer's wife, who was an enrolled nurse, at one stage thought he was dead. As I worked on him all sorts of thoughts were racing through my mind. He was a married man with children; what would his family do if he died? There would be a big enquiry and although it was his own fault in disregarding safety matters (an added factor was his uncommunicative nature), as Master I was accountable for the safety of all on board and I would have the final responsibility.

Turning the patient on his stomach I started the Schafer method of rescucitation whilst at the same time the back of his throat was tickled with my small, thin, silver paper knife, which we had managed to insert between his clenched teeth, in an effort to make him vomit. This treatment proved successful when he suddenly vomitted a large quantity of black liquid and his colour began to change as he started to breathe more easily. I had been unable to detect a pulse and, as I did not know how long he had been starved of air, there was a possibility that he might have suffered brain damage so it was important to get him to hospital as soon as possible. Fortunately we were not far from the entrance to the Klang Strait and I proceeded there informing the agent and pilot at Port Swettenham of my intended arrival. However it was about

8 p.m. on a Saturday night when I arrived and there was no sign of a pilot nor could I contact the pilot station. There was nothing else for it but to continue down the Strait, all the time trying to raise the pilot station, whilst we prepared a lifeboat to take the Chief Officer ashore in case there was no shore boat available. At last there was an answer from the harbour office; they had not received my messages and none of the pilots were at home. I told the chap in the harbour office that I had an extremely ill patient on board in urgent need of medical attention, and that his life depended on the clerk having an ambulance waiting at the New Piers to meet the boat that would be bringing him ashore. I laid it on a bit thick.

After anchoring, the boat was lowered immediately with the patient's stretcher lying on an improvised platform. I gave the Third Officer, who was in charge, the Chief Officer's passport, discharge book and other documents and told him and the Second Engineer Officer not to come back until they had put the Chief Officer into hospital. Whilst the boat was proceeding inshore the amber strobe light of an ambulance was seen on the jetty some distance away, but the feeling of relief turned to doubt as after a few minutes the ambulance appeared to be turning to move off before the boat had arrived. Fortunately the Third Officer had seen the movement and immediately started flashing the signal lamp in the direction of the jetty to attract attention. The clerk in the harbour office had not let me down and I gave him a silent "Well done!"

There were only a couple of labourers on the jetty but they gave the boat's crew a hand to hoist the stretcher up the vertical iron ladder and get the patient into the ambulance. The officers accompanied the Chief Officer to Klang hospital and saw him admitted and then they returned in the boat to the ship. I waited for the ship to swing to the tide and then proceeded back up the Strait and continued the voyage.

The officers and the boat's crew had done very well as had the rest of the ship's crew. Recovering the Chief Officer's apparently lifeless body from its hazardous position in the pumproom bilges, and taking it up approximately forty feet of narrow stairs, had been a hard and awkward task which the sailors had carried out with all speed. Various people contributed to his recovery and cared for him during the short passage to port. In fact it was an all round team effort. However the Chief Officer did not write to the ship to thank his former shipmates for their efforts on his behalf and when I saw him in the London office some weeks later he barely acknowledged me. But then his inability to communicate, and his unsociability, had contributed to his accident.

Chapter 31

An Unexpected End

────

The *Texaco Southampton* was due to be taken out of service in 1985 when new regulations would require her to have dedicated ballast tanks and piping system, i.e. solely for the carriage of clean ballast water and not used for the carriage of oil. The cost of the alterations to the cargo system, and the inevitable reduction in the cargo capacity, meant that the ship would be uneconomical to operate after that date. I therefore expected to stay with her until 1985, at which time I would have reached the age of 62 which was then the normal retiring age.

For economic reasons, in common with other shipping lines, the Company had been gradually reducing the size of the fleet until by 1981 it had been reduced from over thirty ships to about twenty. It was planned that a further three ships would be scrapped in 1982. However at a meeting at Texaco Headquarters at White Plains, New York, in March 1982 our Managing Director received news that nine ships were to be scrapped that year. He received such a shock that it was said that he was still showing the effects of it when he returned to London.

I had been in touch with the office on another matter when I heard news of the nine ships and that *Southampton* and her sister ship *Greenwich* were included in the list of ships to be scrapped. Although her cargo tank bulkheads were thin in places and becoming prone to leaks (which we repaired) the *Southampton* was still in reasonably good condition for her age and could still steam at her designed speed of over 15 knots. We had put a lot of hard work into her, the ships staff carrying out large scale repairs at sea which would normally have been done in shipyard, in order to reduce costs and I fully expected that I would remain with her until I retired.

I had been due to rejoin my ship in April but instead I was asked to visit the London office where I received the sad news that I, too, was being made redundant. It took some time to come to terms with the fact that my sea-going career was at an end and that I was now on the beach for good. At my age there was little chance of getting a command in another company and there were many younger officers being made redundant throughout the industry. The officer who took *Southampton* to the scrap-yard in Taiwan was made redundant at the end of the voyage and within 18 months the fleet had been reduced from twenty ships to a mere five.

However, when I considered the matter I realised that I had been quite fortunate compared to many people who were being made redundant in various industries throughout the country at that time, most of whom were comparatively young with little prospect of finding other employment in the immediate future, and with only a small amount of redundancy payment to fall back on. Several well-known shipping companies had been reducing their fleets and laying off men in recent years and if Texaco had taken similar action at an earlier date (several of the ships had been uneconomical for some time) I would have been in a much more difficult situation. As it turned out I had been lucky to stay at sea for so long and to reach an age where I had accrued a reasonable pension and sufficient years of service to earn a good redundancy settlement.

From an early age I had been very interested in ships, especially those of the Royal Navy, and fascinated by the stories I had read portraying an open-air life, seeing the world and experiencing many adventures, unusual situations and possibly a bit of action. Going to sea at the beginning of the war my expectations were fully realised, both at sea and on shore, during my war and peace-time service in the Navy. It was a wonderful experience which left me with a host of happy memories.

I had also been fortunate in choosing to serve in oil tankers when I returned to sea. The very nature of the trade, the systems and equipment involved in operating the ships meant that there were always problems arising and difficulties to be overcome, which presented a continual challenge and prevented any possibility of boredom. Whilst chatting to the harbourmaster in Newcastle, Australia, I mentioned that I was on my first trip in command to which he replied that I would find that command was '90% boredom and 10% sheer terror.' I could agree with the latter part of his observation but I was never bored.

Altogether I visited one hundred and fifty ports in sixty countries, my one regret being that I did not manage to visit South America or Canada, or pass through the Panama Canal. Apart from that, I feel I could say of my sea-going career that I had 'been, seen and done it all.'

But I never did drive a picket boat with a brass funnel!

BIBLIOGRAPHY

——

The Mediterranean Fleet – 1941–1943. Ministry of Information. Published by H.M.S.O. 1944 (The situation in the Mediterranean leading up to the Battle of Sirte).

Bless Our Ship. Captain Eric Wheeler Bush D.S.O.** D.S.C.R.N. Published by George Allen & Unwin Ltd. 1953 (In relating my experience of the Battle of Sirte, in the interest of accuracy as to the sequence of operations and manoeuvres, I have drawn on the account of the proceedings given by Captain E.W. Bush, the Commanding Officer of HMS Euryalus in his autobiography).

Two Men Who Saved France – Petain and DeGaulle. By Major-General Sir Edward Spears. Published by Eyre & Spottiswoode Ltd. 1966 (The sequence of events during the Dakar Expedition 1940.)